PLATO

Each book in the series GREAT LIVES OF THE ANCIENT WORLD succinctly explores the life, culture and lasting legacy of outstanding figures across the ancient world, including China, the Indian subcontinent, the Middle East, and ancient Greece and Rome.

SERIES EDITOR: Paul Cartledge

Archimedes: Fulcrum of Science   NICHOLAS NICASTRO
Plato: A Civic Life   CAROL ATACK

PLATO

A Civic Life

CAROL ATACK

REAKTION BOOKS

For Malcolm, as ever

Published by
REAKTION BOOKS LTD
Unit 32, Waterside
44–48 Wharf Road
London N1 7UX, UK
www.reaktionbooks.co.uk

First published 2024
Copyright © Carol Atack 2024

Printed and bound in Great Britain by TJ Books Ltd, Padstow, Cornwall

A catalogue record for this book is available from the British Library

ISBN 978 1 78914 946 3

CONTENTS

Plato with statue of Athena, both sculpted by Leonidas Drosis (*c.* 1836–1882), outside the modern Academy of Athens.

Introduction

'The safest general characterization of the European philosophical tradition is that it consists of a series of footnotes to Plato.'[1] That was the verdict of mathematician and philosopher Alfred Whitehead, who was writing around 2,300 years after Plato's life and career while attempting to establish his own overarching theory of the cosmos. Whitehead went on to explain that he did not mean that all philosophers were Platonists who adhered to doctrines derived from Plato's work, but that important pointers to the direction of philosophy, to what counted as philosophical, were scattered through his work. Across his dialogues, Plato asked big questions. These laid the foundations for philosophical inquiry into the nature of existence, the possibility of immortality, the nature of knowledge and how it might be transmitted, and what it might mean to live a good life or to establish a good society.

Plato placed many of those questions in the mouth of his own teacher, Socrates. Socrates himself famously wrote nothing. He now exists as a tradition – a series of conflicting characters used by writers of different genres to communicate their own ideas and their own critique of the project of philosophy. But Plato's work goes far beyond the representation of Socrates; rather, he uses the charismatic figure of his teacher to present his own groundbreaking theories and his synthesis of earlier Greek philosophies and new developments, as he gathered an exciting group of researchers and thinkers in his higher-learning Academy. Plato's own educational enterprise played a key part in the eventual transformation of Athens from political power to international hub for culture and learning, and arguably provided a template for high-level study and research still relevant to today's institutions.

Plato's dominance of the philosophical tradition goes far beyond the narrow confines of academic philosophical research. In creating myths to explain some of his ideas, he produced time-less images which powerfully convey the experience of thinking. In the twentieth century his image of the prisoners in the cave, kept in the dark and confabulating falsehoods from the confusing imagery around them, resonated with the era of totalitarian regimes and new forms of mass media, especially the powerful new medium of cinema.[2] Plato's casual invention of Atlantis, an island empire doomed to destruction by the arrogance and expansionism of its ruling dynasty, took on a life of its own, quite separate from the more scholarly interest in the account of the creation of the universe that accompanies it in his *Timaeus*.[3]

'It's all in Plato, all in Plato: bless me, what do they teach them at these schools?', the professor explains to a bewildered young man confused about his exclusion from the magical land of Narnia in C. S. Lewis's series of fantasy novels for children.[4] The final part of the story, *The Last Battle*, ends with the series' familiar young characters being led after their sudden deaths into another world, where they realize that all their previous experience had been an unsatisfying imitation of the true and eternal realities now revealed to them. The experiences of the captive prince of Narnia in the earlier *Silver Chair* might remind us of the *Republic*'s cave.[5] The presence of talking animals in the first book, *The Lion, the Witch and the Wardrobe*, also points to Plato – to the myth of the Golden Age embedded in the otherwise dry and difficult late dialogue the *Statesman*, one of the dialogues in which Socrates is replaced as main speaker by the much less charming Eleatic Stranger, mouthpiece for the ideas Plato had developed in part from his encounters with the Greek philosophers of southern Italy.[6]

Lewis's use of Plato demonstrates the way in which Platonic idealism had fed into the traditions of Christianity, drawing on the work of pagan philosophers. Perhaps one of the hardest challenges in reading Plato, for anyone educated in the traditions of European and Anglophone academic philosophy, is to step away from a cultural context in which his ideas are so deeply embedded and to encounter them afresh.

Other twentieth-century readers gained different knowledge from Plato. For Virginia Woolf, Plato's writings epitomized a masculine community of education and friendship from which she felt excluded. Reading dialogues like the *Phaedrus* gave her insights into this homosocial community and even into sex between men: 'I had known since I was sixteen or so, all about sodomy, through reading Plato,' she wrote in a memoir.[7]

This 'ancient life' endeavours to reconstruct what we can know of Plato's life and the historical context in which he lived, using all the historical and material sources available to us. It draws from the literary and epigraphic evidence for life in Athens contemporary with Plato; from inscriptions recording political decisions, from the plays performed in the city's dramatic festivals, from surviving historical texts such as the works of Thucydides and Xenophon and the works of other Socratics, fragmentary as many of them are. It looks beyond Athens to the wider Greek world in which Plato travelled, and the complex interactions between cities and peoples, seeing Plato's reflections of his own experience and conversations even in his depiction of Socrates, ostensibly set fifty or more years earlier.

Despite the wide array of sources, it is largely impossible to pin down many key dates, from the year of Plato's birth itself to the timing of his journeys to Sicily and the foundation of the Academy. At significant moments it becomes difficult to order events – did

Plato's first journey to Sicily happen before or after he had set up the Academy? And how were both these activities affected by the changing international situation heralded by the King's Peace of 387, one example of wider political events impacting what types of travel and trade were possible for an Athenian? I have also taken a rather more cautious view on identifying dates than some previous scholars, although I note arguments made in favour of specific dates in important recent work by Debra Nails and Robin Waterfield.[8]

The Mediterranean during the fourth century BCE.

The practice of philosophy has been to extract arguments from the text and remove them from their context. But the common thread through Plato's work is the commemoration of the life and unjust death of Socrates; on the one hand, this offers an overarching narrative, on the other, it obscures Plato's own experiences beyond his interactions with Socrates. In using the dramatic context of the dialogues to reconstruct Plato's thought and experience, one must be aware of his own self-construction through these texts in which he himself is an absent presence.

Perhaps the biggest challenge in writing a life of Plato is the power of his own fictionalization of Socrates and the centrality of his lifelong mourning of his beloved teacher to the structure and content of his dialogues.

Plato's thought appears to offer a systematic idealism, but a single coherent statement of key elements such as the 'Theory of Forms' cannot easily be extracted from initial appearances in the *Phaedo*, the *Republic* or from the difficulties observed and

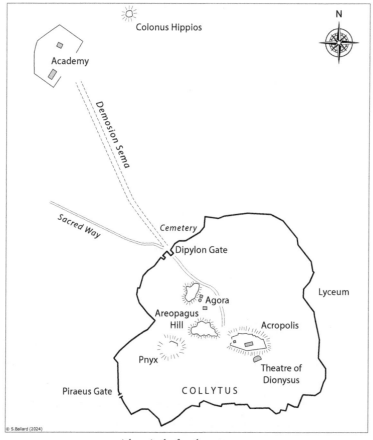

Athens in the fourth century BCE.

modifications proposed in later dialogues, such as the *Parmenides* and the *Sophist*. Even with the baggage of the history of philosophy set aside, the risk of falling prey to what Quentin Skinner labelled the 'fallacy of coherence' is great.[9] In telling Plato's life, and noting both the changing political conditions and intellectual environment to which he responded throughout his long writing and teaching career, one can perhaps come to recognize that it is inappropriate to speak of fixed doctrines, or to identify a particular work – especially the *Republic* – as a final and firm statement.

This book aims above all to show how Plato's philosophy developed from his experiences in Athens and his interactions with philosophers in Athens and beyond. It shows how his upbringing in Athens, during a period of unusual upheavals caused by war, plague and civil strife, contributed to the concerns and topics he explored and how his writing responded to the problems of his own day as well as commemorated Socrates. It shows how even the established Plato, later in his life, was still rethinking and revising his core arguments in response to new challenges. It emphasizes the multiplicity of other voices contributing to the development and refinement of his thought, from his readings and other encounters with the ideas of his fifth-century predecessors to the challenge posed by the arrival into the Academy of figures such as Eudoxus and Aristotle.

The Platonic Corpus: Sources and Problems

Plato's works were transmitted from antiquity through the collection and copying of manuscripts by ancient scholars. There was a recognized corpus of genuine works, along with others the authenticity of which was questioned. Around the turn of the first millennium, the Alexandrian scholar Thrasyllus organized the works into tetralogies, an arrangement which has become standard in modern times, although other arrangements were known in antiquity. This arrangement included a group of *nothoi*, dialogues regarded as illegitimate or inauthentic. There remain many works whose authenticity has been disproven or which remain disputed.

Plato's importance as founder of the Academy is reflected in a wealth of later biographical sources. The earliest is Aristotle's critical history of philosophy, the first book of his *Metaphysics*. This provides important evidence for Plato's connections with and responses to the thought of earlier thinkers, but, while Aristotle was himself an eyewitness to the early years of the Academy, his written account of Plato often appears to draw as much on evidence from the dialogues as from that of any independent sources. Because intellectual genealogy – tracing lines of descent from the founders of schools – was important to ancient philosophers, there are histories of philosophical schools; a history of the Academy by the first-century BCE Epicurean philosopher Philodemus of Gadara survived in partial form in the library of Lucius Calpurnius Piso Caesoninus at Herculaneum. The carbonized scroll was initially unwrapped after its discovery during the initial excavation of the site in the eighteenth century, and some fragments deciphered. Improvements in technology have enabled researchers to use new techniques to read previously illegible sections and to strengthen some conjectural readings. Despite many remaining gaps in what is readable, the text cites earlier sources close to Plato himself, and offers a distinctive account compared to more fanciful biographies from later antiquity.[10]

The most detailed ancient biography of Plato is contained in Diogenes Laertius' *Lives of Eminent Philosophers*, written in the third century CE.[11] Plato is one of two figures whose life is given a whole book to itself – the other is Epicurus, founder of the hedonistic Epicurean school. Diogenes draws together a wealth of material, some extracted from the dialogues, some from other sources in the doxographical tradition, now lost to us. His account, which takes up the third book of his ten-book work, is riddled with anachronisms and chronological difficulty, but is yet valuable as evidence for how Plato was read in later antiquity, as Diogenes draws on material from both favourable and hostile traditions.

Other ancient biographies that survive include Apuleius' *On Plato and His Thought*, written in the second century CE.[12] Apuleius' account seeks to explain Plato's life in order to introduce his work. This approach was followed by the Neoplatonist Olympiodorus, writing in the immediate aftermath of the closure of Athens's philosophical schools in 529 CE and the deprecation of pagan philosophy by the now Christian ruling elite. For Olympiodorus, the anecdotes gathered from earlier sources take on mystical qualities; another, unnamed writer tones down these suggestions in his own version of Plato's life.[13] As Alice Swift Riginos noted in her collation and analysis of ancient anecdotes about Plato, a great deal of biographical patterning is under way in all these works, so that caution, even scepticism, is needed about each of the familiar stories.[14]

Snippets of biographical information, as well as critiques of Plato's writing, dot ancient miscellanies such as Athenaeus' *Sophists at Dinner* and Stobaeus' *Anthology*, and later encyclopaedias produced by Byzantine scholars, such as the tenth-century CE lexicon the *Suda*.[15] Athenaeus depicts a group of sophists/intellectuals conversing about a wide range of learned topics; at one point, Plato becomes their focus. They look for errors in the dialogues and search for Plato's own sources. While many of the anecdotes in these works are implausible, and often chronologically impossible, they do provide some insights into later attitudes to Plato, particularly the persistent view that he was a plagiarist who copied the arguments of others. Given that the sources he is said to have plagiarized are as varied as Protagoras and Philolaus, we can detect a tradition hostile to Plato.

Another genre of biographical writing in antiquity was the letter. We have a collection of thirteen letters attributed to Plato, but even in antiquity the authenticity of some was doubted. 'This letter is not by Plato,' says a manuscript note attached to Letter 12.[16] Other letters purporting to be by Plato were never admitted to this canon, although they are gathered in modern collections such as Rudolf Hercher's huge and magnificent *Epistolographi Graeci*, which presents them, along with Latin translations, in 843 double-columned pages.[17] The problem is that writing letters in the voice of famous thinkers and politicians was a common classroom exercise in later antiquity and also a way in which students and scholars might engage with the ideas of their predecessors.[18] Some scholars, notably Michael Frede, have even argued that no letters attributed to authors from the fourth century BCE are actually by those writers, and that all emerge from this later educational context.[19]

Plato's tendency to keep himself in the background meant that there were plenty of tempting and intriguing gaps to fill. The 'Seventh Letter' can be seen as the most thorough attempt to explain Plato's philosophy in the context of his life. It sets out Plato's biography, providing a great deal of personal information, explaining Plato's motives for choosing certain courses of actions, such as his apparent withdrawal from political life in the wake of Socrates' death, and including helpful if not entirely philo-sophically accurate summaries of his thought. The letter was long accepted as Plato's own work, but early modern scholars started to raise doubts. Perhaps the letters were not by Plato, but by someone who was closely associated with the early Academy in Hellenistic Athens. Or were they, perhaps, much later exercises, associ-ated with the development of Neoplatonism under the Roman empire?[20] To this day there is no agreement; Malcolm Schofield rejects Platonic authorship, but suggests that the letters originate from close to Plato's time, whereas Myles Burnyeat placed them much later.[21]

Plato also appears in letters attributed to other figures, alleg-edly Socrates himself, his own nephew Speusippus and, in perhaps the most charming collection of letters, Chion of Heraclea, a student at the Academy.[22] While these letters clearly cannot be considered as contemporary documentary evidence for Plato and his activities, they tell us a lot about the way later Greek and Roman writers thought about Plato and the Academy; in the case of the *Letters of Chion*, the presentation of the title character as a tyrannicide is intended to counter the persistent worry that the Academy was a school for potential tyrants, radicalizing its elite students into overthrowing the regimes of their cities. The 'Letter of Speusippus to Philip', on the other hand, suggests that the Academy was willing to stay in contact with Philip II, king of Macedon from 359 to 336, at a point when Demosthenes and other orators were depicting him as Athens's most dangerous enemy but prior to his defeat of the city. If genuinely by Speusippus, who took over the running of the Academy on his uncle's death, it would suggest a continuing role for the institution and its members in opposing popular and majority political views.

In reconstructing Plato's life, I follow Michael Frede in seeing the letters as ancient attempts to link Plato to schools of philosophy from across the Greek world, especially the Pythagoreans of southern Italy, rather than as the original work of their alleged authors.[23] That means that I reject the historicity of some of the narratives of the letters and other ancient sources, regarding them as post factum fictionalization, but use them critically to explore the development of philosophy and early responses to Plato and his thought.

1

A Wartime Childhood

As rumours spread that the Spartan army was approaching and the outlying districts of Athens were in danger, Athens's principal leader, Pericles, brought the rural population into the city for safety. Yet the crowded conditions were insanitary and a new and often fatal sickness spread easily through the population. The Athenian historian Thucydides, writing a few years after these events, noted:

> They had not been many days in Attica when the plague first began amongst the Athenians, said also to have seized formerly on divers other parts, as about Lemnos and elsewhere; but so great a plague and mortality of men was never remembered to have happened in any place before. For at first neither were the physicians able to cure it through ignorance of what it was but died fastest themselves, as being the men that most approached the sick, nor any other art of man availed whatsoever. All supplications to the gods and enquiries of oracles and whatsoever other means they used of that kind proved all unprofitable; insomuch as subdued with the greatness of the evil, they gave them all over. [1]

This plague arrived in 430 and roared through the city, taking rich and poor alike, at the same time as the Spartans laid waste to the farmland around Athens. Perhaps, the Athenians wondered, this was a judgement from the gods. They found omens in ancient oracles, which now seemed to warn of their present suffering. Some of those camping in the city had been forced to sleep in sacred areas where ordinary mortals were not supposed to tread. It was impossible to follow the usual religious practices, with desperate survivors throwing the corpses of family members on to any funeral pyre they could find.

The precise nature of the disease that caused this suffering remains unknown; the symptoms Thucydides reports resemble those of other pandemic diseases such as the bubonic plague, but there is no firm evidence. It killed the general Pericles in its second year, 429 BCE, after taking his sons Paralus and Xanthippus in the first wave of infections.[2] The time before the war would come to seem almost a golden age, a time when Athens led the Greek world, received tribute from other cities and reshaped itself with the grand building scheme that produced such incomparable monuments as the Parthenon. But the empire and the glory it funded contained the seeds of the city's decline, as Pericles eventually concedes in the last speech Thucydides gives to him.

Otherwise, Thucydides skates over political controversy within the city, keen as he is to show Pericles as an unparalleled leader of the democracy. Other, later, sources such as the imperial-Roman-era biographer Plutarch tell us that Pericles was lampooned by comedians, and his spending of the city's resources was challenged in the courts.[3] But Plato himself would look back to the years preceding his birth as significant ones.[4] When he imagined Socrates at work in this more glamorous Athens, Plato placed the sons of Pericles in the audience as his teacher argued with Protagoras, a rival Greek educator drawn to Athens from Abdera in northern Greece by the prospect of teaching its young elite the skills they needed to succeed in their political careers.[5]

Ariston, Plato's father, and his young family had a home in the city, in the prosperous central deme (ward or parish) of Collytus.

The wealthy citizens who had homes here were well placed to participate in the assembly of citizens which met on the Pnyx, a nearby hill, and at the Theatre of Dionysus beneath the Acropolis. The latter was also the venue for the annual religious festivals in honour of Dionysus, where officially appointed dramatists competed for prizes, awarded by democratic vote by a citizen jury. An earlier resident of this area had been the tyrant Peisistratus, whose family had seized power during the sixth century and ruled Athens for 35 years before the democracy was fully established in the last decade of the sixth century. The Agora, the commercial marketplace and civic centre surrounded by public political offices, was nearby, making it easy to transact commercial, legal and civic business.

Another tradition, however, places the family away from the city in these critical years, as settlers on the island of Aegina, some 30 kilometres (20 mi.) south of the city's main port of Piraeus, in the middle of the Saronic Gulf that separated Attica from the Peloponnese, and suggests that Plato was actually born there.[6] At the brief height of its fifth-century imperial power, Athens allowed – indeed encouraged – citizens to take up parcels of land in overseas territory that had come under the city's control, and it is possible that Ariston had done this. But there is no evidence to support ancient biographers' claims that the Spartans expelled Athenian settlers from Aegina and sent them back to Athens at this stage of the great Peloponnesian War, which had broken out in 431.

Whether in Athens or elsewhere, aristocratic Ariston and his wife Perictione survived the years in which the sickness killed many of their fellow citizens. Unlike many of the Athenians from outlying districts who had had to camp in the city's sanctuaries and open spaces during the war, they had a home of their own. Two of their children, a daughter, Potone, and a son, Adeimantus, lived through the plague years as infants; another son, Glaucon, was born at its height, perhaps a couple of years before Plato. Because none of these sons bears the name of Ariston's father, Aristocles, it is possible that a first-born son so named had not survived infancy. Athenian citizen men usually, although not always, named their first son after their own father, so that names alternated through the generations. There had been previous holders of the name Aristocles; the name appears in a list of archons, the officials who governed the city, for 605/4. But a third or fourth son might bear the name of a more distant relative, or even a name new to the family; Glaucon was named after his maternal grandfather. Later biographers played with the idea that the child originally received his grandfather's name Aristocles as his given name, and that Plato (*platōn*, 'broad') was a nickname from his youthful training in the wrestling ring that stuck with him into adult life, or a description of his appearance which suited his role as a dignified intellectual.[7]

The exact year of Plato's birth remains unknown but was most likely between 429 and 423. Ancient biographers worked backwards from the date of his death, more securely known to have happened in 348/7.[8] A birthdate in 429/8 would give him 81 years, an elegant square and cube number satisfying to any ancient numerologist, and exemplifying the numerical patterns which, as some of his followers believed, structured the cosmos. Perhaps he had been born at the time of Pericles' death in the archonship of Ameinias, in 429, connecting him to the greatest figure of Athenian politics, as an anonymous biographer in late antiquity insists?[9] Yet that date must be too early, as Debra Nails and Robin Waterfield have argued; it would open the possibility that Plato was old enough to participate in political and military events in 411–409, where the biographical tradition places his earliest political engagement as an adult citizen in 404–403.[10]

The day of Plato's birth also connected him with the divine, according to other sources; he was born on the seventh of the month, the day sacred to the god Apollo, in the Athenian spring month of Thargelion.[11] Other later stories connected his conception to the presence of the god, perhaps responding to the Christian tradition, and imagining that Apollo was Plato's divine father. In these stories, Ariston was warned through a vision of the god Apollo to stay away from Perictione through her pregnancy, and he did so until Plato's birth.[12]

Whether Plato was born in Athens or Aegina, and whatever the involvement of Apollo, his infancy and early childhood within the home of his relatively wealthy family would have been much alike. A few days after his birth, Ariston formally accepted him into the household, carrying the newborn around the hearth in a ritual known as the *amphidromia* (running around).[13] An olive wreath was hung on the door to announce the arrival of a son. Family and friends attended his formal naming on his tenth day of life.

The biographical tradition fills Plato's early life with stories prefiguring his later philosophy, connecting him with divine powers. Cicero reported a story that once, while Plato was sleeping in his cradle, bees had settled on his lips, suggesting his 'future eloquence' and 'unique sweetness of speech'; later biographers embroidered this story to enhance its significance, so that, by the time the author of the anonymous introduction to the works of Plato was writing, he was able to assert that this incident took place while Plato's mother had taken him to Mount Hymettus when she went to perform a sacrifice, and that the bees had filled Plato's mouth with honey.[14]

The ordinary course of Athenian childhood provided plenty of opportunities to engage with the gods, as well as enabling children to take their place in society as future citizens. As a three-year-old, Plato was brought by his parents to a key part of one of the city's most ancient festivals, the Anthesteria, which celebrated the opening of the new season's wine and thanked the god Dionysus for providing it. Each family member had a specific role in the event; while children like Plato were crowned with garlands of spring flowers to introduce them to the community, adult men enjoyed

Unknown maker, *chous* (wine jug) depicting a young child crawling
towards a *chous*, c. 430 BCE, red-figure ceramic.

the communal feast of the Choes ('Beakers').[15] Elsewhere in the
city, the wife of the magistrate in charge of the traditional religious
festivals, the 'king archon', participated in a 'sacred marriage' to the
god.[16] Much of what we know about this festival derives from the
images of its rituals painted on miniature vases for pouring wine;
this kind of jug was known as a *chous*, from which the second
day of the festival got its name. These tiny jugs were placed in the
graves of children who had died before the age of three, the age
at which children could participate in the festival. Reaching this

age was a moment of hope for parents, as the infant had survived into childhood; perhaps as many as one in three infants ordinarily would not survive to their first birthday. In the aftermath of the plague, a child's survival was even more precious.

Outside such occasions, Plato's early childhood was spent among the women of the household. Whether he was nursed as an infant by his mother or a wet nurse, he would have been kept among the women in the interior parts of the household, protected from any harm by amulets and cared for by his family and the city's gods. Plato had vivid memories of the kinds of stories the women told to children. When he sets out the plan for raising and educating infants in the ideal city Kallipolis, developed in his *Republic*, he has Socrates, his own teacher, consider the consequences of mothers and nurses telling impressionable infants powerful and terrifying stories about 'gods wandering at night in the shapes of strangers from foreign lands'.[17] Socrates suggests that it would be much better if these storytellers were 'supervised' and allowed only an official selection of improving stories which would 'shape the souls' of their young charges much more positively.[18] While Plato's thoughts on controlling the arts cover performances and works aimed at all ages, he starts with the stories that women told to infants.

Perhaps Perictione told her young son some of the stories of her own ancient and well-connected family, which had an even grander history than that of Ariston, and reached back through the generations to some of the city's most revered political leaders, eventually finding, as the family trees of the city's traditional elite often did, an origin story featuring heroes and gods. Diogenes Laertius, who as noted wrote a biography of Plato in the third century CE as part of a series of philosophers' lives, was sufficiently impressed by Perictione's grand heritage to begin her son's story with an account of his mother's ancestry:

Plato was the son of Ariston and Perictione (or Potone); he was an Athenian, and she traced her family back to Solon. For he was the brother of Dropides, whose son was Critias, whose son was Callaischros, whose sons were the Critias who was one of the Thirty and Glaucon, whose children were Charmides and Perictione, from whom Plato the son of Ariston was born, in the sixth generation from Solon. And Solon traced his own ancestry back to Neleus and Poseidon. And they say that Plato's father too drew a link back to Codrus son of Melanthus, who according to Thrasyllus are said to be descended from Poseidon.[19]

This account, like many ancient genealogical accounts, emphasizes connections with the famous and divine but skips some details. Diogenes Laertius draws on both Plato and other sources to reconstruct a family tree, but scholars believe that some generations are missed out.[20] The important points, however, are both the link to the distant past and the presence of a divine ancestor as well as the mythical royalty of ancient Athens.

The Athenians told many stories about their origins that emphasized how they had always lived in Attica, the city and its surrounding area, and enjoyed the favour of the gods. These stories were illustrated on the city's public buildings and temples and retold in important public speeches such as the annual funeral oration celebrating those killed in war, and even appeared on the painted pottery that decorated Athenian homes and was used at the dinner parties attended by elite men. Plato disapproved of several of these stories, which indeed today deserve content warnings for sexual violence. First, there was the story of the birth of the king Erichthonius from the ground, which for the Athenians underscored their connection to the land itself, their status as 'earthborn' natives. But Erichthonius was the product of a divine sexual assault. Hephaestus, the limping god of craft production,

The Acropolis, Athens, as seen from the Hill of the Pnyx.

had attempted to rape the virgin goddess of knowledge, Athena, but, as she pushed him away, his sperm dripped from her dress to the ground and the child was born from the earth.[21] For Plato, the idea of gods committing such violence was impious.[22]

Second, the early Athenians were looking for a patron deity to protect the city and gathered together with their king, Cecrops – himself a strange creature, often depicted with a serpent's twisting body instead of legs – to choose one. Both Athena and Poseidon demonstrated their powers. Poseidon, god of the sea, made salt water spring from the rock of the Acropolis, the most sacred site in the city. Athena, however, made an olive tree appear in its unpromising rocky ground. The Athenians chose Athena as the deity who had given them the most useful gift, and they nurtured an olive tree in the shadow of her temple – there is still an olive tree on the Acropolis even now. In this case, Plato disapproved of the idea of gods in competition with each other. Strife was for humans, not the divine; the divine should never be in conflict.

The Athenians believed that their ancient kings played key roles in the development of the city and had fought in its defence. At the time that Plato was writing his works in the fourth century BCE, other scholars, known now as 'Atthidographers', were compiling the ancient stories into histories of the city from its foundation to the present day.[23] None of these works survives complete, but a substantial fragment from the work of non-Athenian Hellanicus (of the island of Lesbos) was quoted by another scholar in an ancient commentary on Plato's *Symposium*. Melanthus was a stranger king, an outsider given the role in thanks for his single-combat victory over a Boeotian hero, which saved the city.[24] His son Codrus also fought for the city: the Spartans had received an oracle that they would capture Athens as long as they did not kill its king; Codrus entered their camp in disguise, picked a fight with two Spartan warriors and was killed. Neleus, his younger son, went on to found the twelve Greek cities of Ionia, connecting them to Athens.

Many elite Athenians claimed connections such as these, which linked them to the gods through their ancestors. Those aristocratic families claiming a link to Poseidon reveal the structural class conflict of Athenian society, setting these ancient families apart from their fellow citizens, who nonetheless could claim equal political status under the city's democratic regime. While Athena was the city's patron, as its myths affirmed, Poseidon also had an important Athenian cult, with a shrine at Colonus just outside the city itself. Poseidon here is a god of horses and so was a particular patron of the wealthy families whose sons made up the city's elite cavalry. Aristophanes, as ever, skewers this division in his 424 BCE comedy about class and power in the democracy, *Knights*, in which the cavalry form the chorus. Plato's ancestry created a political identity for him that was already at odds with the city's democracy, and his wider family would go on to play significant roles in the

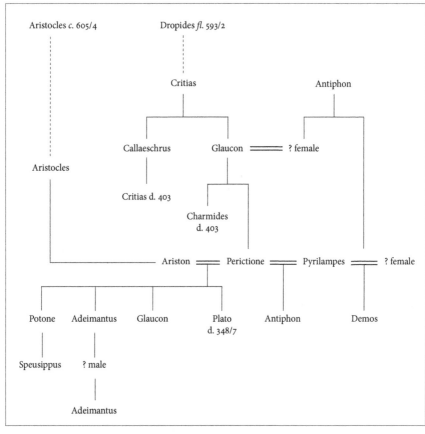

Plato's family tree.

civil conflict that tore the city apart during the period when Plato was studying with Socrates.

In his writings, Plato displays an ambivalent approach to stories of the distant past, dismissing their significance on the one hand and yet incorporating them into his work on the other. But it is significant that, when he offers a new set of Athenian myths to replace the familiar tales, he identifies them as transmitted through his own family, as told to one of his mother's ancestors, Dropides, by Solon himself. Dropides held the key political role of archon (literally 'ruler') in 593/2 and was a friend of and probably related to the great politician and poet Solon, whose reforms set Athens on the path to democracy in the early sixth century BCE.[25] These reforms addressed serious inequalities in the city between property-owning families and wage labourers, cancelling debts and outlawing the process through which indebted citizens could be enslaved by their debtors. This *seisachtheia* (shaking off of burdens) both set the city on the path to democracy and established the analogy between the political freedom of citizens and the status of not being enslaved.

Scholars in antiquity disliked the idea that Plato himself as a child would have heard the kind of stories that he himself had banned from his imaginary ideal city, Kallipolis. They reimagined his family background so as to place philosophical discussion at its heart. Some even depicted Perictione as a philosopher in her own right, aligned with the Pythagorean ideas so often linked by ancient commentators to the work of her son, thereby turning his philosophical heritage into his familial heritage.[26] Fragments (surviving extracts) from two works attributed to Perictione, *On the Harmony of Women* and *On Women*, discuss themes that appear in Plato's own work, reframed to fit the context of women's lives, as this excerpt shows:

> This is how, in my opinion, a woman is harmonious: if she has become full of wisdom and restraint. For such a woman will benefit not only her husband, but also her children, relatives, slaves, and her entire household, which holds her possessions and friends, both fellow citizens and foreigners.[27]

But the language of the first treatise suggests it was written in the third century BCE, long after Perictione herself lived, and that of the second seems even later.[28] What we know of the lives of elite Athenian women of this time suggests that it is unlikely that a woman could access philosophical education outside the home. Women from wealthy families spent their time at home, managing the household in the city and the country.[29] They did not take part in the dinner parties (*symposia*) at which their husbands and brothers might recite poetry and discuss politics and philosophy, or enjoy erotic performances from dancers and musicians. While poorer women might sell goods and produce at the market, such activities were inconceivable for the women of Plato's family. Athenian rules on citizenship, introduced by Pericles, limited citizen status to those who could prove that both parents were Athenian citizens, and this led to greater surveillance of elite women's activities.

Perictione's life, and that of her children, changed dramatically when Ariston died at a young age, while her sons were still children; the exact date is unknown but was between Plato's conception and 424/3. The widow and her children were returned to the protection of her family. Perictione was swiftly remarried to her paternal uncle Pyrilampes, son of Antiphon, in his fifties and perhaps thirty years her senior. This was typical of Athenian marriage practice, which in elite families was largely concerned with the preservation of family wealth. Women spent their whole lives under the legal guardianship of male relatives; first of their father, then their husband. If they were then widowed, they became the wards of any adult sons, or of their nearest male relative. A widow's guardian would arrange a new marriage for her, but if he was currently unmarried, he could also marry her himself. None of Perictione's sons was an adult who could become her guardian and the easiest solution for the family was to pair her up with an unmarried male relative. This was a second marriage for both Pyrilampes and Perictione and suggests that the family was unable to secure a marriage alliance with another family. Plato soon gained a half-brother, Antiphon.

Pyrilampes, now both Plato's stepfather and great-uncle, had an estate in the Attic countryside and Plato may well have spent some of his childhood there. After the years of the plague, and several years of fierce fighting across the Greek mainland, the Athenians had gained an advantage when their general Nicias defeated the Spartans at Pylos in 425 BCE and brought a group of their elite troops back to the city as hostages. A few years of relative peace followed – including, for a while, a complete cessation of fighting under a sworn armistice. This enabled citizens to spend time on their farms and estates, in a return to peacetime normality. Mentions of children's activities in Plato's work suggest time spent in the countryside, most likely at Pyrilampes' estate. Searching for an image to represent a futile search for elusive knowledge, Plato gives Socrates the simile 'like children chasing after crested larks'.[30] The image of the bird, startled from its nest on the ground and rising quickly into the air, as the children run behind it with outstretched hands, vividly conveys the fallibility of human inquiry and the impossibility of grasping knowledge.

Perhaps, at this time, Plato's mother and stepfather, and his older siblings, participated in many of the rituals of Athenian life. Plato's sister Potone was the kind of girl who might have been chosen to 'be a bear' for Artemis at her sanctuary in Brauron, or, as a member of an elite family, carry a basket in a procession for Athena, a highly coveted role for Athenian girls.[31] Perictione would have participated in other ceremonies, conducted by married Athenian women of citizen status. Her background exemplified the 'well-born ladies' whom Aristophanes depicted in his comedy *Thesmophoriazusae*, 'women celebrating the Thesmophoria'.[32] In this festival the wives of citizens took over a male-dominated civic space, camping where the Assembly met on the Pnyx to make offerings to the earth-mother goddess Demeter for the benefit of the growth of crops and the reproduction of the citizen body.

The myths underpinning many of these rituals were among those Perictione's son would question. Was it proper to think of gods behaving badly, squabbling and snatching women? Plato would later use the stories passed down within Perictione's family to explore this question and to offer some alternative stories in which gods and men behaved in a more exemplary fashion. His *Timaeus* features speeches by Socrates, Critias and Timaeus, a visiting philosopher from Locri in Magna Graecia, the Greek-speaking cities of southern Italy. Critias was a much-used name in Perictione's family, although there is much dispute as to whether the speaker in the *Timaeus* is intended to represent Perictione's cousin or her grandfather.[33] This Critias reports a story told to his father during the Apaturia, an autumn festival in which young men were inducted into citizenship, cutting their hair, and passed on in turn to him:

Listen, Socrates, to this story, totally weird but absolutely true, which Solon, the wisest of the Seven Sages, once told. Solon was a relative and friend of my great-grandfather Dropides, as he often used to say in his poems. Dropides told this to my grandfather Critias, as the old man recalled for us the many great ancient deeds of this city, which had become obscured by time and by the decline of humans...[34]

Critias goes on to tell the stories that Solon heard when he visited Egypt, after leaving Athens while his reforms, the foundation of the later democracy, bedded in. The priests there laughed at his idea that there was any ancient history for the Greeks – 'You Greeks are eternal children,' he mocked – and went on to tell a story of a version of Athens unknown to its present inhabitants.[35] The story unfolds to be that of the decadent city Atlantis, destroyed by the gods in a great flood which also washed away the green and fertile hills of the original version of Athens, leaving behind the barren rocky soil of the present day.

The seeds of Plato's complex and ambivalent relationship with Athens's democracy, and the ideology that supported it, lie in his family background. His mother's remarriage brought Plato closer to his maternal relatives, some of whom were deeply involved with the governance of the city, and others who would play leading roles in overturning the democratic constitution. The ageing Pyrilampes was, at his second marriage, a veteran of military and political service to the city and its democracy. He had been a friend of Pericles, under whose leadership the city had extended its power across the Greek world and grown wealthy not just on the exploitation of its silver mines but on tribute extracted from other Greek cities which had sought its protection from the Persians to the east. Pyrilampes had played a significant role in Athenian diplomacy while his friend led the city, making many journeys on its behalf to the court of the Great King in Persia.[36]

It was against the threat of a renewed Persian invasion of mainland Greece, and Persian interference in the Greek cities of the Aegean and Asia Minor, that the Delian League had originally been founded in 478. That had begun on Delos, a tiny island in the Cyclades sacred to the god Apollo. Financial contributions from members of the League were initially stored in treasuries in the god's sanctuary. But as Athens asserted its dominance over other members, in 454 the treasury was moved to Athens and into the sanctuary of Athena on the Acropolis.[37] It was during the period in which Pyrilampes had been most politically active that income from the League was used not just for military adventures but to fund the building programme that included the Parthenon, the great new temple to the patron goddess Athena, which still dominates the Acropolis. Pyrilampes' enthusiasm for the Athenian regime extended to giving his son from his first marriage, born around 440 at the time that Athens was being rebuilt, the name Demos ('People'), the first attested use of the word as an individual name.[38] His ally Pericles dominated politics because of his appeal to and support from the mass of poor citizens, even though he himself was a member of one of Athens's greatest families, the Alcmaeonids.[39]

Athenian politics, however, was almost defined by its volatility and the ease with which great generals and orators could fall from public favour and the people could clamour for revenge against those whom they had previously praised. Even Pericles had been fined and briefly pushed out of public life, some years before Plato's birth. While Pericles quickly returned to favour, others did not. As one of his close associates, Pyrilampes found himself on the sidelines.[40]

By the time the young Plato encountered him, Pyrilampes was past the age at which citizens were required to be actively involved in political office, and his friend and ally Pericles was dead. He was recovering from a serious battle wound acquired fighting for the city at Delium against the Boeotians in 424 – the same campaign in which Socrates distinguished himself for bravery as the defeated Athenians retreated. While Perictione could tell Plato stories from a glorious distant past, his stepfather had memories of more recent glories, of his political and military triumphs, but also of failure.

Plato's first exposure to Athenian democracy was from a man who had played a part in the city's imperial success and who had loyally fought for the city. Now he was sidelined at home, still carrying the physical traces of his service in his battle wounds and watching the Periclean project unravel. The historian Herodotus numbered among his aims in writing history documenting the rise and fall of cities that the great could be brought low and the insignificant could rise to greatness.[41] Pyrilampes could tell that story from his own experiences.

No trace of Pyrilampes' diplomatic achievements during Athens's brief imperial peak survives in the written record. The major successes of Athenian diplomacy in the Periclean period were attributed to the even wealthier Callias, the head of another leading family. He had proposed and negotiated treaties with the cities of Rhegium (a Greek city in the toe of Italy) and Leontini (eastern Sicily) as part of alliance-building in the immediate run-up to the Peloponnesian War, and possibly another truce with the Persians before that, though no secure, near-contemporary literary or epigraphic documentation has survived beyond an oblique reference in Herodotus' histories.[42] However, Pyrilampes had been a key participant in Athenian diplomatic missions to the court of Persia's Great King. Whatever their formal outcome in terms of treaties and decrees, he had been rewarded by the Great King with gifts of peafowl, at least one breeding pair, vivid living symbols of the power of the Achaemenid empire.

The exotic birds came to define Pyrilampes' career for the Athenians. Once a month he opened the doors of his home so that the public could view them; he had after all acquired them while on the city's business. However, there was no public access to the birds beyond that. Despite Pyrilampes' being so committed to democracy that he had named his son Demos, the presence of the birds, symbols of the despotic power of the Great King of Persia, raised suspicion among some Athenians that he had an undemocratic taste for luxury and perhaps a hankering to replace the democracy with tyranny.[43] And others were simply annoyed by the presence of these status symbols: 'I'm fed up with ambassadors boasting about their peacocks,' says one of Aristophanes' heroes, in a play performed in 425 BCE.[44]

The hidden presence and limited access to the spectacle of the birds appears to have run contrary to ideas of what was publicly acceptable behaviour for citizens in a democracy. The question of access to them appears to have ended up in the city's courts, after they had been inherited by Demos; a certain Erasistratos had brought legal proceedings to gain access to the birds and fragments of a speech from the case survive. Plutarch, writing centuries later but drawing on a wide range of sources, links the peacocks to corruption and licentiousness among Pericles' circle, alleging that Pyrilampes used the birds to reward Pericles' lovers, although he also draws on comic poets, suggesting that these stories might be part of contemporary political humour rather than a record of what happened.[45]

What is private and what is public would become a major pre-occupation of Plato's thought. The question of whether ordinary citizens should have access to the family's private estate to see the peacocks, and whether gifts received while serving the city belonged to the city or the individual, finds echoes in the *Republic*. There, Plato designed a society in which the ruling elite would have no private property.[46] His childhood experiences of moving from household to household, and the negative attention that the peacocks brought to his stepfather and stepbrother, might have influenced his developing views as he reached the age when he might study and socialize outside the family home.

By 413 the fabled peacocks had been inherited by Pyrilampes' son Demos and Perictione had been widowed again, barely ten years after her second marriage. This time, her eldest son Adeimantus was just old enough to become the head of the household and assume guardianship over both his mother and his siblings.

Plato's early childhood had been marked by repeated loss – of his father, then his stepfather. But that was in the wider context of the aftermath of the plague and the demands of war, which had left few Athenian families unaffected. The trauma was collective as well as individual. Plato would return to the years of his early life repeatedly in his writings, reimagining the intellectual life experienced by Demos and others in the generation before his own, a life no longer accessible after plague, defeat and impoverishment limited the opportunities for Athenians.

2

Education in a Divided City

E ducation marked a key divide in Athenian life, that between the sexes. While her brothers went out to school, Plato's sister Potone remained at home, learning the duties of domestic management as she was prepared for marriage. At the age when Plato was starting to attract admiring looks from older boys and men at the gymnasium, his sister was married, veiled when leaving home to attend to religious duties but otherwise largely confined within her husband's home. Uneducated women living in seclusion could hardly be equal partners with their older husbands, experiencing the life of the city to the full, and stimulated by intellectual conversation and political debate. Other norms eliminated citizen women from public space even further; it was barely proper for a married woman's name to be spoken in public.[1]

Plato began to follow his older brothers into the masculine spaces of the gymnasium and school in late childhood. His stepbrother Demos, perhaps fifteen years his senior, had already made his mark in the training grounds and groves in which teachers educated Athenians for citizen life. The teenage Demos had become a minor celebrity because of his physical beauty. "'Demos the son of Pyrilampes is handsome (*kalos*)" is scratched on the city's doorways,' observes a character in Aristophanes' *Wasps*, performed in 422.[2]

Demos had been in the final stages of his education in the 420s BCE, a decade during which fault lines in Athenian education had widened as new teachers offered new methods to equip the city's elite for successful participation in its democratic institutions, opening up a cultural divide. Aristophanes had begun to explore these issues in his comedy *Clouds*, performed in 423 to an audience of Athenian citizens at the City Dionysia, an annual festival at which tragic and comic playwrights competed for prizes.[3] Aristophanes took aim at a range of speakers, collapsing the ideas of several controversial philosophers and teachers into his depiction of an eccentric teacher whom he ominously named Socrates.

Aristophanes used the *agōn* (debate scene), which was a central feature of Athenian comedy, to set different forms of education against each other: the established schooling of Athenians in culture and sport against the new ideas about speaking and arguing

Kylix attributed to Douris, depicting scenes from the education of an Athenian youth, *c.* 500–450 BCE, red-figure ceramic.

that visiting teachers from across the Greek world, like Gorgias
of Leontini in Sicily and Protagoras of Abdera in Thrace, were
bringing to the city. He represented traditional education as the
'Stronger Argument' (*kreittōn logos*), who expresses a nostalgia for
a past kind of education focused on lessons in traditional music
and physical exercise. In turn the 'Weaker Argument' (*hēttōn
logos*) asserts the attractions of the methods of new teachers, the
power unleashed by finding flaws in opponents' arguments and
turning them back on themselves.[4] His presentation itself drew
on the rhetorical strategies of Protagoras, seen in texts such as the
Dissoi Logoi (Double Arguments), which took the Greek love of
structured opposition to a new level.[5]

In practice, the different kinds of education were encountered
in successive stages; a *grammatistēs*, teaching basic literacy skills
to younger boys just starting their education, might be more traditional in approach than a specialist rhetorician who worked with
older boys and young adults and incorporated new methods.
Aristophanes represented this as a conflict between generations,
between the traditions of older citizens and the newfangled ideas
of their sons. Plato, starting his education within a few years of
Aristophanes' play, would share his ambivalence towards the
new skills even as he began to demonstrate his own mastery of
language.

Athenian Schooling

By the early 410s Plato had reached the age when he might follow
his brothers to their lessons, accompanied by a *paidagōgos*, not a
teacher but a slave who 'led boys', escorting them between home,
school and the gymnasium. Boys from families like his began their
education outside the home at an older age, attending one teacher
for lessons in reading and writing, including the basics of how to
frame a speech or a letter, a second teacher for lessons in culture

Kylix attributed to the Akestorides Painter, depicting a schoolboy
practising the lyre, *c.* 460 BCE, red-figure ceramic.

and a third for physical training, the three planks of the traditional Athenian curriculum. Another famous youth, Alcibiades,
had studied these three skills, 'letters and to play the lyre and to
wrestle'.[6] Plato's later biographers saw the three skills of literacy,
music and sport as training the reason, spirit and appetite respec-
tively, and although that formulation is retrojected from Plato's
'tripartite soul' account of human psychology the structure might
have shaped Plato's own thought on education and character.[7]

Athenian boys needed reading and writing skills not just to
engage with their duties as citizens but to manage the business of
their family's homes and estates in and outside the city, which might
involve overseeing contracts and other legal business. Pyrilampes as
Plato's stepfather chose tutors and trainers for his stepsons, sending
them to a school run by the *grammatistēs* Dionysius.[8] Unlike in
Sparta, where boys attended classes organized by the city, with

an emphasis on physical training rather than academic subjects, fathers in Athens organized their sons' education themselves. Plato would later give some thought to how successfully they did this, coming to prefer the Spartan way.[9]

Entering this stage of his education took Plato into another world, a masculine and public space, the opposite of the private and feminine world of the internal spaces of his home. Most teaching took place in and around the gymnasia at the edges of the city, in fields and groves outside the city walls, close to water sources. The three main such spaces were the Academy to the northwest of the city, the Lyceum to the east and the Cynosarges to the southeast; they were not just spaces for individual exercise and conversation with friends and students but were used by the city for training hoplites and occasionally even cavalry practice. When first established by the Peisistratid tyrants over a century before, they had been spaces for the city's elite, but the democracy had invested in improvements and opened them to all male citizens.[10]

When boys walked from their homes in the city to the Academy for their lessons, they encountered a series of monuments which communicated important stories about being an Athenian. Leaving the Agora by the processional route, the Sacred Way, travellers passed through the Cerameicus ('place of pottery'), a densely inhabited part of the city, full of potters' workshops, workers' homes and entertainment venues, nestled against the city's walls. They passed through the city's Dipylon gate, where the citizens assembled each summer for the festival of the Panathenaea, celebrating Athens's patron goddess on her birthday with a procession up to her great temple on the Acropolis, with its great frieze depicting this ritual. Another nearby gate led to the sanctuary of Demeter at Eleusis and was used by the procession of initiates walking there, although at the time when Plato became of age to join them the route was closed due to the Spartan occupation of parts of Attica.

Outside the city walls the 'broad road' was lined with memorials and tombs to citizens, a public space in which the Athenians came together to hear the annual funeral oration honouring those who had died in battle for the city in the preceding year.[11] The boys could read the names of the war dead from the inscribed monuments set up in commemoration. Athenians might see the names of their own fathers, brothers, relatives and neighbours, listed by their tribes – the artificial groups created by the reformer Cleisthenes to cement loyalty to the city as a whole rather than to village or family – rather than identified by their fathers' names.[12] These collective monuments to the citizens who had died in the service of their city testified to the city's democratic ethos and reminded Athenian viewers of the rewards of engaged citizenship. There were also memorials to some of the city's greatest generals; that to Pericles, who had died in the plague, the most recent. The route towards the training ground gave boys a lesson in Athenian masculinity and the service that would be expected of them as citizens and soldiers.

The entrance to the Academy was dominated by a shrine to Eros, dedicated by Charmus, a relative of the Peisistratid tyrants of the sixth century, who had transformed the grove, building a wall around its central area. If you stopped to look carefully, you could read the dedicatory inscription:

Eros full of tricks, Charmus set up this altar for you,
At the shaded boundaries of the gymnasium.[13]

The Academy was named after the Athenian hero Academus, whose shrine was at its original heart.[14] The story was that Athens's ageing king Theseus had imperilled the city by abducting the young Spartan princess Helen while she was dancing in a sanctuary of Artemis. Her father, Tyndareus, sent an army to Attica to retrieve her, led by her twin brothers Castor and Pollux. This army would have destroyed the city in its pursuit of her, just as Troy was later destroyed by the Greeks under Agamemnon, but Academus revealed where Helen was being kept, enabled her return and so prevented all-out war between the Athenians and Spartans.[15]

The Academy site was full of reminders of Athenian identity. Its extensive gardens contained an olive grove, whose trees, the 'child-nurturing gleaming-grey olive', as Sophocles had described them, had been grown from cuttings from Athena's sacred olive tree on the Acropolis – descended from a gift to the city from the goddess herself. This grove now provided the olive oil that filled the painted vases given as prizes in the city's Panathenaic games.[16] Young men training nearby might gain inspiration and hope to win one of the precious vases.

Other parts of the grounds had been planted only a few decades previously, at the expense of the politician Cimon, along with an aqueduct to bring water from the nearby river Cephissus.[17] Elsewhere in the grounds were altars to Athena herself, Hermes, Artemis and other gods; before Cimon's improvements turned it into a state training ground, the Academy had been a primarily religious space.

Physical education was an important part of schooling men who would need to fight for their city. Boys met their trainers at the gymnasium grounds to learn how to run, throw the discus or javelin and wrestle. Sports offered a way for young men to earn honour for themselves and their cities by participating in athletic contests which were part of many religious festivals. The most prestigious Panhellenic festivals, such as the festival of Zeus at Olympia, the original Olympic Games, were attended by competitors from across the Greek-speaking world, and simply offered glory and a wreath, although Athenian victors were traditionally given a cash prize and free meals by their city.[18]

As a young man Plato earned a reputation for his prowess in wrestling – an important individual contest at such festival games

– working with the coach Ariston of Argos. Aristotle's student Dicaearchus reported that Plato once competed as a wrestler at the Isthmian Games, which were held in a sanctuary of Poseidon near to Corinth and were included in the prestigious circuit of the top four festivals.[19] As these games were thought to have been founded by Athens's king Theseus, they were particularly attractive to Athenian competitors. Although Athens remained at war, the regular circuit of Panhellenic games continued with Athenians competing. Alcibiades, the glamorous ward of Pericles, had sponsored multiple chariot-racing teams at Olympia – another way a wealthy young man might participate in such events.[20]

There is no doubt about wrestling's importance to Plato. Later in life, he would describe participants in more intellectual contests and arguments as tripping each other up and being unable to get off the floor, as if they were taking part in wrestling bouts. He imagined a pair of coaches in a related discipline, the brutal all-in *pankration*, reinventing themselves as teachers of rhetoric, now tripping up and overthrowing their opponents with arguments.[21]

The homosocial space of the gymnasium, including its practice arena and its changing rooms, was very much an erotic space, a key site for pederastic relationships. *Paederastia* was another, less formal, practice by which young Athenian boys learnt to participate in the social spaces of the city and develop their own networks of friends beyond their immediate family. The young Plato would have been admired by older boys and men, and eventually have accepted the advances of an *erastēs* or 'lover', although the biographical sources only name those whom an older Plato pursued in turn.[22] The culture of pederasty drove individual and collective homoerotic fascination with the young and athletic male body, permeating the spaces in which men exercised together and also those in which they socialized. A good-looking boy like Demos might enjoy a brief period of celebrity in his teenage years and be made famous for being *kalos*; as well as the graffiti Aristophanes mentioned, an adolescent boy's brief moment of fame might be recorded with an inscription on a painted vase or cup to be used at a drinking party.

The Academy's prominent shrine to Eros stood over and licensed erotic pursuit. Daniela Marchiandi has argued that one

Amphora by Andokides, depicting two pairs of wrestlers in training while a trainer to the left watches them, *c.* 525 BCE, red-figure ceramic.

Kylix attributed to Douris, depicting an older man propositioning a younger man, and with the caption *Ho pais kalos* ('The boy is handsome'), c. 480–470 BCE, red-figure ceramic.

fragmentary stone relief panel, probably a metope from the frieze of a building, depicts a man holding a small animal, either a deer or a hare, suggestive of hunting and the exchange of gifts from older man to younger as part of a courtship ritual.[23] Such scenes were familiar from the drinking cups used at symposia.

Aristophanes wove into his depiction of education the homoeroticism that came to the fore as youths stripped to exercise. His Stronger Argument, representing traditional education, reminisces about the modesty of boys in the old days, when it was ensured that their genitalia remained unseen, and recollects the imprint that a youthful bottom might make in the sand of the training ground.[24] Pubescent youths were socially sanctioned objects of desire – older married men still sighed after beautiful boys, who were blooming in the present moment. Those in their twenties, not yet married, might form a close attachment with such a teenager; some older men too, although others frowned on such friendships. Perhaps Plato felt all eyes turn to him as he and his opponent wrestled in the sand; when he came back to the changing room after a wrestling bout, he would anoint himself with oil, then scrape his skin clean. The erotic tone of Plato's dialogues set in gym changing rooms shows his familiarity with the experience of the male gaze.

Music and Culture

The other important aspect of a traditional education was music (*mousikē*), which could denote any kind of poetic or musical performance. The ability to play and perform in both private and public settings was a social asset; citizens performed in the dramatic festivals, and songs sung at symposia reminded them of the deeds of their predecessors. Aristophanes' Stronger Argument describes the place of music in the traditional curriculum:

> Very well then, I will tell you about how old-style education was arranged, back when I was blossoming while speaking words of justice, and decent moderation (*sôphrosunê*) was valued. First of all, the voice of a boy should not be heard at all, no muttering, then boys from the same district gathered together and walked in an orderly group to their music teacher, without cloaks, even if it was snowing flakes as thick as barley meal ... he taught them to know a song by heart, and not to keep their thighs together – songs like 'Clever Athena the sacker of cities' and 'A sound heard from far away', tuned to the mode their fathers had passed down.[25]

But these styles of education and music were already under challenge when Aristophanes' play was staged. The Stronger

Argument goes on to recall the days when the old style predominated, and boys were beaten for introducing new forms of music, different modes (scales to which the strings of a lyre might be tuned) or tunings that were discordant, according to the traditional styles. That moment had already arrived in the 420s, when Aristophanes was writing; musical innovator Damon of Oe, a friend of Pericles, had taught many sons of influential families.[26] Plato's own teachers had been taught by Damon's student Dracon as the new music of such dramatists as the tragedian Euripides took hold.

Plato relished his own cultural education, but his tastes remained traditional. He threw himself into learning the various genres of poetry that were proper to different social and religious occasions, as entertainment at private parties and in the city's festivals. He saw himself becoming a prize-winning poet or playwright, garlanded for his contributions to the city's dramatic festivals. Plato's own first compositional efforts were dithyrambs, marking a devotion to Dionysus as well as his own poetic ambition – and also a taste for the most ancient forms of culture.[27] Dithyrambs predated tragedy as a verse form; while there was something distinctly old-fashioned about them, other creators were producing innovative versions. Plato went on to write lyric and tragic verse; the latter was the verse form most celebrated in the city. Its dramatic festivals brought citizens together to experience performances of stories from the past that commented obliquely or directly on the present.

Athens's playwrights delivered political critique, reflecting current events and arguments by retelling old stories and connecting them to current events and ideas. While it had been decades since playwrights had depicted recent history directly, as Aeschylus had done in 472 in his *Persians*, Euripides had been staging plays that retold Athenian patriotic myth – the stories of the great deeds of past Athenians and their rulers. In his *Suppliant Women*, performed in 423 shortly after the city's defeat at Delium, he presented the great king Theseus as an exemplary model of a democratic citizen, showing individual heroism in helping the people of Athenian ally Argos retrieve their dead from the battlefield after their defeat by Thebes, but always responsive to the collective decision-making of the people.[28]

Now Euripides' plays were questioning military power and highlighting the plight of the defeated, such as his *Trojan Women*. Plato was probably too young to have seen this play, produced in 415 at the City Dionysia. The play showed the plight of victims of war through the story of the royal women of Troy as they are enslaved and allotted to their Greek captors after the fall of their city. The production schedule makes it unlikely that it was a comment on a specific episode of that year – Athens' punishment of the islanders of Melos after their city defied attempts to bring it under their control – and it could be a critique of Athens' rivals. The consequences of defeat were always relevant to audiences in ancient cities.[29] Plato might have seen Euripides' *Ion*, performed two or three years later, which revealed Ion, another Athenian prince and the founder of the Ionian cities of Asia Minor, Athens's key allies in the Aegean sphere, to be the son of the god Apollo.

Plato bridled at the way dramatists were reshaping traditional stories for political purposes, using gods and heroes for political propaganda. He was even more annoyed by the 'new' music they used for choruses and – an increasingly prominent feature – for solo songs performed by actors in character, such as Hecuba's laments in the *Trojan Women*. Euripides' taste for musical novelty had brought him plenty of criticism at the time of performance.[30] In his final work, the *Laws*, Plato looked back to the changes in music in the Athens of his youth.[31] The sound of new music was, he concluded, emblematic of a cultural decline associated with the enthusiasm for fast-paced change fostered by the democracy. The desire for novelty led to a mixing of genres and musical styles, an abandonment of orderly harmonies. Plato's elderly 'Athenian

Stranger' voices these views and lists different kinds of song that should be distinguished; hymns, the paean, a song of praise to Apollo, and the dithyramb, with lyrics about the birth of Dionysus, the god of wine, fertility, metamorphosis and theatre. In this imaginary version of ancient Athens, there was no mixing of genres, no playing a paean in a musical mode appropriate to the dithyramb. Everyone else sat in silence under the threat of a beating, repeating a promise made by Aristophanes' Stronger Argument.[32] What was happening now was that the traditional genres and modes were being mixed up:

> Running wild, allowing pleasure to get too strong a hold on them, they made melodies for the kithara sound like songs for the reed pipe, introducing every style into every other style. Without realizing it, in their folly they were telling lies about music and poetry, saying that there was absolutely no standard of correctness in music and poetry, that the most correct criterion was the pleasure of the person who enjoyed it – however good or bad that person might be. By writing compositions of this kind, and adding words of the same kind, they filled the people at large with contempt for the rules of music, and the effrontery to set themselves up as judges. As a result, audiences who had been voiceless found a voice, as if they knew, in music and poetry, what was fine and what was not. In this way, aristocracy, in music and poetry, was replaced by a kind of depraved theatrocracy.[33]

It wasn't that Plato was an uncritical fan of traditional performance styles. He also experienced the grand performances of rhapsodes, the professional reciters of Homeric epic. Their mannered performances, with their ornate costumes, left him unmoved, as the ironic comments he gives to Socrates in conversation with the rhapsode Ion imply.[34] And they raised further questions – perhaps such traditional forms of education as learning Homeric epic were not quite sufficient for the needs of the present day. Understanding the strategies of Agamemnon, leader of the Greek forces of Troy, was not a firm basis for an Athenian general facing a different kind of war, in a much more complex and fluid political situation, Socrates suggests.

A New Curriculum, New Crisis

Athenians needed to be able to persuade their fellow citizens in the Assembly or the law courts, and to argue convincingly against their rivals. Someone able to deploy the new techniques in presentation and argument might be more likely to win over rivals and attract support from a broader mass of citizens.[35] Education became an arms race to ensure that a young man had the tools to compete and win on the speaker's platform on the Pnyx or in the law courts of the Agora. The traditional physical and cultural skills were no longer enough; you needed to be able to persuade rich and poor citizens alike to support your agenda or support your version of a legal case. Athenian engagement with the intellectual development of the wider Greek world was motivated by potential practical benefits to citizens in their own activities. Rhetoric now formed the final part of a citizen's education, even though some remained suspicious of what they saw as tricks with language. The new teachers became known as sophists, literally 'purveyors of wisdom', a word that was beginning to acquire negative connotations. As mentioned in the earlier discussion of his *Clouds*, Aristophanes parodied the methods of these new teachers as the 'Weaker Argument': 'I have been called the "Weaker Argument" among the philosophers for this reason, for I was the first to think up ways of speaking in opposition to both laws and lawsuits, which is worth more than 10,000 staters, choosing the worse causes and still winning.'[36] The comedian satirized the claim some teachers made, that they could make a weaker argument *appear* stronger and thus win debates from an apparently losing position. Those adopting such arguments were confident of their intellectual superiority, as Aristophanes' personified argument demonstrates. Not all responses to the new teaching were positive, however. Aristophanes' parodies suggest both a sceptical and an opportunistic response from Athenians who would grab the chance to win a dispute while despising the teachers who enabled them to do it.

The Athenians had already shown their indifference to innovative thought, hounding the philosopher Anaxagoras of Clazomenae out of the city for his investigations into the natural forces

Kylix attributed to the Euaion Painter, depicting a youth holding out a kylix to be filled by an older man; both are wearing fillets as if attending a sacrifice, *c.* 460–440 BCE, red-figure ceramic.

underlying the cosmos. The economic prosperity of imperial Athens under Pericles and its need to educate its leaders naturally attracted philosophers and teachers to the city; they received an uncertain welcome. Anaxagoras had arrived in Athens in the 450s, but it is not clear how long he stayed before leaving. Whether his departure was under a formal decree of exile or simply through a good sense of self-preservation is unclear, but the episode suggests that fifth-century Athens was not a hospitable place for independent and innovative thought.[37] When Aristophanes reached for outlandish ideas to mock in the *Clouds*, Anaxagoras' model of a non-anthropomorphic Mind as a causal principle in the cosmos was an obvious choice for amusing an audience. That Aristophanes attached these ideas to a quite different Athenian eccentric, Socrates, would have significant consequences.[38]

Those later labelled sophists were also serious contributors to this intellectual scene. Protagoras too was not just the proponent of catchy ideas about making speeches; his arguments resonate to the present day, although the Athenians were most interested in the possibility that he could teach them to manipulate language and so influence decisively their speech-based political and judicial systems. Plato later focused on the key claim that opened Protagoras' book *On the Truth*: 'Of all things the measure is man: of those that are, that they are; and of those that are not, that they are not.'[39] Did human knowledge reflect an absolute set of values running through the cosmos, or was all such knowledge inherently perspectival? This claim at the core of Protagoras' thought remains controversial now – does it simply acknowledge pluralism, or open the doors to relativism? Plato encountered these ideas through his education, although his most detailed written account of them is in the *Theaetetus*, a work of his maturity.[40]

Although Plato had not himself had the chance to study with Protagoras, Demos was old enough to have had the opportunity at least to hear him speak, and perhaps contributed to Plato's portrait in his *Protagoras* of a 'figure of considerable intellectual complexity' whom Malcolm Schofield observes is sketched with 'a free hand'.[41] But the biographical tradition shows that Protagoras became unwelcome in Athens; his overt agnosticism in his *On Gods* was offensive to conventional thinking.[42] His thought on language was useful – Protagoras was recognized as the first person to categorize and systematize the different tenses. Aristophanes with his own love of language parodied this too, mocking the concern with grammatical gender.[43] But the problematic relationship between language and reality, between words and the world, would eventually develop into a major interest of Plato's.

Another visiting teacher was Gorgias, from Leontini in eastern Sicily, who first came to Athens in 427 as an ambassador for his city, pleading for Athens's help in the endless warring between the wealthy but politically unstable Greek settlements on the island.[44] Cities found it useful to send good public speakers on such missions; Gorgias was already famous for his skill in rhetoric, an art in which Sicilian teachers were pre-eminent. When he arrived at Athens, he addressed the Assembly, dazzling his audience with his use of language – the rhyme and rhythm of his prose, the balanced clauses, the exotic vocabulary. The Athenians also flocked to his paid lectures, which featured controversial and contrarian takes on familiar stories: Helen of Troy was an innocent victim, Palamedes the inventor of writing was not a traitor to the Greeks.[45] He demonstrated that the weaker argument could be made stronger through both reasoning and style, and that a skilled practitioner could have fun while arguing – the final word of his speech in praise of Helen admitted that the work was a 'plaything'.[46] Just like Protagoras, Gorgias was a serious intellectual who engaged with new ideas and theories, yet his role in Athens as a teacher of rhetoric has pushed aside that more serious aspect of his work, as perhaps did his enjoyment of splendid costume for his mannered performances of his display speeches. Perhaps the story that he dedicated a gold statue of himself at Delphi reflects a critical response, an accusation of vanity.[47]

Plato later imagined a conversation between Socrates and Gorgias in which the latter aimed to show not only that rhetoric was a craft in its own right, but that it could displace practitioners of other crafts. A doctor can advise a treatment, but only the rhetorician can persuade the patient to undergo it:

> In competition with any other skilled practitioner you like, the rhetorician would be better than any of them in getting people to choose him, since there is no subject on which the rhetorician would not speak more persuasively before a large crowd, than any skilled practitioner you care to name.[48]

The rhetorician could, in this scenario, displace all other forms of expertise; Plato came to see this as dangerous and corrosive to community and well-being. His response to the threat of rhetoric developed into his own claims about the role of knowledge within the organization and leadership of communities. The power of the philosopher kings he imagined in the *Republic* depends on intrinsic knowledge rather than the manipulation of language.

However, the role of language and manipulation of demotic pseudo-knowledge in Athenian democratic decision-making was also exposed by the events of 415. The young Alcibiades had nearly come to grief on one of his first campaigns, the disaster at Delium in 424, in which Pyrilampes had been injured. He had gone on to be elected a general in 420 when he was barely thirty years old and so only just qualified by age. Yet there was less military action to lead after Nicias together with a Spartan king negotiated a pause in the fighting and an alliance treaty. Typical of Athenian action in this period was a campaign in 416/5 against the tiny Cycladic island of Melos, whose citizens regarded themselves as Spartan colonists and who refused to submit to Athenian authority. Thucydides imagined a debate between the Athenian generals and the oligarchic rulers of the defeated islanders in which the Athenians displayed arrogance and contempt as they informed them that 'the possibilities are defined by what the strong do and the weak accept.'[49]

Not long afterwards, the young and wealthy Alcibiades proposed to the Athenians that they send an expeditionary force in response to a request for help from allies in Sicily, although some suspected he had grander motives, perhaps even an attack on wealthy Carthage on the African coast. He deployed his rhetorical skill to persuade his fellow citizens to fund the scheme and to participate in it.[50] While Nicias pleaded for caution and made clear the vast cost of the proposed expedition, Alcibiades urged boldness and talked about the potential upside of the venture. He played on his background and his recent successes with his chariot teams at Olympia. Plato was still too young to attend the Assembly and hear these debates, but as nobody in Athens was talking about anything else, from the gymnasia to the dining room at home, he would have heard about the debates. While the Athenian pederastic system assumed that the older man pursued the younger, and gave little thought to the emotions of the younger party, Athenians of all ages succumbed to a national crush on Alcibiades, whose wealth, ancestry and good looks were unparalleled and who now promised to lead the city's forces to great glory.[51] Only Socrates, it seemed, was able to resist, at least in Plato's later retelling of Alcibiades' actions.[52]

But even private events could cause public disturbance. As the Athenians prepared to send off the expedition to Sicily, they woke one morning to find that the stone pillar-statues, the herms, which protected the entrances to their homes, had been vandalized overnight: as well as damage to their faces, many were now missing their most significant ritual attribute, the erect phallus with which the statues warded off bad luck.[53] It soon became clear that the damage had been caused by a group of wealthy youths, members of a drinking club.[54] A second scandal was uncovered as the first was being investigated: a witness testified in an Assembly hearing that a related group of privileged young men had mocked the rituals of the cult of Demeter at Eleusis, the sacred Mysteries, by performing a version of them at a private symposium (drinking party), held at the house of Charmides, Plato's uncle.[55] For even ordinary Athenians, being initiated into the Mysteries was a marker of Athenian identity and pride that the goddess Demeter had revealed the benefits of agriculture to them before others. Even worse, this testimony came from a slave, and the participants had committed their impiety in front of slaves who had not been initiated into the cult's secrets.[56]

The elation of Alcibiades' victory in the Assembly and excitement about the expedition turned to suspicion and doubt. Athens's elite faced the prospect of their family business being dragged through the courts as their younger members stood trial, and also the possibility of exile and heavy fines. The fleet sailed anyway, and many of the accused fled the city.

Encountering Socrates

Somewhere in or towards the centre of these doubts was Socrates, long the focus of comic playwrights' critique of new trends in education, the head of the fictional school of Aristophanes' *Clouds*. He had attracted a following of elite young men, while at the same time developing a reputation for annoying his fellow citizens with endless unsettling questions. But he was also another veteran of the Athenian army's retreat from Delium in 424, along with Alcibiades and Pyrilampes. Socrates, street philosopher and amateur educator, would come to play perhaps an even greater paternal role in Plato's life than either Pyrilampes or his birth father Ariston. Plato's encounter with Socrates would be a defining moment in his life, sending it in quite a different direction from that of his brothers. It came at the point at which a youth from a well-connected family might take lessons from specialists in political and military skills, in preparation for launching into public life. Plato may well have studied with such teachers, but it was Socrates' influence which prevailed.

Plato would present Socrates' conversations as resembling neither of the styles of teaching favoured by Aristophanes' two arguments, or indeed that of the *phrontistērion* (thinking place), the school where the *Clouds* depicted Socrates teaching his strange collection of acolytes. The actual Socrates was not really a teacher, emphatically not a professional teacher for pay, but he had been hanging around the places young men like Plato were to be found for many years and conversing with them. He was well known to the city's youth; many of those who would be caught up in the political scandals of the next few years were among his followers.

Unlike the sophists, focused on training young men for conventional success, and in distinct rejection of the ideas of philosophers from Ionia and Italy who asked questions about the nature of the universe and the things it contained, Socrates had started to investigate questions about how to live within a community. He wanted to understand what went beyond the conventional social and religious pieties to really count as human excellence. Rather than expound doctrines or impress with rhetorical flourishes, he asked questions that challenged his discussants to examine the difficulties and inconsistencies in their own beliefs and ideas, and those they had accepted without questioning from their teachers and parents.

Quite how and when Plato himself first came into contact with Socrates remains unknown. The biographical tradition asserts that their meeting happened when Plato was twenty, so, depending on his birth date, somewhere between 408 and 405, around the age at which Plato's education progressed from that of a typical elite

Athenian to that of a developing intellectual. However, it is much more likely that they had met many years earlier, given Socrates' public presence and their overlapping social circles.

Plato must have first heard reports from family members about this unconventional teacher even before the events of 415. Adeimantus and Glaucon or even the older Demos would have had plenty to report about this Socrates who engaged boys in exciting arguments and overturned their preconceptions, showing the gaps between what they had been taught by their schoolteachers and the more advanced teaching provided by the sophists. Socrates was well known to Athenian youths of Demos' generation, if not to their fathers. Plato depicts Socrates' renown among the young – even while he remained unknown to older men – in his dialogue on courage, the *Laches*, set in the aftermath of Delium. When Lysimachus and Melesias, two Athenian fathers, were trying to find the right teachers for their sons, they asked the successful generals Laches and Nicias for their help. Laches expressed astonishment that Socrates had not been included in the invitation, as Socrates and Lysimachus belonged to the same deme and so should have been well known to each other. Forced to think about it, Lysimachus remembered that he had been good friends with Socrates' father Sophroniscus, although he did not know the next generation so well:

A sort of memory is coming into my mind now when I hear these people speaking; for the lads here have often spoken to each other at home, and they've mentioned Socrates and praised him to the skies. But I never thought to ask whether he was the son of Sophroniscus. But, tell me, boys, is this the Socrates you mentioned then?[57]

The boys confirmed that indeed it was. Socrates was well known and much admired among their circles. It was the men of their fathers' generation who were suspicious of the eccentric educator. But Plato, by his late teens, had lost both his father and stepfather. His guardian, for the few remaining years from around 413 until he came of age at eighteen, was his older brother Adeimantus, and Adeimantus was of the generation who knew and admired Socrates. Like Lysimachus' son and his friends, Plato's brothers must have talked about him at home. Their interconnecting networks make it implausible that Plato's own first encounter with Socrates came only when he was a young adult.[58]

Most likely it was at one of the city's gymnasia, talking to a crowd of youths, perhaps including his older brothers, that Plato first encountered Socrates. In his own writing, Plato depicts Socrates talking to youths just starting to venture out to the gymnasia for training, accompanied by slaves to keep them out of trouble and take them home safely again. His *Lysis* imagines such a scene: Socrates is persuaded by a young man, Hippothales, to divert from his walk outside the northern part of the city walls, between the Academy and the Lyceum, and to visit a new gym, where, it turns out, his friend Mikkos is teaching.[59] Hippothales is pursuing a youth called Lysis and Socrates quickly works out that he needs to demonstrate to Hippothales how to pursue the younger boy. Socrates engages first Lysis and then his friend Menexenus in a discussion about friendship, often looking past his young interlocutors to the listening Hippothales as he does so. Perhaps Plato first heard Socrates in a setting like this, long before he made a conscious choice to associate with him. The Socrates of the *Lysis* is kindly if teasing towards his young interlocutors and lets their enslaved minders take them home at the end of the discussion.

Plato later depicted other members of his family among the young men with whom Socrates held intense discussions about ethical and philosophical matters, often in the changing rooms of the gymnasia. He imagined how Socrates might have conversed with his uncle Charmides when the latter was a handsome youth, easily labelled as *kalos*, venturing out into the semi-public world of the gymnasium in the company of his guardian Critias, his older cousin.[60] He imagined a time a few years before his own birth, on another occasion when Socrates had been fighting for Athens. This campaign, in 432 BCE, took Athens's forces north to the Chalkidike peninsula, in an attempt to persuade the citizens of Potidaea, originally a colony of Sparta's ally Corinth, to pay its dues to the Delian League. Athens's actions were a significant factor in precipitating the start of the wider Peloponnesian War, in which Corinth was at times as involved as Sparta.[61] Plato later imagined Socrates, on his return to Athens in 430, visiting the wrestling gym run by Taureas to catch up with his friends and swaps news from the camp for news about the upcoming generation – who is a promising student and who is becoming a beauty?

The answer surprises him. Critias explains that the most promising youth in all respects is his young cousin Charmides, who has reached the critical age in Socrates' absence. Charmides has been complaining of headaches – perhaps Socrates might like to speak to him under the ruse of offering him some remedies? Plato imagines the moment when Charmides and the other youths return from training and enter the changing room, and the older men respond – including Socrates:

> So he arrived, and caused much laughter; for each of us sitting there shoved his neighbour in excitement, so that he might sit next to him, so that the man sitting at one end was made to stand up, and we threw the other off sideways. But he came and sat between me and Critias, and then, my friend, I began to feel unsure of myself, and my earlier brashness, which had made me feel I could converse with him easily, was knocked back. Then, after Critias explained that I was the one who knew the remedy, he gave me a look with his eyes impossible to describe, and everyone in the

gym surged around us in a circle. And at that moment I got a glimpse inside his cloak, and I started to burn up and was no longer quite myself. I thought that in matters of love Cydias was the most wise, who said in giving advice to someone else, when speaking about a handsome boy, 'be careful, if you are a fawn, when approaching a lion, in case you are seized as a serving of flesh for him'. For it seemed as though I had been captured by a creature of that sort.[62]

Given the explicit dramatic date of this dialogue, Charmides must be a teenager, a little older than Lysis and Menexenus but still under eighteen and in need of a guardian. Plato, writing some decades later, seems to have been thinking of his own experiences, both those of a youth attracting admiring glances and those of an older man gazing at boys' bodies. It is tempting to treat the dialogue as autobiographical.

Diogenes Laertius presents the first encounter of Socrates and Plato in rather mystical terms, with Socrates recognizing in Plato the fulfilment of a prophetic dream:

There is a story that Socrates had a dream about a young cygnet sitting in his lap, which suddenly sprouted feathers and flew away, singing a sweet song. On the next day, Plato was introduced to him as a pupil, and he said that this youth was the bird.[63]

This story is unlikely to be true, although it was much elaborated in later biographies. Its function is to connect Plato with Apollo, to whom the swan was sacred.[64] Another version reports Plato's response to his initial encounter with Socrates. The young Plato had been writing poetry and was aiming to complete a tragedy and to compete as a playwright, but after he heard Socrates speaking, he destroyed his poems.[65]

A story told by Plato's Athenian near-contemporary Xenophon, in his own recollections of Socrates, offers another possibility.[66] Xenophon depicts the moment when a young Athenian, Euthydemus, began to speak with Socrates.[67] Euthydemus was obsessed with learning, but was studying by collecting and reading the books (papyrus rolls) of famous poets and teachers. The shy youth heard Socrates' discussions with other young men as he hovered in a saddler's shop at the edge of Athens's marketplace, too young to enter it and conduct his own business, but eager to be involved. Eventually, Socrates lured him into a discussion on how to gain the skills needed to prosper in a political career and poor Euthydemus was rather bruised by the experience, any sense that he knew anything about anything evaporating under Socrates' questioning. Xenophon's Euthydemus may not be Plato – their interests do not exactly coincide – but his and Plato's initial conversations with Socrates may have taken a similar form, whether they took place at the saddler's or at the gym.

Xenophon goes on to show Socrates warmly encouraging his new student in more positive conversation; he insists that the destructive questioning, which Plato formalized as the elenchus ('refutation'), was only the opening stage of a Socratic education. Once he and students were familiar with each other, Socrates' lessons were based on encouragement, a format Plato also depicted in his *Euthydemus*, named after a quite different holder of that name.

Plato's new teacher was not an exotic visitor to the city like Gorgias or Protagoras. But Socrates was not born into the Athenian elite, either; both Plato and Xenophon present him as less wealthy than the young men who followed him, although the biographical tradition links him to elite families by marriage, on the assumption that the name of his wife Xanthippe ('blonde horse') denotes an aristocratic background.[68] His friend and fellow demesman Crito was certainly among Athens's wealthy; Xenophon compares Socrates' property, worth five minae, with that of Critobulus,

Crito's son, which is worth more than five hundred minae.[69] Serving as a hoplite, as Socrates did, required a level of financial resource to pay for armour and weapons, and the costs of owning an enslaved male person for assistance on campaign. Socrates' father Sophroniscus had had his son follow his trade as a stone-mason, but it is far from clear if Socrates still practised this craft as he devoted himself to his personal mission – and unlike the visiting sophists, refused to be paid for teaching. Plato presented Socrates analogizing his own work to that of his mother's mid-wifery, but there is no firm evidence that she practised this work, often undertaken by women who had survived their own childbearing years.[70]

The key to Socrates' project was the search for self-knowledge. Socrates saw himself as embodying the Delphic maxim 'Know yourself'; in his case, the only certain knowledge he could claim was his own ignorance.[71] His rounds of questioning took state-ments offered by others as their starting point and found out their weaknesses without Socrates' contributing any content to the dis-cussion. Life for a human being was not worth living without such questioning, he said.[72] And only ignorance led people to do wrong; with secure knowledge informing their decisions, no one could choose or even want to do anything other than what is right.

The conversations that Plato depicted in his dialogues reflect the consequent search for self-understanding. After Charmides has been drawn into discussion in the dialogue that bears his name, the philosophical business of the dialogue begins – the pursuit of a definition of a character virtue. Everyone had praised the youth for the way his character exemplified the virtue of *sōphrosunē*, a com-bination of moderation and restraint, that does not map precisely to a single English term but is often translated as 'temperance'. But what is *sōphrosunē*? Socrates begins by eliciting a definition from his interlocutor, then exposing contradictions within it through questioning. As the interlocutor agrees to Socrates' points, their

own position is gradually chipped away, their certainty under-
mined, until they have to concede that the confident definition
they gave earlier does not work. Plato depicts Socrates searching for and failing to find definitions for qualities including piety
(*Euthyphro*), courage (*Laches*), temperance (*Charmides*), friendship (*Lysis*), virtue itself as a whole (*Meno*) and, perhaps the most
important virtue of all, justice (*Republic*). When Plato came to
write these dialogues, he was not recalling specific conversations.
And while he reflected his teacher's method and interests, the
conversations he writes of don't give Socrates' interlocutors a fair
share of the discussion, or depict them offering the best possible
responses.[73]

In the *Charmides*, the youth's guardian, Critias, takes over the
discussion when it starts to make some philosophical progress. But
the conversation ends with Charmides on the one hand unsettled
by the demolition of the values he thought he understood and on
the other excited to continue exploring ideas. Does he possess the
quality of *sōphrosunē* and does he need the 'charm' with which
Socrates might cure his headaches?

> And Charmides said 'But, by Zeus, Socrates, I don't know
> whether I have it or whether I don't. For how would I know
> something, when you yourself are unable to discover what-
> ever it is, as you say? I'm not entirely persuaded by you,
> Socrates, but I really do think that I'm in need of the charm,
> and nothing will stop me from being charmed by you for
> as many days as it takes, until you say that it is enough.[74]

Perhaps Plato here is recalling his own early conversations
with Socrates – when Adeimantus (as his guardian) and Glaucon
might have introduced him to the philosopher – and his own
youthful desire to continue to be provoked and unsettled, to con-
front the commonplace ideas with which he was familiar and to

explore ways of transcending them. Plato marked Charmides' commitment to continuing conversation and pointed the way to his own philosophical development.[75] Yet the final exchange between Critias, Charmides and Socrates, with its jokey threats about forcing Socrates to speak to them, also points to a troubling future; already tainted through their involvement in the scandals of 415, Critias and Charmides would go on to play significant roles in the political turmoil to come.

The life stories of ancient philosophers often include a moment of conversion, from which point their choice of life has been set. The biographers' picture of Plato's sudden encounter with Socrates as a young adult settles on this as the moment at which Plato appeared to choose between the political and philosophical life, two models explored and expanded upon by later biographers and historians. Socrates, the eccentric disputant who one might find arguing about the meaning of courage, or silently lost in thought while pondering the directions of his spirit guide (*daimonion*), inspired Plato to reject the life that Critias chose. But the events of the next decade further entangled Plato and his circle in Athenian politics. While they might have given him a motive for attempting to separate himself from the political, his growing intellectual curiosity and development also drove him towards pursuing knowledge rather than power.

3

The Trial and Death of Socrates

The vision of a successful expedition Alcibiades had conjured for the Athenians in 415 did not materialize. Under-resourced, struggling with lack of support from home and contending with strong resistance from the Syracusans and their Spartan allies, the Athenian generals failed to achieve their goals in Sicily. After two years, in 413, the remnants of the expedition were captured and either killed or imprisoned. Thucydides reported the impact on the city of news of defeat in Sicily:

> When the news was told at Athens, they believed not a long time, though it were plainly related and by those very soldiers that escaped from the defeat itself that all was so utterly lost as it was. When they knew it, they were mightily offended with the orators that furthered the voyage, as if they themselves had never decreed it. They were angry also with those that gave out prophecies and with the soothsayers and with whosoever else had at first by any divination put them into hope that Sicily should be subdued. Everything, from every place, grieved them; and fear and astonishment, the greatest that ever they were in, beset them round.[1]

The defeat of the Sicilian expedition left the city threatened from the outside and divided on the inside. Plato spent his time in conversation with Socrates and others against the background of a developing political crisis. The continuing fallout from the twin sacrileges of the mutilation of the herms and the profanation of the Eleusinian Mysteries two years previously had shown deep divides within the citizen body, and these were not healing. A section of the elite was in conflict no longer with political rivals but with the democracy itself. They felt that democratic decision-making processes had failed and so had begun to work to replace the regime with a more tightly controlled one in which they would have a greater voice. The division between old and new styles of education was mapped on to Athens's political arrangements – some speakers began to advocate a return to older practices, to the time when only the wealthier citizens had a voice in the Assembly or held important offices. They labelled this the *patrios politeia*, 'ancestral constitution', eliding the gap between the time of Solon almost two centuries prior and the time of Athens's great historical moment in defeating the Persians at Marathon a hundred years after that.[2]

Using their social networks, their dining clubs and dinner parties held in each other's homes, a group of oligarchic-minded Athenians manoeuvred to restrict the political rights of the mass of poorer citizens, many of whom were away from the city serving in the fleet. The conspirators managed the trick of getting the majority of Athenians able to attend to vote down the democracy. A little to the east of the Academy was the hill of Colonus with its shrine to Poseidon Hippios, the 'horsy Poseidon' beloved of Athens's elite cavalry class, the wealthy section of the population most associated with the growing attacks on democratic process.[3] The Assembly was moved from its usual location on the Pnyx for a fateful meeting in 411, and a group of the city's elite conspired to overthrow the democracy.[4] They established a regime in which four hundred citizens, selected by wealth, would exercise the responsibilities previously exercised by the Council of Five Hundred selected by lot from all citizens.

This regime itself failed to achieve stability and four months or so later a further Assembly meeting – more conventionally held on the Pnyx – put in place a revised constitution extending full rights, including that of office-holding, to 5,000 citizens, so encompassing the moderately well-off. The historian Thucydides approved of this arrangement, describing the 'mixed' (rich-and-poor) regime, which fell somewhere between democracy and oligarchy, as the first time in his life that the Athenians had enjoyed 'good government'.[5]

Plato was too young to be directly involved in these events, but the consequences of the Athenian defeat in 413 impacted his daily life as Sparta restarted physical attacks on Attica and the city. The Spartans built a permanent fort in the town of Deceleia, halfway to Attica's northern border with Boeotia.[6] From there they sent out expeditions against the city itself, which often camped close to the Academy. However, the grove dedicated to Academus was given special treatment by the Spartans: they left it undisturbed when they attacked Athens's outskirts, seizing crops and welcoming runaway slaves.[7]

Plato Stays in School

As the war dragged on and Athens's success began to seem less assured, Plato moved into the prolonged adolescence that kept young Athenian citizen men on the margins of the life of the city, no longer legal children but not yet treated as ready for the responsibilities of being a full adult either. In more peaceful times, such youths might spend time furthering their intellectual and physical training in preparation for political and military glory. But the loss of so many citizen men in Sicily and the continuing difficulties of the war led to other demands on young men. As their first step into adulthood around the age of seventeen, young men joined a troop of *ephebes* (the word means 'on the cusp of adult age') and began military training, including postings to the city's borders to defend against invasions.[8] Plato reached this age between 411 and 407 – challenging years for the city as its restored democracy contended with the continuing Spartan threat. Youths could expect to play a role in the defence of their city.

Plato's late work the *Laws* suggests he may have had youthful experiences as a junior border guard assigned to rural parts of Attica. His main speaker in that dialogue, the unnamed 'Athenian Stranger', sets out the role of young men in the imagined community of Magnesia, a new polis to be founded on Crete, where the discussion takes place.[9] Here young men between the ages of 25 and 30 can be selected to join countryside patrols for two years as part of their transition to adulthood, during which time they are responsible both for strengthening the country's defences and for beautifying the local environment. It is both a form of military training and a rite of passage; the Athenian Stranger thinks that irrigating temple sites and building gymnasia might be rewarding activities for the young conscripts, who spend a month at a time in each of the twelve segments of Magnesia's territory. The details Plato includes here suggest that, while he undertook similar duties at a time when the Athenians' territory was under real threat and partially occupied by the Spartans, his experience was more one of community service than of active fighting. His brothers, however, were now fully fledged hoplites, serving their city. Plato recalled how Glaucon's lover had written poems in praise of his courage when he fought for the city, in 409.[10]

Despite all the difficulties and interruptions, Plato persisted with his studies, finding Athenians with interests matching his own among the followers of Socrates and others, widening his circle of intellectual companions and always hunting for books. He looked beyond Socrates to find out more about the traditions Socrates had rejected. Socrates was unusual in having thrown his predecessors off, pursuing his own interests rather than those of

Socrates, in a standard portrait bust, Roman imperial era, derived from
a Greek original.

cosmologists and scientists. Other companions and teachers represented distinctive intellectual traditions and heritages, introducing
him to other philosophical perspectives from the stern views of
the Eleatics to the bewildering pronouncements of Heraclitus. It
was Cratylus – most likely a little older than Plato, but younger

than Socrates – who introduced Plato to the complex and paradoxical thought of Heraclitus, in pursuit of questions of language
and meaning.

Aristotle described how Plato learned from Cratylus[11] and
through him was introduced to the work of earlier thinkers: 'As a
young man Plato first became acquainted with Cratylus and the
ideas of Heraclitus, that all perceptible things are continuously in
flux and that there is no scientific knowledge of them; and he held
to these views later.'[12] Diogenes Laertius insists that Plato associated with Cratylus after Socrates' death, but his much later account
is dependent on Plato's work, while Aristotle's independent and
more contemporary testimony suggests that his involvement with
Cratylus pre-dated the death of Socrates.[13]

The conflicting views about language and definitions held by
Cratylus and Socrates provided Plato with a way of dramatizing
his own intellectual journey. Socrates' search for definitions ends
in an impasse if the gap between language and reality itself gets
in the way of attaching words to objects. Much later Plato looked
back to this time and imagined an encounter between the two
thinkers, in which Cratylus' views about the importance of names
could be set against Socrates' interest in definitions. Socrates' friend
Hermogenes is the interlocutor.[14] As David Sedley has shown,
Socrates and Hermogenes' discussions in this dialogue suggest
Plato's views about the way in which philosophy should be studied
and the order in which students should encounter topics.[15] What at
first seems like an undivided list of etymologies turns out to be the-
matically arranged, moving from the structure of the cosmos, and
the divine beings and natural bodies it contains, to the ethical vir-
tues. Plato's presentation of the encounter offers a mature reflection
on the different views he encountered from Socrates and Cratylus.

Through Cratylus, Plato encountered the thought of Heraclitus
of Ephesus, who had been active in that Asia Minor city a century previously. His comprehensive insights into the cosmos and

human life emphasized the experience of instability and change, yet also encompassed that change within a cosmic order. Heraclitus expressed his thought in enigmatic aphorisms, such as 'you cannot step in the same river twice.'[16] At least, that was how his ideas had reached Plato, whether from hearing friends quote Heraclitus or through reading a copy of the philosopher's book. Plato and his colleagues summarized it even more concisely than Heraclitus himself had done: 'everything flows.'[17] Cratylus himself eventually took this further, reaching the view that it was impossible to pin language to reality, or to produce meaningful speech, and that one could only make indications by pointing. He painted himself into an intellectual corner from which it was no longer possible even to step into a river once.[18] Rigorous adherence to philosophical worldviews could be dangerous and counter-productive.

Amid the fast-moving discussions and changing views, Plato found the seeds of what would become his major philosophical project: getting beyond changing impressions gained through the senses to grasp at underlying persistent realities which could not be directly perceived but accessed only through rigorous thought. The conclusion of the *Cratylus* points to his answer to this difficulty; Socrates makes a final speech, aimed at rebutting Heraclitus' account of change, before the discussants part on good terms.[19] He argues that the instability of Heraclitus' sensible world precludes knowledge; what is needed is an account of 'the things which always are':

> If it is always changing, it is not stable knowledge, and from this account there would be no knowing and no becoming known. But if there is always that which knows and that which is known, there is the fine, there is the good, there is each of the things that exist, and it seems to me that these things are not similar to the things we were just talking about, to flowing and decay.[20]

Plato set Socrates' insistence on definitions against the instability of Heraclitus' vision. It would have been easy to go along with sophistic views, as he depicts Hermogenes doing, and to accept a version of Heraclitean flux and Protagorean relativism, so that each man's argument has as good a chance as another's of being right at any given moment.

In the course of their discussion, the group agrees that some people are better name-givers than others; such a person is a *nomothetês*, the same noun used to describe the founding lawgiver of a city. The way he presents this conversation shows Plato adapting the thought of his teachers and friends and synthesizing a new direction, in this case one of the major underlying structures of his philosophy, known to us as the 'Theory of Forms' although never named as such by Plato himself.

Socrates had turned away from cosmological thought to focus on ethics and the search for the morally/ethically, not only politically, good life. But other thinkers insisted that both forms of enquiry should proceed hand in hand, as difficult as it seemed to take the most abstract questions about the nature of existence as fundamental to more practical concerns about how to live. Another important thinker whose writings Plato encountered incorporated both the big picture and the smallest possible elements into the vast sweep of his thought. Democritus of Abdera (b. *c.* 460 BCE) was an atomist, who believed that all matter was constructed from tiny and indivisible particles, but also an ethicist concerned with how society should be organized and the ways in which its members should live good lives. He and his teacher, Leucippus, produced works on the organization of the cosmos, which like the work of many other philosophers were aimed at making sense of the disconcerting thought of the Italian Eleatic thinkers.[21] But Democritus was also much concerned with the organization of society and how individuals might achieve happiness within it. His goal of creating a complete philosophical system that could explain everything may have caught Plato's attention.[22] Later sources would suggest that Plato tried to buy up and remove those works from circulation, to replace them with his own grand model, and would also draw parallels between the lives of Democritus and Plato. But whether discussing with his friends or reading papyrus scrolls, Plato was learning about the ambitions of other thinkers and the ways in which they expressed their systematic thought.

Other figures Plato had first encountered through their teaching of rhetoric to ambitious youths turned out to have deeper intellectual scope and to be engaged in these same discussions. The Athenians had been keen to apply Protagoras' teaching to public speaking but the rigorous work that underlay it had broader aims. In the same way, Plato had encountered Gorgias' display speeches, whether hearing them in person or reading circulated copies. Gorgias' powerful use of language had a lasting effect on intellectual life in Athens. But there was another side to his work, much more engaged with the projects of the philosophers who interested Plato than with attempts to grasp political power through the manipulation of language. Gorgias' interests extended to important metaphysical questions and his contribution to developing philosophical debate was characteristically paradoxical and combative. His treatise *On Nature* was organized into three sections; one report states: '[Gorgias] says that (i) nothing exists; and (ii) if it does exist, it is unknowable; and (iii) if it exists and is knowable, it is not communicable to others.'[23] Nobody was quite sure whether Gorgias was serious about taking on the philosophers. Was this a considered critique of Parmenides' thought, or just another language game? Gorgias had plenty of students in Athens and beyond – he never stayed long in the same place. But his teaching was in demand; in Thessaly at this time he taught Meno of Pharsalus, who would later follow Socrates and meet both Plato and Xenophon; in Athens Gorgias had taught Isocrates.

What Plato took from Gorgias' work was its engagement with the challenge opened up by Parmenides, that only what existed could be the object of thought. Gorgias, with his skill in language, could easily suggest counter-examples to show that it was possible to think and speak about the non-existent. But his treatise carefully worked through the argumentative possibilities, nodding to the ideas of the other Eleatics Zeno and Melissus.[24] It took up the distinction between eternal objects and those that are generated, which come to be and are subject to change. Plato was alert to this distinction, wherever he found it. Gorgias' book led him back to the Greek philosophers of southern Italy. While his conversations with Socrates were focused on questions of definition, Gorgias pointed to discussions in which the possibility of definition – of using language at all – was itself under question.

The puzzle of how words acquire meaning and how nouns refer to the objects they name had been of great interest to the sophists of the preceding generation, including Protagoras and Prodicus of Ceos, who wrote a treatise and gave public lectures on the question.[25] Aristophanes had mocked the technical discussion of language in the *Clouds*, attributing similar interests to Socrates.[26]

Plato's major project later in life would be to insist that political life could prosper only if underpinned by the conceptual frameworks that philosophers were developing; there was no hope of coherent civic life without reference to the stability of eternal truths. One might see his search for stability as a response to his experiences during his late adolescence and early adulthood, as his city's political life repeatedly collapsed into crisis, and a defeated Athens was eventually starved into submission. But while the young Plato was navigating his way between his duties as a citizen and his intellectual interests, Socrates' inquiries into ethical and political values were running into trouble.

Warning Signs Large and Small

When Plato looked back on this period, he saw clear warning signs that all was not well and that his teacher had made enemies. Plato was becoming much more aware of the changing political climate. Since his stepfather's death, his mother's ancient family had loomed larger in his life, connecting him to democracy's well-heeled critics. Now that Plato was old enough to join his brothers at symposia at home and at the homes of other friends and relatives, he heard Athenians talking who were critical of democracy and contemptuous of the city's poor, calling the demos the mass (*plēthos*) or mob (*ochlos*). Sometimes he heard Alcibiades, who had finally returned from exile in 407 after being recalled to the city to serve once more as a general. Xenophon depicted his arrival within the city as a moment of excitement, though one tinged with tension, as the citizens gathered at the Piraeus to greet him when he disembarked on the day Athena's statue was ritually washed – a disconcerting moment.[27] For Socrates' younger followers, it was an exciting opportunity to meet a living legend.

His teacher had had a combative relationship with the city's political leaders for some time. Although Socrates too tried to keep his distance from political machinations, he was committed to serving his city when asked. Before Plato met him, he had served as a soldier, with some distinction in the rout at Delium. But the operation of the lot drew him into the heart of politics, when he was selected as a councillor (*bouleutēs*) in 406.[28] The council operated as the executive of the Athenian Assembly, arranging its agenda, chairing its meetings and administering urgent affairs in between the full meetings of Athens's citizen body. Each year, fifty citizens from each of the ten tribes were chosen by lot to serve on the council.

Leadership – particularly the role of chairing meetings – was rotated through each tribe in turn during the course of each year, with one of the presiding tribe's citizens selected by lot to lead each meeting; during this period the councillors from that tribe stayed in the city and ate together in the *tholos*, a round building in the Agora, close to the law courts. It was in this way that Socrates found himself in the chair of a notorious meeting of the Assembly, at which the Athenians decided the fate of the generals apparently responsible for a great loss of life at sea after a naval battle around the Arginusae, a group of islets between Lesbos and the coast of Asia Minor.[29] This was not Socrates' great moment, however. He was unable to prevent the overriding of law and customary practice, which led to a group trial of those generals who had been foolish enough to imagine that they might receive justice from the city they served. Those generals, six out of the eight concerned, were convicted and later executed. Alcibiades, despite the enthusiasm at his return, quickly fell from favour when the Athenian fleet under his command was defeated by the Spartan admiral Lysander at Notium, also in 406.[30]

Plato could see how this had happened, although he carefully depicted Socrates' most challenging discussion with a non-Athenian who had died before Socrates did. Meno had been killed by the Persians after joining the mercenaries supporting Cyrus' bid for the throne.[31] In his dialogue *Meno*, Plato presents Meno as a handsome young man from Thessaly who has studied with Gorgias, fighting back against Socrates' method as they seek to establish a definition of virtue. The discussion has circled round repeatedly; when Socrates asks Meno for a definition, the youth replies with a list of examples, describing what virtue is for different types of people, not the single, unified definition applicable in all cases that Socrates wants. The discussion becomes increasingly bad-tempered; Socrates accuses Meno of being spoiled because of his youthful beauty, which makes him behave like a tyrant. Meno becomes monosyllabic in his replies until he finally cracks and accuses Socrates of being like a 'stingray' who numbs his prey. The articulate Meno, who has given countless speeches to demanding audiences, is transformed into a sulky child. He closes with a threat: 'And I think you are well advised in not going away on voyages or spending time abroad, because if you were to behave like this as a foreigner in another city, you would soon be arrested as a magician.'[32]

Included in the audience that Plato imagines for Socrates' conversation with Meno is Anytus, who would later become one of Socrates' accusers. Socrates turns to Anytus to continue the inquiry into who might be teachers of virtue.[33] Anytus is critical of professional teachers and claims that any Athenian citizen would be a better educator. Socrates counters with an extended set of examples to show that the greatest citizens were not the greatest educators, ranging through the less successful sons of the city's greatest leaders, Themistocles, Pericles and Aristides, whose son Lysimachus is a mutual acquaintance. His final example is Meletus, son of a Thucydides distantly related to the historian of the same name, who had been educated well in wrestling but had not developed the skills needed to succeed in verbal or intellectual contests. Anytus amplifies Meno's earlier threat, as he warns Socrates to 'take care' and that it is 'easier to harm people than to benefit them' in Athens, before storming off.

Athens's precarious political and economic position worsened after the city was defeated by Lysander's Spartan fleet at Aegospotami, close to the entrance to the Black Sea at the Hellespont, in 405. This closed off the critical trade route through which grain arrived at the Piraeus to feed the city's population. Xenophon echoed Thucydides in describing the arrival of the news in the city:

> When the Paralus arrived at Athens in the night, they began
> to speak about the disaster. The wailing passed from the
> Piraeus through the Long Walls up to the city, one man

announcing the news to another, and nobody slept that night, not just mourning the dead, but even more mourning themselves, thinking that they too would suffer what they had done to the Melians, as Spartan colonists, defeating them through a siege, and to the Histiaeans and the Scionaeans and the Toronaeans and the Aeginetans and many other Greeks. On the next day they held an assembly, in which they decided to block all their harbours but one, to put the walls in good order, to position guards, and to get ready for a siege in every other respect. And that is what they did.[34]

A year or so later, what the Athenians had feared took place. The Spartan fleet controlled the trade routes from the Black Sea to Athens, and Lysander was able to besiege the city remotely. But this time, the political response was one of division, not unity:

Theramenes and the ambassadors who were with him brought these terms back to Athens. A great crowd (*ochlos*) surrounded them as they entered the city, fearing that they had come back without completing their task. For there was no longer any time to delay, on account of the number (*plēthos*) of people dying from hunger. On the next day the ambassadors reported the conditions under which the Spartans would make peace; Theramenes argued for the deal, saying that it was necessary to obey the Spartans and take down the walls. Some people spoke against this, but a much greater number joined in agreeing to them, and it was decided to accept the peace terms. After this Lysander sailed into the Piraeus, the exiles returned, and, thinking that this day was the beginning of freedom (*eleutherias*) for Greece, they eagerly tore down the walls as flute-girls played.[35]

Socrates had struggled to keep himself out of politics, but after the Thirty took power it became impossible. Now the regime was run by men whom he had at some point or other taught, and they were not prepared to let him stay in the background but found ways to test his loyalty.[36] For Plato, the new regime was a source of great anguish and personal conflict between loyalty to his family and to the values of civic life he was being taught to respect. A later writer voiced the thoughts Plato might have had about the opportunity the new regime offered him, in the pseudo-autobiography contained in the 'Seventh Letter':[37]

> When I was a young man I was afflicted by the same thing as many are – I thought that as soon as I became master of my own affairs I would go straight into public life in the city. And some opportunities in the business of the city fell my way as follows. Since many people reviled the city's constitution, there was a change of regime, to one in which 51 men held leading roles as officers, eleven in the city, ten in the Piraeus – each of these groups was responsible for administering the marketplace and the citizens – and the Thirty were established as an autonomous group to rule everyone. In fact some of these men were relatives of mine and known to me, and they summoned me at once as though on matters proper to our relationship. I experienced emotions which were unsurprising given my youth. For I thought that they would lead the city from a kind of criminal existence and administer it in a just way, so I paid keen attention to them and what they might do. And as I watched these men they soon demonstrated that the former constitution had been a golden age.[38]

Plato and his brothers were closely connected to the new regime through the involvement of members of their extended family in key executive roles and with clear responsibility for the regime's brutal actions. One of the leaders of the board of Thirty to whom the Spartans handed over the city's administration was Critias, the cousin of Plato's mother Perictione. Later scholars speculated that Critias had been a lover of Plato's brother Glaucon only a few years previously.[39] His maternal uncle Charmides, Critias' former ward, was appointed to the board of Ten who were to control the Piraeus, Athens's port, a part of the city with a long-standing tradition of support for democracy. As a naval base and centre for trade, the Piraeus had a more diverse population, with a greater proportion of free non-citizens, than the city of Athens itself. Charmides, the one-time quietist, found himself part of a brutal campaign of repression in the centre of opposition to the Spartan-backed regime.

However, it was in the Piraeus where Socrates' circle would see the regime's cruelty demonstrated. The Piraeus, as a port, had long been home to immigrant traders and entrepreneurs. Some of them, such as the Syracusan businessman Cephalus, had come to the city at the invitation of Pericles; Cephalus had established a slave-run factory to make shields, contributing to the city's imperial power and military capacity. Cephalus' family had helped with other ventures, such as Thourii, Pericles' colonial project in southern Italy, and they had both paid the taxes levied on non-citizens and performed the liturgies appropriate to their wealth, sponsoring dramatic productions and kitting out warships. The business was now managed by Cephalus' son Polemarchus and the family's wealth caught the eye of the tyrants.[40] Polemarchus' brother Lysias, now working as a speechwriter, told the story of the brutal attack on his family in a later court case; he himself survived only by bribing his captors, while Polemarchus was not so lucky. The tyrants expropriated their factory, homes and all their possessions – even snatching the gold earrings that Polemarchus' wife was wearing – and then ordered him to drink hemlock.

Socrates might have expected to be treated well by the new regime. Yet his former students did not treat him kindly, or even just leave him alone. Xenophon reported one incident, emphasizing that, whatever lessons Critias and the like might have learned from Socrates in the past, they had now forgotten in their lust for power.[41] Socrates was a liability to them, still wandering the city encouraging his fellow citizens to examine their thoughts and preconceptions. He also criticized the regime's executions and the continuing impoverishment of the citizens: deploying the herding analogy, he observed that it was a poor herdsman who made his flock smaller and less healthy.[42]

Inevitably, these remarks were reported back to the oligarchs. Critias and another leader of the regime, Charicles, hauled Socrates in and suggested that he stop speaking with young men and encouraging critical thinking.[43] Xenophon presents Socrates putting up a rather sophistic defence, quibbling about what qualified as young – under thirty, the minimum age to serve on the Council. Perhaps the oligarchs had half a mind to separate their relative Plato, who was still in his twenties, from his beloved teacher. Perhaps Critias realized that Socrates' teaching might produce political rivals. He himself had shown a talent for independent and provocative thought in his political writings and poetry.[44]

On another occasion the oligarchs set Socrates up, calling him along with four other citizens into their council chamber and ordering them to participate in the arrest of a fellow Athenian, Leon of Salamis, so that he could be put to death. But whatever the oligarchs' provocations, Socrates' commitment to doing nothing that was wrong meant that he would rather face death himself than be involved in the execution of an innocent citizen.[45] Socrates had no difficulty in ignoring these orders and fully expected to be summoned and executed himself.

Socrates was not the only citizen of the narrow oligarchy to dislike the regime. But others took more decisive action, actively working to overthrow the tyrannical rulers rather than simply failing to cooperate with them. Theramenes, previously a moderate oligarch but unpopular with the Thirty, was executed after he became disenchanted with the regime and spoke out against the executions.[46] Xenophon recorded him transcending his earlier reputation for inconstancy with his bravery in facing death; as he drank the hemlock, he gave a mocking toast to Critias and the regime. His former collaborator Thrasybulus survived to emerge as the hero who led the resistance movement into an all-out civil war; Xenophon praised him for his efforts to reunite the citizen factions. The actions of Plato and his brothers during this period are not recorded but their uncle Charmides and his former lover Critias were killed in the fighting.[47]

The Charges against Socrates

The restoration of democracy in 403 did not bring immediate peace to the city, despite the citizens' oaths and commitments to renewing their community in peace. Many were still suspicious of those who had supported the other side; some of the oligarchy's supporters had left the city anyway, as they had been allowed to move to Eleusis, on the western border of Attica. As part of the agreement by which democracy was returned, the citizens agreed a formal amnesty for misdeeds under the oligarchy. They were barred from prosecuting each other for wrongs committed during this time or from mentioning actions from that time as character evidence in other court cases. Surviving court speeches suggest that citizens used a great deal of ingenuity to circumvent the amnesty and to 'remember the bad things' (*mnēsikakein*) they were supposed to forget.[48]

Plato with his close connections to leading oligarchs was naturally under suspicion, as was Socrates. The 'Seventh Letter' suggests that Plato had considered taking an active part in the new regime, until it turned on his teacher.[49] Some of Socrates' associates left Athens. Xenophon, who had enjoyed his service in Athens's cavalry in the run-up to the civil war, thought that his economic and political prospects were better outside the city and went off with his Theban friend Proxenus in 401, joining a group of renegade Spartans and other Greeks, including Meno of Pharsalus, in what turned out to be a doomed attempt to put Cyrus the Younger on the Achaemenid throne.[50] Xenophon's adventures as the stranded Greeks made their way home, recounted in his *Anabasis*, have thrilled readers from antiquity to the present.

Plato stayed in Athens, however, continuing to spend time with Socrates and meeting visiting philosophers. He might even have considered another attempt at entering political life; the author of the 'Seventh Letter' imagines that: 'Not much later the regime of the Thirty fell and the whole constitution as it then was; and the desire to take part in communal affairs and politics took hold of me again, though more hesitantly than before.'[51] As the letter's writer noted, the restoration of democracy did not lead immediately to the peace that citizens hoped for; there was 'nothing surprising' in people taking revenge for the wrongs they had suffered under the oligarchy. The new arrangements created opportunities for past enmities to be pursued even as the formal amnesty was declared.

Socrates on Trial

Socrates himself was bemused by the charges brought against him in 399 by three of his fellow citizens, Meletus, Anytus and Lycon; he had never been in court before as either defendant or prosecutor, perhaps unusually in a city where individuals regularly litigated a wide range of grievances against their neighbours and collectively policed each other's contributions to the democracy through the courts.[52] While his friend Crito was a constant target of more or less vexatious accusations, framed with an eye to his wealth, Socrates was neither rich enough to be worth pursuing nor concerned with pursuing cases on his own behalf.[53]

The charges were not at all straightforward. According to Xenophon, they were that Socrates 'is guilty of not recognising the gods traditionally recognized by the city, and of introducing other novel divinities: he is also guilty of corrupting the young men'.[54] These charges were brought under laws relating to impiety, so the indictment had been lodged with the 'king archon', responsible for the city's religious life. The case would be tried by one of the city's courts with a large jury panel of 501 citizens, a mark of its importance.

Plato was unsure that the Athenians could even say what impiety was. He later imagined Socrates in conversation with another eccentric Athenian, Euthyphro, who met Socrates while visiting the archon's office to lay charges in a prosecution of his own. His evaluation of a complex situation led him to prosecute his own father for murdering a former employee who had in turn killed one of the family's enslaved members. Euthyphro's father had tied up the killer and thrown him into a ditch and the man had died overnight as Euthyphro's father pondered what to do. Prosecuting one's father was unthinkable in the context of Athenian culture, in which reverence for one's elders was a cultural commandment. In Plato's imagined version of Socrates' conversation with Euthyphro, the question of whether the notoriously religiose Euthyphro was impious in filing charges against his own father leads to a discussion in which it proves impossible to identify or define piety itself. While there is lots of philosophical interest in the search for a definition of piety, Plato's message is that any prosecution for impiety rests on shaky ground.

No one imagined what the outcome of Socrates' trial might be. Under the previous democracy there had been other prosecutions of intellectuals who held unconventional views, under the Decree of Diopeithes.[55] Often the mere hint of a possible indictment was enough to make a sophist think about how long he wanted to stay in the city. Protagoras had withdrawn from the city without any formal proceedings and had died on another journey without being able to return.[56] The philosopher Anaxagoras, whose ideas had inspired then disappointed Socrates, had been prosecuted for his religious views, for his identification of the divine with natural forces.[57] Socrates' friends were aware that many Athenians did not distinguish clearly between the views expressed by different philosophers, all equally outlandish to the traditionally minded. Socrates' case had not been helped by the comic poets' treatment of him. It was more than twenty years since Aristophanes in the *Clouds* had put some unpopular ideas – about divine forces and their operation in the cosmos – into Socrates' mouth.[58] Plato thought that this amounted to a first attempt at prosecution and makes a rebuttal of this conflation, the first plank in Socrates' self-defence.[59]

Looking back in later life, Plato constantly returned to these weeks, setting some of his philosophically most significant dialogues within the pre-trial period, as if those final weeks represented a perfected and complete Socrates, philosophizing at a higher level. When Socrates leaves the discussion at the end of the *Theaetetus*, it is to go to the archon's office, where the discussion scenario of the *Euthyphro* takes place. The *Sophist* and the *Statesman* are presented as conversations of the two following days. Perhaps Socrates did feel an urge to wrap up his affairs, facing the possibility that he might be exiled for a while and to conclude his discussions with his wide circle of followers. Plato, who had already lost two father figures, Ariston and Pyrilampes, was understandably anxious for his teacher.

He encouraged Socrates to take the forthcoming trial seriously and to prepare his defence. These were the circumstances in which many Athenians hired speechwriters, to help prepare their defence and to construct a case for them to present. Socrates already knew a successful speechwriter – Lysias, the Sicilian whose family had been torn apart by the oligarchs and who was now earning a living as a speechwriter for hire, offered to write it.[60] Lysias' democratic connections and his understanding of Athens's legal system might have been invaluable, had Socrates accepted. However, Socrates refused all offers of help, trusting to his *daimonion* (spirit guide), which reliably warned him against pursuing dangerous courses of action. But his wisdom did not extend to the art of persuading a jury to acquit him, or even of persuading them to accept his proposed penalty.

The trial itself was a significant enough event that several of Socrates' followers wrote about it, reporting his speeches in his defence, although only two versions survive, of which only Plato's version can claim to be an eyewitness account.[61] Xenophon had not returned from his Asiatic adventure, and his version of the event relies on the testimony of Socrates' follower Hermogenes.[62]

Socrates first addressed the charges laid against him. Plato separated out the rumours and gossip around Socrates, the half-remembered version of Socrates whom Aristophanes had mocked, and set out carefully how Socrates was engaged in a different project. But perhaps Socrates' presence in the court-room and his questioning of his accuser Meletus were a powerful reminder of just how irritating Socrates had been to the civic body. It seemed that many disliked the way in which their conversations with Socrates left them feeling confused about the matter at hand and with a lingering sense that they had somehow been talked down to. From politicians to craft workers, many Athenians had had these discussions. While, for Plato, Socrates' deconstruction of preconceptions liberated him to reconceptualize knowledge itself, the *Apology* suggests that that was not the usual response. When Socrates repeated the story of how his friend Chaerephon had consulted the oracle at Delphi and been told that Socrates was the wisest of the Athenians, even their residual affection for the memory of the popular and democracy-loving Chaerephon was not enough to damp down a resurgent annoyance with Socrates.[63]

The first vote led to Socrates' conviction on the charges. It was at this stage that the Athenian legal process offered scope for negotiating down the punishment. Both accuser and defendant could propose penalties and the jury of 501 allotted citizens would vote secretly for a second time. It was an opportunity for the convicted man to show contrition and evoke pity from the jury. Plato, Crito and others had a plan for this part of the trial; Socrates should offer to pay a fine, in the hope that the jury would find this preferable to sending him into exile.[64] However, the accusers were trying to game the system too. They proposed that Socrates should be condemned to drink hemlock, and so executed. The stakes were significantly raised.

Socrates responded badly to this; he declined to enter a penalty. He mocked the process first and proposed that he should be treated as a civic hero, given permanent dining rights among the city's councillors, an honour more usually accorded to Olympic victors and others who had performed some significant deed of benefit to the city. The majority of the Athenians did not perceive Socrates' activity as a benefit to the city or see him as a heroic figure. His eventual suggestion of a small fine he might pay was hardly convincing, even as his supporters got him to propose a large sum – thirty minae, the equivalent of several years' wages for a craft worker. Socrates' gambit failed spectacularly and the vote for his execution was passed by a larger margin than the vote to convict him in the first place.[65]

Socrates Imprisoned

Socrates' disastrous bluff landed him in custody until his sentence could be carried out, but the gods whom the Athenians thought he had discarded gave him a few weeks longer. The Athenians did not carry out impure actions on sacred days and executions like all deaths were considered to generate impurity. As a sacred embassy was currently visiting Apollo's sanctuary at Delos, the sentence could not be carried out until it returned. Socrates continued to be grateful to Apollo, who had recognized his work through his oracle at Delphi. He amused himself by trying to write hymns of praise to the god, a new activity for him.[66] Unlike Plato, he had not been educated to write verse in the conventional forms of lyric poetry with their strict metre.

In this situation, there remained acceptable ways to avoid execution. Many Athenians facing a severe penalty would take themselves off into informal exile before any trial could take place; that was what several of Socrates' circle had done in 415, when faced with prosecution over the profanation of the Mysteries (see Chapter Two). Generals often took a considered view as to whether it was safe to return from an unsuccessful or controversial campaign – two of the Arginusae generals had avoided execution that way. Plato imagined Crito trying to persuade his friend to escape from prison, leave the city and stay a safe distance away, in Thessaly to the north.[67] But Socrates refused to be rescued. He argued that his commitment to the rule of law in Athens meant that he should not attempt to evade punishment, when he had lived his life benefiting from the stability of Athenian society under its laws.

The centrality of Socrates' final weeks in Plato's writing suggests that it was a turning point in the younger Athenian's own life. His act of literary commemoration is at its most profound in his *Phaedo*, a conversation he depicts between the visiting philosophers with whom he and Socrates had recently been working and some of Socrates' old friends, on the day on which Socrates' punishment was carried out and he drank the hemlock. In this scene Crito of course was there, quietly bribing the jailer to admit Socrates' friends to his cell. Others present included other discussants familiar from the dialogues: Crito's son Critobulus,

Jacques-Louis David, *The Death of Socrates*, 1787, oil on canvas.

Apollodorus, Hermogenes, Aeschines and Antisthenes, and Ctesippus and Menexenus among the younger men. Simmias from Thebes, along with Cebes and Phaedondas, represented a Pythagorean viewpoint, and Eucleides and Terpsion the Megarian school, two approaches to philosophy which played an important role in Plato's later thought.

The list of characters suggests the influences on Plato's own thinking on the cusp of his full adulthood. But he kept himself out of his presentation of Socrates' final conversation, depicting himself as absent at the critical moment. 'I think that Plato was ill,' Phaedo the non-Athenian narrator of the dialogue notes, after listing those present.[68] Socrates' final act is to request that a sacrifice be made to Asclepius, the hero-god of health; perhaps for Plato's recovery, perhaps more likely an acknowledgement that reaching the end of life was a release from its suffering.[69]

Immortality

The discussion that Plato imagined he had missed concerned a pressing question for Socrates: the immortality of the soul. There were differing views in Greek culture on what the experience of the soul in the afterlife would be like. The Homeric view was that whatever was conveyed down to Hades ('The Unseen') on an individual's death was not equivalent to the fully embodied person who had lived, but a feeble shadow. When Homer describes the souls who emerge from the underworld to speak to Odysseus, they report a shadowy, incomplete existence, requiring blood to animate them enough to be able to converse instead of merely gibber and squeak; Achilles says that he would rather be a hired labourer working for a poor man and alive than a king in this underworld.[70]

In his *Apology*, Plato showed Socrates imagining two other possibilities after death: 'either the person who has died does not exist and has no perception of anything, or, according to the stories, some kind of change occurs and the soul moves its home from this place to another place.'[71] While Socrates acknowledges that non-existence cannot be bad, but simply a dreamless sleep, he explores the idea of a change of location in more detail:

> But if death is a kind of relocation to another place, and the stories are true, that all the dead are in that place, what could be better than this, jurors? For once someone arrives in Hades, and, in exchange for those who claim to be jurors here, finds those who are truly called jurors, who are said to make judgements there, Minos and Rhadamanthys and Aeacus and Triptolemus and any other demi-gods who were just in their own lives, would this be a bad change of place?[72]

In this personal afterlife, Socrates would be able to track down and talk to figures from the past with whom he felt a connection, poets and thinkers and those who had suffered injustice, like Palamedes. This view of the afterlife was familiar to Athenians because it was recognizably similar to that which the Eleusinian Mysteries promised to its initiates, an afterlife in which the individual soul persisted. Being initiated into the Mysteries was almost a required rite of passage for young Athenians – Plato's words here suggest that both Socrates as speaker and he as writer were initiates. It was likely that Plato had taken part in the rituals before Socrates' death, participating in the annual procession to Eleusis and perhaps, as an ephebe, accompanying it. In Athenian myth, Triptolemus was the youthful recipient of the goddess Demeter's gifts to the city; including him in the list of figures Socrates hoped to encounter in the underworld suggests that Plato was thinking of the afterlife promised by the Mysteries.

The initiation rites for the Mysteries took place over several days in the harvest month of Boedromion. Plato would have joined other candidates for initiation – anyone who could speak Greek and pay a small fee, men, women, the free and the enslaved, not only Athenians – in the Agora, to hear the proclamation that began the ceremonies. The following day, would-be initiates went to bathe in the sea at Phaleron, accompanied by the piglet they were about to sacrifice as a personal offering. This purification was followed by two days of ritual seclusion at home before the main event, the grand procession from the city to the cult centre at Eleusis. Thousands might take part in this each year; perhaps not as many as the ghostly 30,000 who appeared to the Persians as they ravaged Attica during the Persian Wars, but still a substantial number.[73]

The ceremony had originated as a celebration of Demeter's gift to the Athenians of grain and the skill of agriculture, after an Athenian had helped her to find her daughter Kore (as the

Athenians named Persephone), lost in the underworld. That
remained important; young soldiers swore an oath to honour
the city's main crops – wheat, barley, olives, figs and grapevines.
But as it developed, knowledge of the underworld and the afterlife had become an important part of the cult's offer to initiates. It
offered consolation to Plato, as he grieved for Socrates, but, just as
he depicted the Theban disciples Simmias and Cebes being dissat-
isfied with Socrates' account of immortality, so Plato too wanted
to know more. He would continue to seek out mystery cults and
their information about the afterlife.

Afterwards

By Socrates' death Plato was once more deprived of a father
figure at a key point in his life, the transition into the full adulthood which Athenian male citizens reached at the age of thirty,
a time when many married and established their own household for their family. Women were married at puberty; Plato's
sister Potone had long since been married to Eurymedon and his
nephew Speusippus was beginning his own education.

However, there is no record of Plato marrying and no anecdotes about his family life, in a biographical tradition in which
the home lives of philosophers were treated with often prurient
curiosity, drawing on comic stereotypes. Socrates' wife Xanthippe,
who had been sent away from his prison cell while he passed his
final hours with his philosophical companions, was presented as
a 'difficult' woman, a scold, angry and abusive.[74] Xenophon's love
for his wife was satirized by Aeschines in a dialogue.[75] Diogenes
Laertius relates the details of the marriages and relationships of
Socrates, Xenophon, Aristotle, Speusippus and many others. The
Cynic couple Crates and Hipparchia each get their own biography; there's also a collection of pseudepigraphic letters telling their
story.[76] There are no such stories for Plato. One late source, the

Byzantine encyclopaedia the *Suda*, asserts that he neither married nor had any physical relationships.[77] Others list his lovers – mostly men.

Marriage was the norm, although not compulsory, in Athens. In other cities, unmarried men might be denied some forms of respect; Dercylidas, a leading Spartan commander who had led campaigns in the Peloponnesian War, remained unmarried and once suffered the indignity of not being given a seat to watch the procession at a civic festival, the Gymnopaedia or festival of Unarmed Dancing.[78] A younger man declined to give his seat to a man who, he pointed out, had no son who might yield his seat in return. Spartan concern about the dwindling number of elite citizens made marriage and the production of legitimate heirs a key social concern.

Full adulthood also meant increasing responsibility as a citizen. Plato had reached the age at which citizens became eligible to participate in more political offices, such as serving on the Council.[79] Perhaps his sense of the injustice suffered by Socrates might have led him to engage fully with the political life and throw himself into the activities of Athenian institutions, helping to reshape the re-established democracy. The author of the 'Seventh Letter' imagined Plato's thoughts on the possibility of taking an active role in politics:

> As I looked at these events, and the men who were active in political business, and the laws and practices too, the more I looked at them and the further I advanced in age, the more difficult it seemed to me to administer political matters correctly; for it was impossible to do anything without friends and trustworthy allies, and it was not easy to find men of that kind, for our city was no longer administered according to the customs and practices of our ancestors, and it was impossible to find new allies with any ease.[80]

However, this is offered as a counterfactual. The author goes on to describe Plato's disenchantment with the state of politics in the city and to make this the point at which he chose to disengage from the civic life. But Plato's immediate response to the situation was a more individual one. Plato's time with Socrates had connected him to philosophers and teachers from around the Greek world, from the intellectual traditions of southern Italy and northern Africa to groups of thinkers based in nearby cities like Megara. His own philosophical conversations could continue, both in Athens and beyond the confines of the city.

4

Plato outside Athens

The ancient biographers imagined Plato travelling extensively and continuously in the period after Socrates' death but elided his responsibilities as an Athenian citizen. The tradition of the wise man as traveller was a familiar one; Plato used the stories of Solon's travels to Egypt and the Near East, for example, in his own *Timaeus*. Knowledge of other lands and their intellectual traditions was a powerful claim to philosophical authority; one of Cicero's characters notes how Pythagoras, Democritus and Plato 'travelled to the furthest parts of the earth because of their desire for learning.'[1]

Cicero described Plato's travels in his dialogue *De Republica*, itself a homage to Plato's *Republic*, presenting them in a speech given by the Roman general Scipio Africanus:

> I suppose you have heard that, after Socrates' death, Plato went on journeys, first to Egypt for purposes of study, and later to Italy and Sicily in order to become acquainted with the discoveries of Pythagoras; and that he spent a great deal of time in the company of Archytas of Tarentum and Timaeus of Locri, and also got possession of Philolaus' notes. And, as Pythagoras' reputation was then great in that country, he devoted himself entirely to that teacher's disciples and doctrines.[2]

Cicero knew and cared a great deal about Plato's work and reproduced passages from it in his own dialogues. The Plato who travelled was an ideal model for Cicero's own project of bringing Greek philosophy to a new, Latin-reading public and of arbitrating between different schools, but Cicero's account emphasizes one tradition, the Pythagoreans, over others, and is dependent on Plato's writing to the extent of including the fictional Timaeus among the philosophers Plato visited.

Diogenes Laertius also drew on Plato's own works to reconstruct his actions after Socrates' death, involving philosophers and schools mentioned in the dialogues, and partly reliant on them:

> When [Socrates] was gone, [Plato] approached Cratylus, the follower of Heraclitus, and Hermogenes, who practised philosophy after the teachings of Parmenides. He was then 28 years old, according to Hermodorus, and he went abroad to Euclides at Megara, along with the other followers of Socrates. Then he went to Cyrene, to Theodorus the mathematician, and from there he went to Italy, to the Pythagoreans Philolaus and Eurytos. After that he went to Egypt to see the priests who interpret the gods.[3]

Diogenes' account, like Cicero's, has such severe chronological difficulties that it cannot be a true historical account of Plato's travels. For example, he suggests that Plato travelled with the tragic playwright Euripides, who had died in 406, some years before Socrates. If Plato did meet Theodorus of Cyrene, it was more likely before Socrates' death than after it, given that the mathematician himself died in 398. But what this and other accounts really do is to tell the story of Plato's expanding intellectual interests in spatial terms.

Later biographers extend Plato's travels further, adding 'Phoenicia' (roughly modern Lebanon) to the list of destinations so that Plato could be connected to the Magi, the wise men of the Persian tradition. Olympiodorus admits that war curtailed Plato's travels, so imagines him meeting the Magi on the Mediterranean shores rather than inland in Asia.[4] But these accounts too are means of establishing intellectual connections – and the authority drawn from meeting important predecessors – rather than precise records of actual journeys.

Whether Plato's encounters with the scholars of the wider Greek world took place in Athens or elsewhere, in the years after Socrates' death he continued to build a network of international connections and knowledge and understanding of philosophical scholarship and practice across the known world. This intellectual journey is best documented in his own writings, where many of these scholars and their ideas are featured, often placed in conversation with Socrates, and occasionally even being voiced by him. The dialogue form provided a way in which Plato could set ideas against each other and synthesize them, although modern readers are perhaps better equipped to be alert to his fictional constructions than his ancient readers were.

It was quite usual for elite Athenians in political or personal difficulty to take themselves away to another part of Greece and wait for public opinion to change – precisely the plan Crito had offered to Socrates and which he had rejected. The Socratics might well fear further political retribution and it made sense for Plato and his colleagues to stay out of the Athenian limelight.

The Philosophical World beyond Athens

Plato went to Megara, home of friendly philosophers who had been a regular presence around Socrates in the last years of his life. Megara, just west of Athens's border at Eleusis, was on the road to Corinth and the Peloponnese, a strategic location which had embroiled it in regional conflicts. Its site along this route had made travel between the two cities to meet Socrates difficult at times; one story has Euclides, the city's leading philosopher, evading Athens's ban on citizens of Megara by sneaking into the city dressed as a woman.[5] This story is chronologically implausible: the principal Megarian Decree of 432 BCE, banning Megarian merchants from Athens and its harbours, was in force when Euclides was a child, not an adult. The 30-kilometre (20 mi.) journey between Megara and Athens had been made difficult from time to time during the Peloponnesian War, with Spartan invasion and occupation. But after the end of the war, under the restored democracy, passage between the cities was opened up and Euclides could easily have made the journey then. Plato presented Euclides as someone who visited Athens often, particularly during Socrates' final months, and who was present at his death, along with his colleague Terpsion.[6] Now, it was just as easy for Plato to continue travelling west of Athens, past the shrine of Eleusis where he had been initiated into the Mysteries.

The Megarians were developing an approach to philosophy that sharpened up argumentation and developed a technical approach and a language for describing its processes. Critics such as the Athenian educator Isocrates labelled their rigorous questioning and demolition of others' arguments 'eristic', full of strife.[7] Others, including Plato, however, appreciated the intellectual power of this new method and labelled it 'dialectic' ('skill in argument'). This dialectic was the next stage in philosophical discussion from Socrates' elenchus, although other philosophers, including the Megarians, were concerned with how to systematize the activity of philosophizing. Dialectic opened up new ways of testing ideas and advancing knowledge, of turning discussion into a powerful tool for evaluating and discarding propositions. Whereas Socrates' searches for definitions had often become stuck in aporia, an inability to progress from the rejection of hypotheses, these new methods offered the hope of making reliable progress, with theses tested and affirmed as the conversation progressed.

Through Euclides, Plato had learned more about the ideas of Parmenides of Elea and the way he had emphasized the importance of truth uncovered by argument rather than reliance on opinion.[8] Parmenides' austere philosophy set out a vision of the cosmos quite distinct from the views of Heraclitus, which had previously been introduced to Plato by Cratylus. Later philosophers attributed many important ideas to Parmenides: that he was the first to declare that the earth is spherical and the first to recognize that the morning and evening stars were in fact the same heavenly body.[9] However, such claims act as analogies for the totality of Parmenides' highly individual overview of the cosmos and of human experience. Analogies might well be needed to understand it. Parmenides' model – that what existed was itself a single and constant entity – was difficult to comprehend, given that it was completely at odds with ordinary perceptions and experience, and indeed regarded them as fallible. Parmenides' insistence on the singularity of everything that existed, the cosmos and what others saw as its separable contents – his radical monism, in the later technical language of philosophy – was hard to grasp and the more you thought about it, the stranger its consequences became. How to account for day-to-day reality, if multiplicity and change are impossible?

Parmenides' major work, an epic poem of which a few fragments survive as quotations, described an encounter between a young man and a mysterious goddess, who exhorts him to recognize the true nature of reality.[10] Parmenides set out some of the key puzzles about identifying the real, that which exists, and differentiating it from the false, which does not exist. The goddess shows a path that leads to the truth: 'There remains only the word of the path – "Is", she says.[11] The goddess goes on to warn the young man of the impossibility of speaking of that which is not, of non-existence and falsity, and she contrasts the way of truth with the way of opinion – conventional ideas about the nature of the universe.

Plato had encountered Parmenides' ideas in Athens and Megara, through the responses of the thinkers he already knew; through Gorgias' brilliant argument that 'Nothing exists'; most likely a response to Parmenides' poem and the fierce and destructive arguments of Euclides and his followers. The significance of Parmenides' thought was in the way that it specified the focus and limits of philosophical activity. Parmenides' poem marks a shift in the object of inquiry; it moved the centre of philosophical activity away from the inquiries into nature made by the earlier generation of Ionian 'scientists'. Rather than seeking a universal underlying substance as the basic building block of every material substance or being, as his predecessors had done, Parmenides thought that there was only one indivisible entity, so the question of an underlying kind of matter did not arise. He was more concerned with the possibilities of knowledge about the cosmos and being able to describe it truthfully. Those who did not follow the path set out by his goddess would condemn themselves to incoherence and irrationality. Those who did would be engaging in what later became known as metaphysics, the emerging discourse of abstract entities rather than physical materials underlying the cosmos and its structure.

Parmenides' followers approached other puzzles in a similar fashion. Zeno was famous for his paradoxes of motion, that Achilles could never catch up with the tortoise and that an arrow which appeared to be in motion was actually at any given moment at rest.[12] Plato might too have encountered the work of the last of the three great Eleatics, Melissus of Samos, in Athens. Melissus was both a philosopher and a leader of his own community and had had his own encounter with Athens as the general who had led his city's forces during the Pericles-led campaign against the island in 440 – and defeated Athens's great general.[13] He argued that what existed was a unity, ungenerated and indestructible.

Parmenides' ideas provide a provocation for Plato's own thinking, possible anchors for stability and persistence against the

political change of democratic practice and the existential instability produced by the thought of Heraclitus. Plato readily adopted
the grand scale of the Eleatics' vision and the possibilities for philosophical inquiry that they opened. His studies with Socrates,
who himself had turned away from natural science, had introduced him to the idea that what unified the cosmos was a principle,
which could be explained, rather than a form of physical matter,
which could be identified. Yet Parmenides' poem – and paradoxes
like those set out by Zeno – offered a way of conceptualizing the
world, but did so in a way that seemed too rigid and simple to
account for the phenomena of reality. Perhaps – as Gorgias' critique
demonstrated – Parmenides simply offered an outlandish theory
that could be presented as a *reductio ad absurdum,* in which the
absurdity took the front seat and so could be dismissed. For Plato,
however, the Eleatics' works created a space in which he could
develop his own account of the way in which everything that exists
instantiates qualities that are not subject to change. It confirmed
him as a metaphysician.

Megara was therefore an ideal early stopping point on Plato's
philosophical journey, giving him access to new tools for criticism
and argument as well as a renewed experience of philosophical
community. It also gave Plato a further opportunity to explore the
ideas of the Eleatics – Euclides was an expert on their thought.
Together they could bring Eleatic metaphysics into dialogue with
Socratic ethics. Plato's earlier experiences had exposed him to
wider currents in Greek thought, the ideas which other teachers
brought to Athens and Socrates had rejected. The seeds of future
research – and travel – were sown. But there was also business to
attend to at home in Athens.

Plato was now a full adult and fully liable as a citizen for duties,
which included military service. By 395, when he was in his early
thirties, the city found itself at war again and many citizens were
called up for service. The end of the Peloponnesian War in 404

had not meant an end to rivalry between Greek cities. The fragile peace between Sparta and its defeated rivals had not held, and Athens was once against embroiled in a war against the city-state. Joining other cities including former allies of the Spartans, the Athenians attempted to wrest hegemony of the Greek world away from Sparta, ostensibly the dominant power in Greece but a poor custodian of Greek interests and incapable of maintaining peace. Athens allied with its neighbours the Boeotians (led by Thebes), Argos and Corinth to resist its dominance.

The younger Socratics were of age to fight for their cities – or for others. Xenophon had ended up in the service of Sparta's king Agesilaus II in Asia Minor. The Spartans recalled Agesilaus to the mainland when it became clear that other cities were mobilizing against them. In 394, Xenophon returned to mainland Greece with the king and fought alongside him – even against his own city.[14] Yet most Athenians, however much they idealized Sparta and its political and social arrangements, did not go so far as to join its army.

There is no firm evidence that Plato served his city as a hoplite, but it is inconceivable that a physically able citizen with the means to equip himself as a soldier could have avoided doing so. Plato's experience as a wrestler would have prepared him well for those hoplite encounters, which at a certain phase were more like rugby scrums than pitched battles. The earliest testimony, from Peripatetic philosopher Aristoxenus, reported that Plato served in three campaigns, fighting at Tanagra, Corinth and Delium, but this confuses Plato's and Socrates' military service; the third of these was not a battle in the Corinthian War (395–387/6).[15] However, if Plato did fight for his city in this war against the Spartans and their allies, he might have found Xenophon, formerly his fellow student, fighting for the opposite side, as he did in the Battle of Coronea in 394.

Plato Commemorates Socrates in Writing

There was business to attend to in Athens itself. While the city was often caricatured – by Plato as much as anyone – as the home of relentless cultural innovation, there were important changes during this period. As the city's democracy re-established itself with a flurry of written documents, writing began to feature more and more in the intellectual life of Athens itself. An early act was the standardization of the Athenian alphabet, agreed in 403/2. This formalized the general practice of inscribing public documents and pointed to the growing importance of the written word for the private as well as the public life of the city.[16] From now on, the Attic dialect of Greek had a standard written form, becoming the classical Greek alphabet as we know it, with its distinctive long vowels eta (η) and omega (ω).

The first oligarchy had established a commission aimed at collating and codifying the city's law, but it was making slow progress.[17] The city's orators were starting to look beyond performance in courts and political meetings, and to circulate written copies of their best speeches. The circulation of copies of legal speeches, as examples for teaching rhetoric or as problems for discussion, was becoming an established practice; Lysias, the younger brother of Polemarchus, may have been an early proponent of such publication.[18] For another teacher of rhetoric, Isocrates, a lifelong competitor of Plato's in the education of elite youth, such publications indicated the importance of teaching in his work.[19]

Publication was a slow and informal process.[20] Writers drafted their works on wax tablets, scratching their words with a stylus into a thin layer of wax poured into a wooden frame; these were usually found in hinged pairs that could be fastened together for protection. These notes could then be transcribed onto papyrus rolls, by students or well-trained enslaved workers. The completed work might be copied multiple times for sale and circulation; papyrus, which was imported from Egypt, was occasionally hard to come by when conflict interrupted access to trade routes, an issue arising at various points in the fourth century. Xenophon's critiques of Plato's presentation of Socratic thought suggest that copies of his dialogues were circulating beyond Athens while both writers were still active. But few copies were made of any works and older texts were hard to find, unless you had access to the personal collections of established scholars.

Socrates had treated the written text with suspicion, as a source of weak understanding, of knowledge not fully grasped. He was not the only early thinker to hold back from writing, and Plato, writing much later, put clear doubts into his mouth:

> You know, Phaedrus, that's the strange thing about writing, which makes it truly analogous to painting. The painter's products stand before us as if they were alive: but if you question them, they maintain a most majestic silence. It is the same with written arguments (*logoi*); they seem to talk to you as though they were intelligent, but if you ask them anything about what they say, from a desire to be instructed, they go on telling you just the same thing for ever. And once a thing is put in writing, the composition, whatever it might be, rolls around all over the place, getting into the hands not only of those who understand it, but equally of those who have no business with it. It doesn't know how to address the right people, and not address the wrong. And when it is mistreated or unfairly abused it always needs its father to come to its help; for it is unable to defend or help itself.[21]

Plato saw that writing could be dangerous to the writer too; expressing controversial ideas in writing might prove even more dangerous than expressing them in speech had been to Socrates, and others. The danger of speaking out runs through his dialogues; the visiting teacher Protagoras of Abdera, represented as addressing a highly privileged audience of the Athenian elite, nonetheless noted his worries about expressing new ideas in Athens as a visitor, a precarious situation. The biographical tradition suggests that Protagoras' worries had been well founded and that he left Athens hurriedly to avoid prosecution – although we can never be sure whether such stories are merely echoing Socrates' fate.[22]

Reading was a problematic source of instruction. Xenophon depicted Socrates' student Euthydemus – and, as we saw, perhaps a little of Plato himself has crept into this portrait – as an enthusiastic book-buyer. Xenophon suggests that owning books did not grant wisdom and was not a substitute for learning through the active mode of Socratic conversation.[23] Antisthenes told a student upset about losing his notes that he should have committed them to memory, not to writing.[24] However, such written notes (*hypomnemata*) might form the basis of a published work; the word is the Greek title of Xenophon's Socratic dialogues.

The increasing presence of the written word made it impossible to hold to Socratic ideals about not writing. Soon after his death, Socrates' followers began to commemorate him by writing speeches and dialogues, attempting to capture his arguments and character.[25] This seems to have begun early and as a response to critics – a speech presented as Meletus' accusation from the trial was written by Polycrates, possibly in the 390s, and motivated Socrates' friends and followers to publish their own responses.[26] Fragments of works by, or attributed to, several of them survive, as well as lists of works now lost: in addition to Plato and Xenophon, authors include Aeschines the Socratic, Aristippus, Phaedo and Antisthenes.[27] The last, perhaps twenty years older than Plato, had already published display speeches rather like those of Gorgias, defences of Homeric heroes, and had also published dialogues involving characters common to the writing of many Socratics. The first, Aeschines of Sphettus, roughly Plato's contemporary, wrote witty dialogues showing encounters between the Socratics and a wider circle, such as Pericles' partner Aspasia in conversation with first Xenophon and then his wife, on the nature of love. A surviving fragment illustrates key features of the developing genre, a focus on topics such as Eros and a disdain for chronological probability. Aspasia was probably already dead when Xenophon was old enough to marry.[28] The dialogues feature an interlocking cast of characters – not just the Socratics but their contemporaries, past students of Socrates like Alcibiades and other educators. They discuss similar examples, positive and negative: long-dead politicians like Themistocles and the kings of other countries, like Cyrus the Great, king of Persia.

If commemoration of their master and rebutting his critics motivated the Socratics to start writing, their works soon became vehicles for debates and disputes with each other, as their own ideas moved beyond those of their teacher. Fragments of dialogues from other Socratics – and it is impossible to know who wrote or published first – confirm that each writer presented their teacher in a way that reflected how their own thought had developed; they also used their own 'Socrates' to criticize others' ideas.

Xenophon himself tried to capture the spirit of Socrates and his engagements with his fellow citizens; in his *Memorabilia* he depicted Socrates in conversation with followers like Antisthenes, rival philosophers, members of Athens's elite such as Critobulus, the son of Socrates' friend Crito, and also craft workers such as the painter Parrhasius.[29] Plato, on the other hand, made extensive use of crafts such as medicine and architecture as analogies for intellectual endeavour (the craft analogy), but did not set Socrates in conversation with lower-status craft workers. Xenophon, despite testimony that he was a pioneer of the genre, appears to have joined this conversation relatively late, after a rapprochement with Athens late in his life.[30] His dialogues often comment on and criticize Plato's writing – sometimes explicitly, sometimes implicitly, such as when he depicts Socrates conversing with Plato's brother Glaucon and chiding him for his attempts to contribute to political life without having the experience or knowledge to be useful to his fellow citizens.[31]

Although it is conventional to classify Plato's surviving works as early, middle or late, on both philosophical and linguistic grounds, even the works classified as early appear to be the product of a mature thinker with a wide knowledge of the ideas of his contemporaries, and a fully worked-out philosophy of his own. Perhaps, as Danielle Allen has argued, it was rivalry with orators over intellectual leadership in the city's culture that inspired him to abandon Socrates' reserve and to start writing.[32] Plato must have started writing for circulation in the 390s, if not before; there is an anecdote about him showing a draft of the *Lysis* to Socrates and receiving a stern critique of its representation of his teacher.[33] But whether the Platonic corpus we have contains those first writings, or the products of his later years, remains unknowable, as does the exact order in which they were written.

Plato may have begun by writing his own version of the defence speeches Socrates had made at his trial, echoing the style of the courtroom speeches Lysias was writing. But rivalry with other students and followers of Socrates may also have played a part. The *Apology* includes Socrates' three speeches from the trial, reflecting his approach at different stages of the case, and even a short passage of dialogue as Socrates questions his accuser Meletus to demonstrate that his accusation is incoherent and that Meletus has brought him to trial on frivolous grounds. He then launches into a *reductio ad absurdum*, aiming to force Meletus to concede that jurors, councillors and Assembly members in turn all provide positive role models for the city's youth – can it really be the case that Socrates, and Socrates alone, damages them?[34] However convincing readers find Socrates' demolition of Meletus' position, these arguments failed to win over the jury. While its members don't speak, Plato has Socrates acknowledge the uproar at his claims, a literary touch that suggests an assured and confident writer.[35] Xenophon, in his version of Socrates' defence speech, makes even more clear Socrates' rhetorical failure.[36]

Perhaps Plato's depiction of Socrates in conversation with a performer of Homeric epic, the rhapsode Ion of Chios, has a better claim to being an 'early' work.[37] Its abrupt beginning and the similarly brusque treatment Socrates gives to his interlocutor suggest an early stage of the development of Plato's literary skills, when his primary concern remained the defence of Socrates. Plato set the scene with an opening exchange:

> Socrates: Greetings, Ion! From where have you just travelled to us? Was it from home at Ephesus?
> Ion: Not from there, Socrates, but from Epidaurus, from the festival of Asclepius.[38]

Just as in later works, the opening words introduce the dialogue's themes – the relationship between poetry, its performance and divine inspiration – and we might note the economy with which they do so.[39] Plato sets out a critique of the use of Homeric epic as a source of practical wisdom. Ion passes on the contents of the poems he performs without any real understanding of their content; he can recite Homer's battle scenes but cannot instruct anyone in how to fight a battle himself. Plato was clear that knowing about the mythical Agamemnon's exploits in the Trojan War was hardly going to equip a young captain on the battlefield or a defendant in the courts. Socrates' conversation reveals how Ion experiences poetic inspiration at second hand, so that even the spark of the divine creativity of the original is a dull copy – although Plato's description of the process and his analogy with magnetism are themselves inspired.[40]

Capturing Socrates' character and interests was a challenge. Xenophon's Socrates is often pragmatic and sympathetic to the domestic and business difficulties of his interlocutors, offering helpful suggestions to solve their problems and enable them to live more fulfilling lives. But it is difficult to reconcile him with Plato's depiction of his teacher and mentor, itself subject to development and change. In the *Ion*, Socrates is far from kind towards the rhapsode. His questioning of the bewildered performer is abrupt and unsympathetic. He makes some questionable argumentative moves as he browbeats Ion into agreeing that, given his firm belief that he can speak authoritatively on Homer but not on other poets, he doesn't really know about poetry more generally. Socrates suggests that performers like Ion make their claims through the influence of a divine power, acquired at second hand from the poet in a chain stretching back to original inspiration by the Muse. Ion is moved by Socrates' description, with its image of a chain held together by the force of magnetism. 'You turn out to be interpreters of interpreters,' Socrates concludes about Ion and his fellow rhapsodes. They transmit material they don't really understand and do so without any deep knowledge of the skills of the characters whose adventures they relate. Ion and others make no original contribution of their own.[41]

Dialogue openings remained important, but Plato began to develop scene-setting introductions and to write dialogues from the perspective of a narrator.[42] This enabled him to develop the setting of his discussion, to introduce more characters and to lead readers through discussions and the philosophical arguments they contained from the perspective of a specific character, often Socrates. Plato began to incorporate more complex scene-setting and multiple interlocutors, with these characters talking to each other in crowded semi-public spaces such as the changing rooms at gymnasia. The *Charmides* is a good example of this development. We have already seen how the opening scene of this dialogue emphasizes Socrates' experience as a citizen soldier and exploits

its location, the changing room of a gymnasium where youths and older men mingle after training, for erotic impact.

By using multiple speakers, Plato could skilfully grade the discussion; even though the dialogue might formally end in a failure to find a definition, the conversation itself has progressed in the depth and insight the discussants have developed. In the *Charmides*, the inexperienced youth Charmides soon exhausts his capacity to contribute to the discussion after an initial round of questioning and turns to his guardian Critias for help. Switching to the more experienced Critias as an interlocutor enables Plato to move the discussion up a gear: the mature and educated Critias can take harsher questioning from Socrates and explore more difficult topics than the young boy who is only just beginning his advanced studies. Plato's own developing philosophical experience and knowledge of other thinkers' ideas needed an outlet in his writing. Nonetheless, even an expanded cast of characters still failed to find a definition of the key virtue of *sōphrosunē*, and the difficulty of translating that word into English – temperance, moderation, self-control – perhaps indicates the challenge.

Plato's Philosophical Encounters in Italy

Plato's initiation into the Eleusinian Mysteries had begun a long-term interest in other cults that promised knowledge of the eternal world of the gods. Perhaps after the end of the Corinthian War, around 386 or a little later, Plato travelled to the cities of Magna Graecia and Sicily, where the Pythagoreans were transforming a religious cult founded by the mysterious Pythagoras into a way of life; meanwhile the Eleatic philosophers were developing ideas about the permanence of an underlying reality, which also appealed to Plato's desire for stability.

This was a different kind of journey than that to Megara, one that required days of travel by sea rather than simply taking to the road for a long day's walk. Although such voyages were central to Greek life, the open sea was still a cause of huge anxiety for travellers. While travel by land might require navigation through or around conflict zones, especially at flashpoints like Corinth, travel by sea was always dangerous. Nobody travelled during the winter if they could help it, when a storm at sea might overwhelm what were still small wooden sailing boats, often with open decks. Would-be travellers regularly consulted the gods for advice on whether they really needed to make their journeys or if it was safe to do so. Sometimes excitement got in the way of that; years earlier, Socrates had rebuked Xenophon for failing to ask the right questions of the Delphic Oracle and assuming that he should travel to Ionia to join what turned out to be the rebellion of Cyrus.[43] Xenophon was now an exile, in consequence of that journey, although he had at least survived it. Plato too would have been mindful of his teacher's advice. He might have sought the approval of an oracle for his travel plans and would have made an offering before his departure.

Voyages to Italy took a predictable route up the west coast of Greece and then across the Adriatic. Ships hugged the shore, their

Silver *nomos* of Tarentum, Taras, 365–355 BCE, depicting a youth on horseback and Taras riding a dolphin.

helmsmen aiming for the shortest possible crossing of the open sea. As Plato travelled west from Corcyra (Corfu), his journey took him to the cities of Italy's south coast, travelling onwards from city to city: Tarentum, Metapontum, Locri. These were substantial and powerful cities, each home to different groups of thinkers.

The Eleatics were not the only group of philosophers in southern Italy. Another group was the Pythagoreans, who in various ways traced their ideas back to the semi-legendary figure of Pythagoras.[44] While Pythagoras himself had lived in the sixth century, by Plato's time he had become a figure of legend, as if he personified the circulation of ideas from the eastern to the western Mediterranean that had accompanied the shift from physical science to metaphysical philosophizing. Pythagoras had been born on the island of Samos, on the Ionian coast, but had been part of a wider migration to the western Greek world in the mid-sixth century during a period of

Painting from the 'Tomb of the Diver', 5th century BCE, depicting men
at a symposium, fresco, Paestum, Italy.

political turmoil.[45] After travels to Egypt and Crete among other
places (most likely mythical), he established himself in Croton
in southern Italy and a community of adherents grew up around
him. These Pythagoreans followed his mode of life and teachings, known as *akousmata*, or 'things which are heard', so called
because they were transmitted orally between full members of the
community and not circulated in written form. While later biographers imagined what these precepts might have been, there is little
trustworthy evidence. But they do seem to have covered dietary
restrictions – vegetarianism, with the exclusion of beans – and the
avoidance of traditional religious activity such as animal sacrifice.

Nonetheless, Pythagorean learning spread beyond the
small group of adherents, as some followers began to integrate

Pythagorean ideas with wider philosophical and scientific concerns and to communicate these developments in writing. Philolaus was an almost exact contemporary of Socrates and an old man by the time Plato reached Sicily. He had endured a tumultuous life; while political strife was baked into civic life in southern Italy, the Pythagoreans with their strange ideas were an easy target for communities looking for scapegoats. There had been a wave of expulsions in the 450s, shortly before Athens had been involved in the refoundation of Thourii. At some point, possibly while avoiding local conflict on a visit to mainland Greece, Philolaus had taught Socrates' followers, the Thebans Simmias and Cebes.[46] Plato had therefore already encountered Pythagorean teaching at second or even third hand and was keen to learn more. Other Pythagorean teaching concerned the cycle of life and reincarnation – the return of souls from the afterlife into new bodies. That had an appeal for a young man in mourning.

Being a persecuted cultural and religious minority had not led the Pythagoreans to cohere as a community of their own. There were tensions between those who were interested in a lifestyle governed by the teachings of Pythagoras and those interested in developing his mathematical and cosmological thought. Philolaus was one of the second group, developing from the ideas of the tradition a view of an ordered cosmos. One of his speculations was that the earth 'moves in a circle', around the fiery centre of this cosmos.[47]

Only fragments of his treatise survive, including what might be the opening: 'Nature (*physis*) in the world-order (*cosmos*) was fitted together out of things which are unlimited and out of things which are limiting, both the world-order as a whole and everything in it.'[48] Scholars still dispute exactly what Philolaus meant by 'limiting' and 'unlimited'; at its most simple, this might represent a contrast between odd and even numbers, or at a more complex level the difference between matter, with its unlimited potential, and form, which provides a shape and thus limits to that matter.[49]

It was an opposition which Plato incorporated into his own thought and which eventually emerged in his later work.

It is likely that Plato also met his near-contemporary Archytas of Tarentum on this journey, beginning a relationship that would be of profound importance to him. Archytas, unlike Plato, was a politically active citizen, holding office repeatedly in his city, which was rising in power and wealth in the early fourth century. Like many of the cities of Magna Graecia, Tarentum, originally a Spartan colony, had faced conflict with the indigenous people and many of the founding aristocrats had perished in these struggles. Archytas was part of a new, democratic regime, in which he would eventually be held in such esteem that he was elected as a general seven years in a row, despite the established custom being that the office be held for only a single year.[50]

As he met with Archytas to discuss philosophy, Plato may well have felt himself to be an under-achiever in that respect as well as in politics. Archytas was in any case well ahead of him in mathematics. While Plato had held back from political involvement in Athens – although the taint of his family's association with the Thirty, and of his own association with Socrates, had made that a reasonable choice – he could not yet point to any significant achievements of his own, in either politics or philosophy. Perhaps it was the recognition of the advances made by Archytas that prompted Plato to pursue his philosophical goals more vigorously.

As more written texts circulated around the Greek world, Plato was able to keep up with the Italian philosophers' works more easily. His rivals and enemies would point to Plato's supposed purchases of their texts as evidence that he plagiarized the ideas of other thinkers.[51] But that is to underplay the significance of Plato's development and synthesis of ideas from disparate philosophical traditions, and the way in which he remained open to new ideas and to criticism.

Literary Development in the *Gorgias*

While the technical language of the Pythagoreans took its time to appear in Plato's writing, broader Pythagorean themes start to appear much sooner. One is the afterlife, the frequent location for the mythical narratives that he was starting to embed in his dialogues. Even the *Apology* concludes with Socrates picturing himself in the underworld conversing with figures from the past.[52] At this point Plato still drew more on Eleusinian than Pythagorean eschatology. He closed the *Gorgias*, like the *Apology*, with a vision of the underworld as a place of judgement, with more emphasis on punishment. But subsequent returns to the underworld, such as those in the *Phaedo* and *Republic*, would incorporate features from Pythagorean cosmology. Critics from other philosophical traditions, the earliest of them the sceptic Timon of Phlius in the third century BCE, said that he had plagiarized the Pythagorean works and that his cosmology in the *Timaeus* was merely copied from the Pythagoreans.[53]

Other educators, rather than unlearned youths, began to people the dialogues. Plato looked back to figures influential while Socrates was active in Athens, setting his teacher in discussion with them, even when the content they discussed spoke more to Plato's own present day. The *Gorgias* is an ambitious work with multiple speakers and a long, developing argument. It shows Plato developing his psychological thought and once more replaying Socrates' trial.[54] But its dominant concern is to show that rhetoric is not a worthwhile or coherent skill and that it should not be the dominant feature of a young man's education. We might see here Plato's sense of himself as a competitor with other educators for the attention of elite Athenian youth. There was no definite moment when Plato shifted from being a student to becoming a teacher; just as for research students in the present day, both identities are possible. In these years Plato began to attract a following of his own – young men who would listen and respond to him as he strolled around the gardens of the Academy and the city's other gyms. He had vital points to make about how they should live their lives as citizens and criticisms of the political culture of the renewed democracy to which they belonged. Some were no doubt eager to hear about the places he had visited and the thinkers he had met.

As the *Gorgias* progresses, Plato points to the problematic consequences of persuasive speech pervading political culture. Gorgias promotes a practice which (according to Plato's Socrates) corrodes rather than develops public life, and the attitudes of his student Callicles allegedly show the political consequences. The *Gorgias* is an angry work, featuring an angry Socrates fighting back against his rivals. In its opening discussion, Plato wittily imagines Socrates getting his friend Chaerephon to ask Gorgias 'what he is', simultaneously demanding a Socratic definition and a denial of his own nihilism, before Socrates goes on to argue that rhetoric itself does not exist as a skill.[55] Throughout the dialogue, the question of what rhetoric is and how it impacts the quality of political debate is explored. If persuasive speech could override citizens' capacity to make reasoned judgements on the basis of the evidence before them in the courts or Assembly, it was a threat to the community. And if it enabled new ideas to be adopted and the demos to be unified, it was a threat to the elite.

Two further characters demonstrate the impact of Gorgias' teaching in education and in politics. For much of the dialogue, Socrates argues not with Gorgias but with Polus, another teacher of rhetoric, who comes from Acragas in Sicily, and Callicles, an Athenian whom Plato presents as the lover of his own stepbrother Demos as well as the embodiment of the views Thucydides had attributed to 'Athenians' in the Melian dialogue.[56] There is no firm trace, outside the dialogue, of these characters, who may represent Athenians who died too young to achieve the kinds of positions recorded in inscriptions that would provide evidence for their lives.[57] Demos himself had been killed on campaign in the Corinthian War, commanding a trireme; Socrates was far from the only friend or family member Plato commemorated in a dialogue.[58] E. R. Dodds suggested that Callicles represented the kind of person Plato himself might have become if he had not met Socrates and turned the course of his life away from political participation.[59] No doubt many of the young men with whom Plato had been educated had expressed such views in the years before the city's defeat and been tempted to support the oligarchic regimes.

Polus, who steps in early to answer on Gorgias' behalf, turns out to be an enthusiast for powerful and charismatic rulers as well as for the art of rhetoric, on which he has written a book.[60] He also speaks up for the perhaps traditional view that respect from one's peers is the ultimate social good, rather than the good of the community itself. Socrates corners him into a detailed discussion of the morality of tyranny; Polus enthuses about the power enjoyed by the kings of Macedon, while Socrates asserts his ignorance of the tyrants and their court.

Socrates' criticism of Callicles used this dialogue to set out a further critique of Athenian democracy and the educators whom he held responsible for its defective character. Callicles' views align with the ferocious arrogance and confidence in the power of their position that Thucydides had attributed to the Athenians at Melos in 416, just before the disaster of Sicily and the city's defeat.

Plato shows how such views were in conflict with Socrates' stern morality. The dialogue concludes with Socrates telling a myth, showing the Athenians how their judgement of him was mistaken. Better judges would be found in the afterlife. As we saw, life after death had been a theme of Plato's writing from the start, also closing the *Apology*. This time, he focused on the punishment of wrongdoers, with the judges of the underworld demonstrating how they were able to provide a better judgement than the

Orphic gold leaf tablet, *c.* 350–300 BCE. The text is a conversation between
an initiate and a spring in the underworld.

Athenians had on Socrates. They see souls as they really are,
stripped of the bodies which might conceal their true qualities.
But these souls are condemned to brutal punishment, while the
souls of philosophers are sent to the Isles of the Blessed.[61] Plato's
description of the underworld and what happens in it suggests that
he had been investigating the cults of the western Greek world,
from the Pythagoreans to the Orphics with their secretive guides
to reaching a happy life after death. Just as the *Ion* offered a bitter
critique of Athenian education and culture, the *Gorgias* offered a
bitter assessment of Athenian politics and looked to the eternal
world of the gods as a place where philosophers might – unlike
Socrates – be judged fairly.

Plato and Sicilian Politics

Even more than the southern Italy of the Pythagoreans, the island
of Sicily developed a powerful place in Plato's imagination. For

Athenians who had grown up during the Peloponnesian War, Sicily would always be connected with both the loss of the Athenian fleet there and the chaos that had engulfed the city's politics as a result. The Athenians had first gone to help Sicilians when the sophist Gorgias of Leontini had led an embassy to Athens in 427, close to the time of Plato's birth. That had embroiled Athens in its first expedition to Sicily, when Hermocrates of Syracuse had led Sicilian resistance.[62] Gorgias had continued to visit Athens, to give display speeches and to teach the young and wealthy; he taught Isocrates, who was perhaps a decade older than Plato and who would emerge as Plato's greatest rival as an educator. He also taught Antisthenes, Plato's greatest rival as heir to the Socratic tradition, before he took up with Socrates.[63]

Athenians continued to be fascinated by the power and wealth of the Sicilian tyrants, including those who since 405 had controlled Syracuse, the city whose forces had outwitted their great expedition. These Sicilians themselves looked towards the mainland of Greece for honour, participating in – and often winning – the most prestigious events in the great Panhellenic festivals at Olympia. They commissioned leading poets to write odes commemorating their victories; Hieron, tyrant of Syracuse, had commissioned Pindar to write in honour of his victories in the single-horse race in the Olympic Games of 476 and the Pythian Games of 470.[64]

Syracusan society had long been dominated by a wealthy aristocracy, the descendants of the original settlers who had arrived from the mother city of Corinth in the 730s BCE, displacing indigenous people, who took back control for a brief period until the settlers reasserted their dominance with the help of Gelon, the ruler of nearby Gela, early in the fifth century.[65] Gelon's brother Hieron then ruled the city, although there was no lasting peace. Even during periods of ostensible democracy, members of elite families, such as the general Hermocrates, played key roles as politicians and generals. Hermocrates had opposed the Athenians in both 424 and 415. But while Hermocrates had fallen foul of the city's democracy, in 405 Dionysius I, the general who had played the greatest part in the city's other long-running conflict, that with Carthage, overthrew the democracy and seized power for himself. Dionysius, who was only three or four years older than Plato, used his position as tyrant to reorganize the city and its *politeia*, granting rights to 'new citizens', including freed slaves, to counter the status of the established citizens. He also turned Ortygia, the small island that protects the city's great harbour and was the original site of the settlement, into his own personal palace fortress, in which the favoured elite were almost captive.

It was not unheard-of for Athens's leading cultural figures to travel to Sicily, whose wealthy cities offered considerable potential for patronage and support. Playwrights could put on their plays in theatres often grander than that of Athens. The tragedian Aeschylus was said to have died during a visit to the city of Gela, killed when an eagle dropped a tortoise on his bald head, mistaking it for a rock with which it might shatter the shell.[66]

Plato had come to Sicily in search of its philosophers and their knowledge, but a meeting with a young Syracusan aristocrat, Dion, drew him into its politics. Dion was still a teenager, but in a powerful position as the brother of Aristomache, one of the two wives of Dionysius. However, he was out of tune with the luxurious life of the Syracusan elite:

> Dion was quite young at that time, but the best student of all those who spent time with Plato, and the keenest to answer the call to virtue, as Plato himself wrote and the events provide evidence. For although he had been brought up in a submissive culture under a tyrant, and in a way of life that lacked equality and was full of fear, accustomed to service to new wealth, the nurturing of amoral luxuriousness, and a lifestyle disposed towards treating pleasure and greedy

acquisition as the good, when once he tasted argument and a philosophy which led to virtue, his soul was immediately set alight.[67]

Just as with stories of Plato's meeting with Socrates, this is a suspiciously patterned narrative of the 'moment of conversion' type, but the connection between Athenian philosopher and Syracusan aristocrat is widely testified. Plutarch follows the pseudo-Platonic 'Seventh Letter', telling how Dion took Plato to meet Dionysius and encouraged him too to turn to the virtuous life.[68] The hedonistic life of the Syracusan elite, secluded from scrutiny on the fortified island of Ortygia, was perhaps even more shocking to Plato at a point when he had been immersing himself in the ideas and works of the austere Pythagoreans. The opulence of Dionysius' court impressed on Plato the possibility of the endless satiation of the most extreme physical appetites. Setting out his political ideas some time later, Plato would identify the life of the tyrant as the morally worst possible life, subject to endless competing and uncontrollable appetites:

Whenever the resources of his mother and father are exhausted for a man of this sort, isn't there already a great swarm of pleasures gathered together in him? Won't he first grab hold of someone's house, or the cloak of a late-night passer-by, and after this plunder some temple? And in all these actions, values newly liberated from slavery, spear-carriers for erotic desire, will defeat within him the values he used to hold from childhood, regarding what is good and what shameful, the values regarded as just – the values which at first were let loose in his sleep, when he himself was still under the democratic control of his father and the laws. But when the tyrant Eros took charge, he has become while awake the kind of person he often was previously in his sleep, and he doesn't hold back from any terrible bloodshed or food or deed, but Eros lives as a tyrant within him without any control or regulation, and since it is the sole ruler of him, as a city, it will lead him to every act of daring, then will nourish him and the disorderly crowd around him, both whose which have come from outside, from bad company, and those which have come from inside, let loose and liberated by his own predilections. Or isn't it a life like this?[69]

The contrast between the luxurious life of Dionysius on Ortygia and the austere ideas of the Pythagoreans disturbed Plato. His critical and vocal evaluation of the lifestyle of the Syracusan elite made him an increasingly unwelcome guest there.

There are several different versions of the final events of Plato's first visit to Syracuse.[70] Multiple versions of the story give conflicting details. Most suggest that when Plato gave a speech in Syracuse criticizing tyrants and extolling justice as a virtue – the most detailed account seems suspiciously like a summary of themes from Plato's *Republic*, quoted above – the tyrant lost patience. In one version of the story, Dion recognized that Plato needed to leave town quickly and found him a place on a trireme about to sail away. In another version, Plato was taken on to the ship heading back to Greece by Pollis, a Spartan ambassador, with instructions from the tyrant to sell him as a slave once the ship reached its destination, Aegina, an island just south of Athens and then at war with the city.

Either Pollis took Plato to the slave market in Aegina, or his presence in the city as an Athenian enemy led to his being taken captive and put up for sale. The man who would become the Greek world's leading intellectual was close to being lost to a life of enslavement.[71] In another version, Anniceris of Cyrene recognized him and ransomed him for a substantial sum – twenty or thirty minas, around three years' earnings for a typical Athenian worker. He refused to accept repayment from Plato's friends at home, saying 'The Athenians aren't the only ones who deserve to take trouble on Plato's behalf.'[72]

One version of this story ends with Plato's Athenian supporters using surplus funds to help him, on his return to the city, to buy the premises which became his Academy. Another version has Dion offering to repay Anniceris. Some versions have Archytas playing a role in negotiations to get Plato away from Syracuse safely, writing on his behalf and joining in the negotiations.[73] Other versions postpone all these details from the first visit in the 380s to a second one in the 360s and set Plato against the younger Dionysius; others, less plausibly given that the anecdote rests on Plato's fame, move it to earlier in his life. But both travel to Italy and a return to Athens marked a decisive point in Plato's life; he had learned more about those philosophies and cults that were informing his own developing thoughts and he was ready to engage more productively in a life of philosophical conversation on his return.

5

Establishing an Academy

Plato returned from Sicily to an Athens that was adjusting to the loss of its leading status among Greek cities, compared with its imperial heyday under Pericles' leadership. Athenian successes in the Corinthian War had threatened Sparta's claim to dominance over the Greek cities of the Aegean world. This instability, and the possibility of a resurgence in Athenian imperial ambitions, brought the Persians back into the conflict, at least in Asia Minor, in support of Sparta. As with the later stages of the Peloponnesian War two decades previously, Persian financial and logistical support strengthened Sparta and shifted the balance of the conflict. By 387, Athenian ambassadors were forced into conceding the terms of the 'King's Peace', in which the Achaemenid king Artaxerxes II secured Persian dominance over Greek cities in the eastern Aegean and Asia Minor.[1] The settlement also constrained Athens from re-establishing its empire, by forbidding the building of alliances and leagues. Sparta was confirmed in its role as the dominant mainland Greek city, policing the agreement, while the alliance that had attacked it was dissolved, as were the Boeotian federal state and the pioneering, revolutionary isopolity agreement between Corinth and Argos. Athens's hope of returning to regional hegemony was put on hold as Sparta aimed to divide and rule its neighbours.

The humiliating terms of the King's Peace were not well received by Athens's commentariat. Isocrates imagined himself giving a speech on the topic, attempting to persuade the Athenians to reassert hegemony over the Greek cities and to campaign together even with Sparta against the Persians.[2] Among the claims he made for Athenian pre-eminence was the rather bold suggestion that innovative teaching had helped to build the political institutions that had made the city outstanding. His intellectualist claim that Athenians' appreciation of the power of speech reflected the importance of reason as the unique capacity of humans was a fairer reflection of the city's political culture.[3] However, subsequent periods of greater regional stability enabled the expansion of Athens's new cultural industry, allowing visitors to flock to the city's festivals and students to hear its famous teachers.

Back to the Sacred Grove

Plato had long met with teachers and friends in and around the public training ground of the Academy. After his travels to Sicily, he acquired a property at the Colonus edge of its site and began to use it to meet friends and students, and perhaps to store his growing collection of books.[4] It may at this early stage also have been his home. The beginning of this philosophical enterprise is usually dated to 387 and linked to the King's Peace of 387/6, another turning point in Athens's post-war history.[5] But this may be one of the invented synchronisms common in ancient historical sources, and if, as Robin Waterfield suggests, the journey to Sicily post-dated the King's Peace, so did this venture.

Plato's new base was not a formal learning institution, but a place where those interested in learning might gather for discussion, or head for a stroll around the training ground – or its own smaller garden – together. They might visit the shrine of the Muses in the public grounds, in which Plato had placed further dedications.[6] Plato, following the example of Socrates, did not charge fees to students.

Athenians coming from the Agora to meet Plato had plenty of reminders of conflict on their walk. New monuments bearing the names of the city's war dead, now including Plato's own contemporaries, lined the broad road leading to the Academy from the city's Dipylon gate.[7] There were also individual memorials among the tombs along the Sacred Way, including a grand one to the handsome Dexileos, a young cavalry rider who had been killed in the fighting around Nemea in 394–393. Attending the annual funeral speeches delivered at these civic memorials had become a habit for Athenians. Plato had mixed views on their patriotism and the myths they told about Athenian victories past and present. And now everyone compared the speeches each year with past versions. You could buy papyrus copies and read them: not just the speech Thucydides gave to Pericles in his *History*, but Lysias' more conventional attempt, which included stories of Athens's mythical

Foundations of fourth-century BCE gymnasium building at the Academy, Athens.

great deeds, such as the defeat of the Amazons, markedly omitted by Thucydides.[8] Plato satirized both approaches in his *Menexenus*, in which the bulk of the dialogue is taken up by a funeral speech which Socrates retells while claiming that it was written by Aspasia, Pericles' partner, who is here presented not only as his teacher of rhetoric but as the author of the funeral speech given by Pericles.[9] The chronological complexities of this 'dialogue of ghosts', in which Plato's character Socrates comments on events that took place several years after the death of the historical Socrates, have long concerned commentators but do at least suggest a composition date.[10] The *Menexenus* twists Athenians' stories about themselves, presenting the city's recent years of mixed success as though they were continuing triumphs, even as the peace settlements restricted Athenian power. Plato, who had seen the growing wealth and power of cities like Tarentum and Syracuse, could see that Athenian exceptionalism was now on shaky ground.

Growing Competition

Plato was not the only Athenian educational entrepreneur. Other Athenians were starting up businesses as educators of elite youth from the city and beyond; together, these ventures transformed the city's appeal to the international elite. Some of Socrates' companions, like their teacher, eschewed formal teaching arrangements, although they had eager audiences. Antisthenes, older than Plato and without his privileged background, had no formal school but an eager and growing audience, readers of his dialogues and treatises.[11] He based his activities in the Cynosarges gymnasium, less prestigious than the Academy but more welcoming to those, like Antisthenes himself, not of citizen status.[12] The Cynosarges was a good location from which to critique Athenian ideology even more sharply than Plato had done: for instance, the Athenians' claim to be 'earthborn' made them no better than snails or locusts,

Antisthenes observed.[13] Isocrates, another of Gorgias' pupils, had already moved from writing speeches for litigants to teaching rhetoric and providing training in public speaking. If he had fixed premises the location remains unknown, but he was already in business when Plato began teaching.

All recognized that the intellectual landscape was changing. Isocrates explained how the state of education had moved on from the days of the first sophists and philosophers in the days of the empire, and worried about newer developments. He thought the Megarians had taken teaching in the wrong direction, an intellectual dead end of unproductive argument. Too many educators, he felt, spent their time quibbling over linguistic minutiae for monetary gain rather than 'pursuing the truth' and providing sound practical guidance:

> But these men have no other concern than making money from younger men. This 'philosophy' of disputes can do this; for these men, who care nothing either for private or public business, take a particular delight in arguments which are of no real use for anything.[14]

Isocrates was most likely writing around 370 BCE, three decades after the death of Socrates and well after Plato had begun teaching. Isocrates found himself competing for students against those like Plato, who had studied with the Megarians and brought their fierce style of argument back to Athens. Isocrates also recognized Plato's contribution, the development of a form of *philosophia* which was not so much about the practical accomplishments needed by a political leader as about a pure investigation into knowledge itself, how we understand the universe in which we live.

Plato himself reflected this debate in the *Euthydemus*, a dialogue whose action takes place in a changing room at the Lyceum gymnasium. He presents a pair of sophists, the brothers Euthydemus and Dionysodorus, who used to teach the *pankration*, a kind of no-holds-barred wrestling, but have moved on to teach its verbal equivalent.[15] Socrates' friend Crito is looking for a tutor for his son and so Socrates describes his bruising encounter with them. He tells how the brothers dragged him and his young friend Cleinias through a whirlwind of fallacious argument, in which what appeared to be logical arguments generated perplexing conclusions. The careful reader will recognize that these apparent jokes introduce important philosophical questions. Is Socrates wishing Cleinias dead when he wishes him to change for the better, as the sophists insist, conflating a change of quality with a change of existential state? Games with words and meaning were becoming more sophisticated; through these dialogical characters Plato challenged readers to consider how past and future selves are connected. Between the slapstick episodes of fast and fierce argument, Socrates sets out the case for the importance of pursuing knowledge as a means to achieving what he counts as virtue. These speeches set out a kind of educational manifesto which, as Plato's own activity centred more and more around education, became the theme of more of his writing.

Developing the Drama of Dialogues

The *Euthydemus* demonstrates how Plato was developing the dialogue form to encompass more complex structure and argument, while still using Socrates' circle of friends and students as the dramatic context for exploring questions of education. This enabled him to critique his rivals without naming them; Isocrates thus appears at the end of the *Euthydemus* as an unnamed Athenian whose work sits somewhere between philosophy and politics. Plato was now building on more complex dialogues like the *Gorgias*, which featured multiple characters and investigated connected themes, linking together his views on personal excellence, education and politics. Although he remained critical of Athenian democracy, and occasional moments of bitterness persisted, he could give the views of others a more sympathetic presentation. The *Protagoras* took a different approach, though it had a similarly ambitious scope, from the range of characters it included to the range of arguments it covered. Here Plato presents a gathering of great teachers in Athens, at the house of wealthy Callias, in the presence of a crowd of youths, their potential customers, set at an unspecified date before the arrival of the plague of 430. This provides the background to a debate between a younger Socrates (perhaps in his thirties) and Protagoras, the great teacher from Abdera, a Greek city on the coast of Thrace.

While Plato had turned away from the theatre, he could use its methods to great effect. This time, he drew on the conventions of comedy, and possibly specific plays in which Protagoras had been a character, to launch the dialogue's narration with a scene between two characters, Socrates and the young Hippocrates, who announces that Protagoras has arrived in the city and is staying at Callias' house, and that they must find out whether he would be a suitable teacher and worth paying.[16]

Plato uses Socrates to put forward his serious discussion points – what kind of education is best? What are the risks of signing up for the wrong kind of teaching? – as the pair encounter the weary doorkeeper, who is reluctant to admit any more sophists. Socrates' narration becomes almost cinematic as the pair finally enter the main courtyard of the house, where Protagoras is being feted by his hosts.[17] The great crowd scene, in which he describes the cream of Athenian youth surrounding the great sophist like a chorus wheeling around a leading actor, is explicitly theatrical.[18]

But Plato also presents this entrance as a *katabasis*, a descent to the underworld in which Socrates becomes a kind of Odysseus and Protagoras an Orpheus, living figures among the dead.[19] The dialogue itself goes back in time to reimagine an Athens before the plague, the war, and so much loss, for the city as a whole and for Plato. Both the main characters, Socrates and Protagoras, were already dead when he wrote this dialogue and so were many of the supporting characters, from Alcibiades, whose fleeting youthful beauty is noted in the opening exchange, to the sons of Pericles, who had died during the plague.[20] Callias, the host, is depicted as bereaved; he has only just inherited the family home from his father Hipponicus.[21] Despite the elaborate details, various anachronisms point to the fictionality of the conversation; this isn't a report of one of the historical Protagoras' actual visits to Athens.[22] Nor are the arguments which Socrates makes towards the end of the dialogue his own. Plato was starting to use the cast of characters from the world of the Socratic dialogue to present his own ideas.

In support of his claim that excellence *can* be taught, Protagoras presents two kinds of intellectual authority, those of tradition and of poetry, represented first by the myth of Prometheus, in which Zeus gives all humans justice, the ability to live in a community, and second by Simonides' poem, in which he analyses why being good is difficult.[23] Through these case studies, Plato sets out a positive case for democracy, for valuing the views and votes of all citizens, as well as another view on virtue to set against Socrates' account. Although Socrates argues powerfully against Protagoras' model, in which all humans can develop their personal excellence through education, nonetheless Plato here is gentler in his treatment of the democracy he criticized so fiercely in the *Gorgias*. Some people suggested that Plato was actually plagiarizing the historical Protagoras' arguments, although such claims were often motivated by rivalry and political hostility.[24] The powerful speech he gave Protagoras, with its myth of the development of society, still serves as one of the most significant arguments in favour of democracy in classical literature.

The final stages of the *Protagoras* suggest both Plato's continuing desire to capture Socrates' often paradoxical ideas and also the way he was moving beyond them. A central point of a complex argument, in which Socrates engages not just Protagoras but Prodicus and Hippias, seeks to establish what is pleasant. Here Plato sets out one of Socrates' most important claims, that no one does wrong willingly. If the pleasurable and the good are the same, and the painful and the bad, and if no one intends to inflict pain on themselves, then no one willingly does wrong.[25] This idea, that wrongdoing was a symptom of ignorance rather than evil, is central to Plato's depiction of Socrates.

The dialogue closes with a return to another of its key questions: can people learn to be good? If, as Socrates has argued, virtue is knowledge, then perhaps it is teachable, as Protagoras has argued. As Socrates and Protagoras emerge from the dialogic underworld, their positions look closer than they seemed at the start. Even the final words reverse the normal ending of a Socratic dialogue; it is Socrates, not his interlocutor, who declines further discussion and announces that he needs to be somewhere else.[26]

Critics have noted the weak points of this dialogue.[27] It is hard to see the connections between the separate passages of its argument, particularly the shift to the discussion of pleasure in its final stages. Some topics are rushed through rather than explored in the depth of later dialogues; for example, when Socrates uses the difficulty of assessing what is large and small as an analogy for assessing pleasure and pain, Plato hints at topics and themes that would be explored more extensively in his own later work.[28] But despite the glitches within the structure of the *Protagoras*, the dialogue shows Plato's ambition and increasing capability of setting out his developing thought, and in using Socrates as a character and his conversations to set out his own method and argument rather than simply recollecting what Socrates himself had said.

Plato's literary skill even extended to breaking the 'fourth wall' constructed by the narrated dialogue. In both the *Euthydemus* and the *Phaedo*, after the opening discussion has settled down into the narrator's account of a philosophical conversation, the listener interrupts the narrator at a key point in the philosophical argument to query whether the narrator's account is accurate, or to express support for the argument being made.[29]

Writing enabled Plato to circulate his own ideas beyond the Academy. The dialogues he was now writing represented Athens's historical political culture and advertised his connection to Socrates, but they also engaged with the debates of the present day, acting as a kind of prospectus for his teaching and the community he was building. These debates are not just local discussions, disputes with competitors like Isocrates, but also place Plato and his Socratic heritage in a wider context.

Looking beyond this World: The Soul in the Cosmos

Modern scholars have identified a distinct shift in the dialogues Plato was now writing; they demonstrate a growing confidence in handling big questions and finding answers to them. There is no absolute divide between the earlier dialogues and those identified by scholars as 'middle period' works; the *Euthydemus*, for example, has features of both periods and any dates absolute or even relative can only be speculative.[30] But his writing increasingly drew on ideas encountered on his journeys to Italy, those of Pythagorean thinkers, and also of Italian mystery cults such as Orphism, which offered even more hope for the afterlife than the Athenian-based Panhellenic cult at Eleusis did. They also perhaps reflect an increasing confidence in the possibility of philosophical discussion and argument, as Plato and his companions and students began to feel some sense of philosophical progress.

One of the most significant doctrines of the Pythagoreans was their insistence on the immortality of the soul, as something existing separately from the particular body into which it has been born. On this account, souls migrate repeatedly between this world and the afterlife, returning for life after life until they reach a level of perfection that spares them from further experiences of mortal life.[31] The idea of reincarnation had attracted Plato's interest as he continued to mourn his lost teacher, family and friends. He now used his writing to explore how his ideas fared when compared with those of the Pythagoreans, giving their ideas to characters who, while not explicitly Pythagorean, had some knowledge of their teachings and could use them to answer the questions that earlier works had failed to settle – how do we acquire knowledge? How might we become good?

One claim, known to modern scholars as the 'Theory of Re-collection', appears in the *Meno*, a dialogue which begins in the typical style of the Socratic searches for definitions Plato had written before.[32] Parts of the dialogue clearly show his continuing distress about Socrates' treatment by the Athenians. But the work turns towards Plato's developing philosophical agenda when Meno, a Thessalian aristocrat and student of Gorgias who is currently living in Athens, fights back against Socrates' questioning. Talking to Socrates is like being attacked by a stingray, he complains. Plato drew out an intriguing point from this argumentative stalemate, 'Meno's paradox': how can you know that you have found what you are looking for, if you do not know what it is?[33] Plato created a dramatic setting in which the historical Socrates' ideas could be challenged, and answered, by the Socrates he had created, giving voice to his own developing thought.

Socrates sketches a model in which souls, prior to becoming embodied in a human life and over the course of multiple lives, possess knowledge of the cosmos and its contents. They lose access to this knowledge when they are born as a mortal, but they can be reminded of it through sense-perception triggered by objects:

> Seeing that the soul is immortal and that it has been born
> many times, and that it has perceived all things, both in

this world and in Hades, there is nothing which it has not learned; so it is no wonder that it is able to recollect the things which it formerly knew, both about excellence and about other matters. For, since all nature is of the same kind, and the soul has learned everything, nothing prevents those who have learned one thing alone – for humans call that learning – from discovering everything else, if they are brave and do not falter in their searching. For searching and learning are simply recollection.[34]

Socrates draws a distinction between the 'eristic' approach pursued so far in his conversation with Meno and learning through recollection. The negativity of the argumentative approach leads people to give up seeking knowledge, whereas recollection holds the prospect of more successful enquiry and so encourages them to continue. Socrates demonstrates recollection by showing it in practice, with an uneducated person solving a maths problem through some kind of innate recognition of the principles involved. He encourages an enslaved member of Meno's household to find the length of the sides of a square whose area is double that of a square with sides that measure 2 feet long.[35] This problem might nod to the work of Archytas, whose most celebrated achievement was to solve the problem of doubling the volume of a cube.[36] Plato's interest in mathematics and its practitioners was a developing feature of his work and Archytas' work on proportions would be useful to him in the future.

Around the same time, Plato turned to a dramatic setting he had used before to explore the question of immortality further: Socrates' prison cell. The importance of the philosophical content of the *Phaedo* is underlined by Plato's chosen scene – Socrates' final day of life, ending with his death by taking hemlock – and by the cast of characters he assembles to witness Socrates' final words.[37] This emotionally powerful setting also provides an occasion on which Socrates' friends and followers might gather for a discussion. Here, Plato drew together multiple strands of his writing – including three of the most significant, commemorating Socrates, exploring the possibilities of human knowledge and placing that knowledge within the context of a divinely ordered cosmos – in a single dialogue.

The dialogue opens with a discussion between Echecrates, who wants to learn about the day's events, and Phaedo, who will narrate them to him. Echecrates of Phlius was another student of the Pythagoreans, who had established a community at that town in the Peloponnese. Phaedo was from Elis, another city in the Peloponnese; he would later return there to teach philosophy.[38] Plato has Echecrates interrupt Phaedo's narration at a significant point, to emphasize that the key point of the argument has been reached. This is where Plato's own theories contribute to an argument to prove the immortality of the soul intended to be more convincing than that which Plato had learned from the Pythagoreans and from the mystery cults of southern Italy.

Within the main dialogue, Plato puts Socrates in conversation with two young students of philosophy from Thebes, Cebes and Simmias. They are identified as students of Philolaus, rather than as Pythagoreans themselves, but the ideas Socrates discusses with them show that Plato was thoroughly versed in Pythagorean teaching.[39] Socrates describes how he has taken to writing hymns and, although he claims that this makes him like a swan, which sings its finest song just before its death, it is his argument for the immortality of the soul rather than his attempts at poetry that turn out to be his swansong.[40]

Socrates explains that he is not afraid to die since he knows that his soul will survive his death and indeed continue, not in the half-life of Hades as presented in traditional Greek myth, but in a fuller form, in a Hades in which his disembodied soul will be able to encounter knowledge fully, not hazily recollected as by the embodied soul in life. Towards the end of the dialogue, Socrates gives a detailed account of the world and the underworld, starting with the Mediterranean, which he describes as a 'hollow' in which people dwelt 'around the sea, like ants or frogs around a pond.'[41] He goes on to describe the geography of the underworld. While other souls endure a lengthy journey through the labyrinthine underworld, and repeated cycles of embodiment, the souls of the 'extremely pious' have a different destination, moving up to the earth's true surface:

> But those who seem to be different in respect of living pious lives, these are set free and separated from these places within the earth, as if from prisons, and they arrive in the pure dwellings above and live on the earth. And those of them who have been purified sufficiently through philosophy live without bodies entirely for the rest of time, and arrive at even more fine dwellings, which it is not easy to describe and for which the present time is not sufficient.[42]

Plato then goes on to describe Socrates' death. Socrates himself, he implies, would be accounted one of the pure philosophers, who enjoyed a better afterlife more akin to an idealized vision of embodied existence. This was the afterlife promised by cults like Orphism to their initiates; but Plato tied it to the possession of philosophical understanding of the connection between the changeable world of mortals and the everlasting, unchanging cosmos, home of the immortal gods and of human souls between each of their lives as embodied mortals. Those who had gained such understanding could be considered 'purified' and ready for promotion to a better afterlife.

Buried within the series of arguments which Socrates deploys to convince Simmias and Cebes is a section that goes beyond the claims of the *Meno* to identify the knowledge that is recollected as knowledge of 'Forms'.[43] This is the first time that Plato gives a full picture of a key plank of his metaphysics, now known as his 'Theory of Forms'. He had alluded to Forms in previous dialogues, to there being 'pure essences' of qualities, not accessible from the sensible world but apprehensible only through the operations of the mind, and enabling the mind to know and make sense of its disordered and jumbled perception of the sensible world.[44] Here he set out his vision of a world of stable and eternal 'Forms' or 'Ideas'. He sometimes calls them Forms (*eidē*), but often identifies them with a formula such as 'The Equal' (*to ison*) or 'The Equal itself' (*to ison kath'auto* or *to ison auto*). Whatever Forms are and in whatever way they exist, they provide a means for individuals to make sense of the qualities of changeable or unclear objects they perceive through reference to something that holds its qualities fully and without mixture or dilution. They offer a kind of blueprint through which the individual can recognize how a real object in front of them displays or instantiates a quality.

The dialogic context meant that this is not a straightforward exposition; Plato never produced one and the discrepancies between his partial accounts, each with a different emphasis, make it dangerous to produce a simplified overview. But the long and detailed argument of recollection in the *Phaedo* goes beyond the *Meno* account to show that what the embodied soul recollects are the Forms. Seeing two sticks of apparently equal length, for example, prompts the soul to recollect the Equal itself, which it knew when it was between lives. For Plato, the ability to access knowledge of a stable and unchanging reality underpinned all forms of intellectual activity. While his account of just how Forms were or might be connected to real-world objects was hard to grasp – and remains difficult to interpret – this was the framework that dominated Plato's writing from this point on.

Plato's increasing confidence in his own arguments, practised and developed through discussion with his followers in the

Academy, left his fellow Socratics behind as he moved away from the Socratic focus on ethics to explore the nature of knowledge, how it might be structured and how it might be acquired. The other Socratics were themselves going in different directions. Antisthenes retained Socrates' focus on the ethics of everyday life and on developing a model of an ethical life that did not look to the city for its values or law to enforce moral choices. He argued that the wise man should live in accordance with the laws of virtue, not those of the city.[45] While Xenophon was not based in Athens, his Socratic dialogues emphasize practical decision-making and commitment to civic participation; he depicts other Socratics, such as Antiphon, criticizing Socrates for his austere theorizing. Plato could expect a lively and critical response to his developing ideas, both within his own school and beyond it.

Imagining the Ideal Society

While Plato and his students were debating the Forms and attempting to access eternal and stable truth through reason, Athens's political situation appeared to be stabilizing. Despite the King's Peace of 387, low-level hostilities between cities had continued, often provoked by Spartan aggression, such as the 382 invasion of the citadel of Thebes and establishment of a garrison there. In 378 a rogue Spartan commander, Sphodrias, had attempted to invade the Piraeus, although the Athenians had easily rebuffed him.[46] In response, the Athenians reactivated their imperial ambitions with the foundation of a new league of allies – the Second Athenian League – making explicit their opposition to Spartan imperialism and abuse of power and also watching out for Persian interference.[47] Sparta's actions made idealization of its culture and political arrangements harder to sustain and perhaps drove the Athenian elite to rethink their political ideals, given the failures of Spartan hegemony. A renegotiated treaty, a second Common Peace, was

Eirene, goddess of peace, holding the infant Ploutos (wealth). Imperial Roman version of a statue by Cephisodotus, erected in Athens in the 360s BCE, marble.

established in 375 and renewed four years later, celebrated with the erection of a statue of Peace, a female maternal figure holding the infant male Wealth, in the Agora.

Plato's concern with immortality and the soul, and with the process of accessing eternal truth through reasoning, did not represent a complete rejection of realistic, real-world politics. The *Phaedo*'s account of the afterlife set out the consequences of wrongdoing through its depiction of the punishment of violent criminals.[48] While the *Gorgias* and *Protagoras* had seen him critique other thinkers' accounts of ethical and political action, and the preparation of young men for political life, he now set out his own thought in his most ambitious work yet. In the *Republic*, he wove another element into the capacious framework of the Socratic dialogue, the *politeia*. This was a genre more associated with political pamphleteering, short treatises which explored how to organize collective life by imagining the political and social arrangements of a city, one key meaning of the word *politeia*, the work's traditional Greek title. This could be a real city with admirable political institutions – Sparta had been a favourite for Athenians – or an imagined one in which new ideas could be tried out. Xenophon, for example, praised Sparta's social arrangements, including the collective upbringing and education of children and the eugenics practices that permitted extramarital sex in the interests of a stronger new generation, but he criticized present-day Sparta for failing to live up to its ancient ideals.[49] A *politeia* could even focus on Athens itself, as with the fifth-century pamphleteer familiarly nicknamed the 'Old Oligarch' and his grudging respect for democratic practices. Plato drew inspiration from his own experiences of both Athens and other cities. Tarentum's democracy – and Archytas' pre-eminent status within it – offered a model of how a philosopher could rule, while Sparta remained an obvious model for parts of Plato's political thinking.[50]

This work was on a grander scale than anything Plato had attempted before, spreading out across ten papyrus rolls and covering multiple themes along the way, linking together topics he had previously tackled separately. Plato's success in this was a major achievement, although there are some discrepancies across parts of the work, notably differences in the accounts of Forms in the central books and book 10. The later account appears a little less abstract; one of its examples, the Form of a couch, suggests that Plato envisages Forms of objects and not just qualities, unless the discussion is intended to be an analogy.

The *Republic* begins as an inquiry into the definition of justice, returning to the pattern of Plato's earlier short dialogues. Its first book introduces this topic, through a series of graded discussions with interlocutors – this time of decreasing age, but perhaps increasing argumentative skill. The dramatic setting introduces the dialogue's themes – Socrates is visiting the Piraeus, the home of radical elements in Athenian democracy, where the resistance to the Thirty had been centred. As he and his party, who have come to watch a new festival organized by migrant workers to celebrate the Thracian goddess Bendis, set off back up to the city, they are invited by resident alien Polemarchus to his family home, so that they can attend a further night of festivities. While the *Phaedo*'s interest in death was explicit, that of the *Republic* is initially less so. But Socrates' journey to the Piraeus was a *katabasis*, a word that could also be used to mean a descent to the underworld and, at the time Plato wrote the scene, almost all the participants in the conversation were already dead.[51] Polemarchus, like Socrates, had been unjustly put to death, also forced to drink hemlock, although by the Thirty rather than the democracy; Cephalus had died a natural death some years previously. It is possible that Plato's brother Glaucon was already dead.

Plato uses this setting to introduce two standard definitions of justice in circulation in late fifth-century Athens. After Cephalus,

Polemarchus' aged father, declines to engage in the discussion, being more concerned with completing a sacrifice,[52] Polemarchus takes over, offering a conventional account of justice: 'Helping friends and harming enemies'. He cites the poet Simonides in support of this definition. However, Plato is clear that Socrates cannot accept this idea, because doing harm to others can never be just, even if the victims are themselves unjust. This definition of justice, according to the exposition in Plato's scene, could be deployed only by those who were themselves unjust.

Socrates' claim provokes a violent response from Thrasymachus, a visiting sophist who is also part of the group. He roars into the argument with the sophistic claim about justice, that it is 'the interest of the stronger', and a fierce critique of Socrates' method.[53] Socrates' response suggests that working out what this interest is might be a more complicated endeavour than the sophist has considered – the stronger party might be incapable of knowing what is in their interest. Plato thus begins to centre knowledge as the basis of ethical collective life by showing Socrates countering Thrasymachus' definition with arguments that present how acting justly is in the interests of all.

Plato's mastery of the definitional dialogue in this initial discussion was so convincing that many scholars have argued that *Republic* 1 was originally a stand-alone work. But its language and imagery are tightly integrated into the ten-book whole and provide evidence for Plato's maturing literary skill. Rather than the disappointing conclusion of the early dialogues, with the discussants leaving off with no definition in hand, the *Republic* presses on as Glaucon and Adeimantus, Plato's brothers, insist that Socrates provide a better argument to show that justice is a better goal for individuals than injustice. And so begins a long, highly structured, journey that weaves together multiple strands from Plato's earlier work – the Socratic interest in definitions and use of the craft analogy, the importance of virtue – with a full exposition of his own mature thought, which both emphasized the importance of knowledge and set out a route through which it might be achieved.

Running through the work is an analogy between the soul and the city as locations where justice is a desirable state. This immediately raises a problem for some readers: surely the interpersonal negotiations of citizens are very different from any internal debate by an individual? Plato's political thought ran the risk of not being at all political. There are other paradoxes; despite the rejection of Homeric epic as a model for education, allusions to the *Odyssey* permeate the *Republic*, linking Socrates to the great but complicated hero Odysseus. Both are drowning men, attempting to swim to the shore.[54] Socrates' eventual capture of the definition of justice is presented as a boar-hunting expedition. And even the way in which Plato tells that story, holding back the revelation of the definition, echoes Homer's art in telling the story of Odysseus' youthful hunting adventures before his old wet nurse recognizes him by the scar one boar gave him.[55]

Plato had started to think of the human soul as being comprised of three distinct parts, each with its own responsibilities and qualities. The lowest level was physical and economic appetite for material things, with spirit, the desire for action and honour, above it. Both should be dominated and kept in balance by the highest level, reason. The analogy between city and soul is first introduced as a heuristic device – it will be easier to identify justice at the larger scale of the city – but Plato linked it to the established image of the 'body politic', the idea of the head ruling the body.[56] In the soul, reason rules passion and appetite; in the city, those with knowledge should rule those motivated by passion and greed. That the concept of justice is applicable in the same way to both individual and community is accepted by Adeimantus without any discussion; as this permits Plato to develop the analogy between city and soul, that is perhaps unsurprising, but it is a weaker moment in the argument and connects with the worries some scholars have expressed that Plato's analysis of politics doesn't quite connect with real-world politics.

The first *politeia* Socrates sketches is a simple community, one that can satisfy the simple wants of its handful of citizens.[57] An element that ensures harmony in this and all the models Plato develops is the principle of specialization: each citizen performs his own specialist task and leaves others to their own work. Plato took this idea from Athenian history, the view that the polis was functioning well when its citizens could attend to their own business. Glaucon dismisses this oversimplified model as a 'city of pigs' – what about the luxuries of life? Socrates adds more complexity to the mix until the simple model has been transformed into an 'unhealthy city', full of the goods that characterized a city like Athens.

Plato imagined a way in which an existing society might be transformed into the model city he was sketching, which is usually identified as Kallipolis ('city of beauty'). This involved expelling all the adults and rebuilding the city with a new population, in this case the children under the age of ten at the city's defeat.[58] Such transformations were a phenomenon of ancient war. He knew of enough individuals whose home cities had undergone complete change; the Syracusans had emptied Gorgias' home polis, Leontini, of its population, while citizens of the joint colony of Thourii who had an Athenian affiliation had been expelled – that event had brought Lysias and Polemarchus back to Athens.[59] Athens itself had removed the populations of cities it defeated and punished during the Peloponnesian War, notably that of the island-city of Melos.[60] The remaining youngsters would be led to accept the new arrangements through a patriotic myth. Plato recalled how the kinds of story he had heard in his nursery had made a powerful impression on his own young mind. This story sets up the class system in his imagined city, persuading the young that their class assignment is akin to or even based on the presence of a specific metal in their soul, placed there in their autochthonous underground gestation. These determined which part of their soul predominated and so which class they would by nature belong to: gold for the guardians, silver for the auxiliary soldiers who support them and bronze for the craft workers.[61] This 'Noble Lie' was less perturbing for ancient readers, used to their own cities' foundation myths and patriotic stories. This story persuaded the city's future rulers that it was both beneficial and necessary that they dedicate themselves to unpaid public service.

Scholars have disagreed on how seriously Plato intended his readers to take this imaginary city. Does Kallipolis offer a blueprint to follow in reforming readers' own communities, or is it an elaborate thought experiment or even a joke designed to provoke further and more serious reflection?[62] In the dialogue, Socrates emphasizes the 'triple wave' of shocking details of the society of the guardians in Kallipolis – the abolition of the family, the elimination of private property and the rule of philosophers – with the ultimate intention of focusing attention on the third of these, and the extensive education that produces them.

In Kallipolis, the philosopher-rulers, those who have emerged from a long education for which they were selected in childhood, carefully arrange for the strongest and best of the citizens to be selected for breeding. Socrates knows that his interlocutor, Plato's brother Glaucon, bred hunting dogs and the selective breeding of hounds suggested a way in which the human stock of the city might be improved, just as Spartans took a pragmatic view on extramarital sex when in the interests of producing healthy children.[63] Hunting also provided a familiar metaphor for the pursuit of knowledge and definitions, as the discovery of the definition of justice showed.

Plato had some fun setting out features of his city and especially the communal lives of its ruling class, who held no property and did not have families. He imagined women participating on the same basis as men, with communal nurseries rearing the children born from temporary unions designed to breed the best possible citizens. Perhaps Plato was recalling another of Aristophanes' plays, his *Women at the Assembly*, performed circa 391 and memorable for its depiction of an Athens where women take over the political institutions and abolish private property and the family.[64]

But the most shocking of Plato's innovations for political reform, the last and greatest part of the 'triple wave', was that philosophers should be the rulers:

> Unless, I said, either philosophers rule as kings in cities, or those who are currently called kings and exercise power practise philosophy genuinely and successfully, and that political power and philosophy become the same thing, while the many natures of those, who now pursue each separately from the other, are compulsorily blocked from doing this, there will be no rest from troubles for cities, my dear Glaucon, nor for all humankind.[65]

Such kings offer an alternative to the failings of democracy, in which power and knowledge are problematically separated. Plato wove his criticism of Athenian democratic culture through the work; images of the democracy as a ship on a voyage where nobody on board trusts or obeys the helmsman, the only person who can bring them to port safely, or as a beast which its trainers can scarcely control, illuminate the steady case he builds for rule to be based on knowledge. Philosophers, who have gained access to knowledge of the Forms through their education, are uniquely suited to rule, when ruling is characterized as establishing and maintaining order in human affairs in a reflection of the divine order of the cosmos.

Over the course of a long argument Plato demonstrates that it is their ability to exercise good judgement, arising from their

knowledge of the Forms, that enables (only) the true, Platonic philosophers to rule. Those who have accessed the highest level of his
training and have grasped the Form of the Good will make the
best rulers, and enable Kallipolis to flourish, staving off change
and decline. Plato did not suggest that Socrates had achieved this
himself – the Socrates of the dialogue admits that he is only specu-
lating about the Good and has not reached the highest level of the
developmental scheme Plato sketched out. This scheme is shown
through a series of images; the Good operates in the realm of eternal being in the same way that the Sun operates in the ordinary
world, illuminating and activating, bringing forth life. The process of coming to learn this is represented by a line that connects
four separate levels of knowledge, from uninformed imagining
and more justified belief rising through structured thinking to full
comprehension.

Plato criticized the state of knowledge generated by Athenian
democracy through another powerful image: the everyday political life of a city like Athens as an underworld, a cave in which
citizens are restricted from movement, able only to perceive the
flickering shadows of objects paraded out of their sight, cast on
the wall by a fire. Ordinary political debate was likened to these
prisoners trying and failing to make sense of what they see. True
knowledge and understanding could be achieved only by breaking
out of the cave, and even then, it would take time for those emerging to understand that they do not encounter reality directly when
they emerge but their first perceptions are of images of it – as one
might see reflections of the sun in a pool. It is tempting to think
that the cave's representation of the revelation of objects in a dark-
ened space owes something to the initiation ceremony at Eleusis,
where initiates gathered in the great hall and were shown sacred
objects by torchlight; others have been reminded of Athens's silver
mines at Laurion, where slaves extracted the ore that had created
the city's wealth.[66]

Plato's critique of the rule of the spirited – timocracy – shows a shift away from Sparta as an ideal and a recognition of the weaknesses of Spartan hegemony and the growing evidence that its military power was fragile. Xenophon noted indiscipline and cruelty in the Spartan forces at Corcyra during this period; moreover, when the Thebans under their charismatic leader Epaminondas defeated the Spartans at Leuctra in 371, the famed 'Spartan mirage' was fading and the city was no longer attractive as an ideal regime.[67] In Plato's exploration of the deficiencies of different types of constitution and the psychology related to each, Sparta seems the target of the account of timocracy, a regime characterized by excessive love of honour, and the dominance of the spirited part of the soul, equally a tendency of the kind of elite youth who might, in Athens, have idealized Sparta.[68]

The *Republic* began with a descent to the Piraeus and concluded with a further descent: Socrates' retelling of the account of the afterlife given by Er, a man who appeared dead for twelve days but revived just before his body was placed on the funeral pyre. This story further revises Plato's account of the afterlife, connecting the emphasis on judgement found in the *Gorgias* with the mechanics of reincarnation more connected to the *Phaedo*. After journeying to the heart of the cosmos, the souls of the deceased reach the home of the Fates and must select their next life. Er sees many great figures making choices that reject the heroic life. Odysseus makes a final appearance as he selects for his next life a soul that lives quietly and takes care of its own business, exemplifying the Socratic ideal.[69]

Plato at Home in Athens

Plato's own life, however, was not one of quiet separation from the everyday. He set his dialogues in Athenian spaces, from the public location of the *Euthyphro*, outside the office of a leading magistrate, to that of the *Symposium*, the home the poet Agathon shares with his partner Pausanias. This latter dialogue is set immediately after a civic dramatic festival at which Agathon's plays have won the first prize in the competition; the historical Agathon's victory dates to the Lenaia festival of 416. But the dialogue's themes point to Plato's own lifestyle during the Academy's early years, his creation of a space in which men could philosophize together in a sociable setting.

Many of the historical details scattered in passing through the text relate to the 370s, the period of Thebes's rise as a political power and opponent of Sparta under its dynamic leader Epaminondas, who like Plato never married, and the formation of the Sacred Band.[70] Plato became fascinated by the Thebans and their Sacred Band, the elite battalion comprised of pairs of lovers, older and younger men whose love for each other would inspire them to fight more fiercely. He depicted Phaedrus, introduced as the 'father' of the discussion and the first to give his speech, enthusing about the possibility of such a force creating a well-ordered city

Kylix attributed to the Foundry Painter, depicting diners at a symposium – some of whom look like satyrs – playing with their wine cups, *c.* 490–480 BCE, red-figure ceramic.

or camp, and inspiring its members to demonstrate their courage.[71] Plato in turn demonstrated through the dialogue that the homoerotic space of the Academy was one in which true personal excellence, and access to the eternal being of the cosmos, could be acquired.

The dialogue's theme is Eros; the cult of Eros at the Academy was one inspiration, but the topic may have been rendered timely by personal events we cannot know, or perhaps the advent of peace.[72] The conversations about love in its idealized household, perhaps drawn from Plato's own home or social circle, provided the place for a new account of how an individual could transcend the mundane and the bodily and come face to face with beauty itself, and through it the Good. While heavy drinking, rude songs and erotic entertainment were more normal fare at a private Athenian symposium, the dinner guests Plato depicts agree to send away the enslaved women who would have provided entertainment and to amuse themselves instead with a series of speeches in praise of Eros.[73] This enables Plato to set up a series of explorations of love as the driver of human action – including, in the myth the character Aristophanes tells, a longing for a lost half of a former double self – before Socrates exploits this theme, not as a metaphor for the pursuit of knowledge but as the actual means by which knowledge might be achieved. He recounts what he learned from the priestess Diotima of Mantinea about the power of Eros; her name, which means 'honoured by Zeus of the place of prophecy', suggests that she comes from Plato's imagination, not the historical Socrates' experience.

Diotima explains how, while love between man and woman produces physical, mortal babies, love between the souls of men produces wisdom – sometimes, as in the case of Lycurgus and Solon, the laws of cities – which can attain the status of immortality. Just as in the image of the line and the ascent from the cave in the *Republic*, Diotima outlines a programme through which it

The arrival of the drunken Alcibiades during the discussion of love by Socrates
and his friends, Pietro Testa, 1648, etching.

becomes possible for the lovers to ascend to knowledge of true
virtue. Where Plato's model in the *Phaedo* did not specify the
objects whose perception might trigger the process of recollection,
in the *Symposium* he granted a special role to the apprehension of
Beauty in the context of the kind of pederastic relationship pursued
in the gymnasium.[74]

Plato re-emphasized the role of erotic love in the pursuit of
virtue in his *Phaedrus*, in which Phaedrus (a guest and discussant
in the *Symposium*) and Socrates swap speeches about the nature
of a lover on a walk outside the city. Again, the notional setting is
historically impossible – Phaedrus, another of Alcibiades' generation caught up in the scandal of the profanation of the Eleusinian
Mysteries, had been in exile between 415 and 407, and Lysias,
whose speech on love Phaedrus recites, had not begun his speechwriting career before then.[75] Perhaps the two characters, teacher

and student, represented a version of Plato's own relationships – with Socrates, his teacher, and Dion, his favoured student.[76]

Socrates responds to the speech of Lysias with another myth of ascent, this time of the human soul, borne aloft by a chariot pulled by horses whose unruly passions will drag it back to earth. The soul itself grows wings under the influence of the right kind of love and can find its way upwards to the immortal heavens. Socrates and Phaedrus flirt on the riverbank on a hot afternoon, and the dangerous power of Eros is in play from the start of the dialogue as they discuss whether this is the place from which the wind-god Boreas snatched the Athenian princess Oreithyia.[77] This abduction story demonstrated to the Athenians their close connection to the gods; a sculpture of the scene topped the Athenian treasury in Apollo's sanctuary at Delos. For Plato, his characters' invocation of this myth both affirms their commitment to Athens and demonstrates their lack of precise knowledge about the city's heritage.

The Academy and Regime Change

While Plato was inescapably involved in Athenian politics and culture, the international appeal of the Academy involved him in politics further afield. In 367, the older Dionysius of Syracuse was succeeded as tyrant by his son (also Dionysius). Plato's friend Dion became a powerful political player in Syracuse as an adviser to the young tyrant, his nephew.[78] Dion may have had plans to ensure that his famously undereducated and debauched nephew was re-educated in virtue, following a programme along the lines of his own. Plutarch, writing much later, appears to be following Sicilian historical sources, as well as the 'Seventh Letter', in writing that Dion's hopes of reforming his nephew and Syracuse's political culture led him to invite Plato to provide Dionysius II with a crash course in philosophical kingship.[79] In this version of events, Plato, accompanied by some of his students, set out to Syracuse.

If Dion had had serious plans for this project, or for establishing a new colony to become a real Kallipolis, as Diogenes Laertius suggests, they were a complete failure.[80] Plato encountered a court even more febrile and 'full of faction' than that he had experienced when visiting the older Dionysius and was swiftly disabused of any thought of encouraging the young ruler to virtue.[81] Instead, the 'Seventh Letter' imagines Plato struggling to maintain the goodwill of the capricious young tyrant and work out how he might extricate himself from his stronghold on Ortygia in safety. The biographical tradition includes several violent episodes; in one, Dionysius threatened to cut Plato's throat, but his student Xenocrates intervened.[82] Other sources focus on Plato's education of Dion himself, and the political intrigues that led to the latter's fall from favour and his exile from Syracuse. Many of the stories explore the later trope of the encounter between the philosopher and the tyrant, probably retrojecting it into Plato's biography.[83] Such meetings were well established in ancient literature: Herodotus depicted the Athenian lawgiver Solon meeting the Lydian tyrant Croesus, Xenophon the praise-poet Simonides meeting Hieron of Syracuse.[84] But it became a more compelling theme under the re-emergence of monarchy as a regime type in the Hellenistic world, in which professional educators might act as advisers to a king.

Historians give a significant role in the events of Plato's visit to Archytas, now leading his home city of Tarentum. When the young Dionysius sent an embassy to Tarentum, Archytas voiced criticisms of monarchical luxury and Dionysius' court. Some sources credit him with rescuing Plato from his predicament in Syracuse on this visit.[85] The historical record does not extend to any meeting between Plato and Archytas on this journey, although Plato would have had the opportunity to put into Tarentum on his voyage from Athens. Yet the opportunity to reconnect with the Italian philosopher must have been part of Plato's motivation in leaving Athens again.

Syracuse was not the only city that connected the Academy with tyranny. Some of its students came from wealthy and powerful families that played dominant roles in their home *poleis*, and even became tyrants themselves.[86] Clearchus of Heraclea, a Greek city on the Black Sea, manoeuvred his way into becoming tyrant of his home city in 365, after its ruling oligarchy failed to maintain a hold on power.[87] Athenians suspected that the Academy was supporting the disruption of other cities and their regimes.

Others resisted tyrants – Dion was noted in this context – while Clearchus himself was assassinated by another former Academy student, Chion of Heraclea.[88] Dion himself came to Athens during his exile from Syracuse after he failed to dislodge Dionysius II from power; while the 'Seventh Letter' gives Plato a significant role in these events, other historical sources do not.[89] Plato's affection for his student involved him in a complex political situation which provided material for his detractors, who suggested that the Academy supported its elite students in attempts to change the regimes of their cities, echoing the role of Plato's relatives in the Athenian oligarchy. The extent of Plato's actual involvement in any of these events is unknowable; the sources are either hostile or seek to defend Plato against the allegations of hostile sources.

6

The Academy Flourishes

Whatever Plato did on his second trip to Sicily, the Academy was well enough established by then that it flourished in his year-long absence, and continued to do so on his return. This became one of the most productive periods of Plato's life. The students and scholars arriving to experience his teaching inspired him to develop his thinking and to write new, philosophically richer dialogues. As the Academy's fame spread and philosophers and students alike travelled to join its conversations, Plato began to subject the ideas of his 'middle period' dialogues – the *Phaedo*, the *Republic* and the *Symposium* – to critical re-evaluation. Socrates' legacy began to slip into the background as Plato's own philosophy developed in the rich intellectual environment the younger philosopher had created, evolving as it did in response to his colleagues and students. Now he turned to large-scale theorizing about the cosmos and the establishment of regimes built on replicating the order of that cosmos.

Attracted to Athens

Plato's growing fame drew others eager to pursue the new learning. Many of those making a commitment to a long and all-encompassing period of study were from wealthy backgrounds. Matthias Haake describes the Academy as providing 'social capital' for such students; being able to spend years engaged in study rather than

Plato, in a standard portrait bust, Roman imperial era, derived from
a classical Greek original.

productive labour, or managing a family estate, was a powerful
symbol of wealth.[1] Others were ambitious intellectuals themselves
and, if not of independent means like Plato, hoping to scrape a
living from teaching and the patronage of their students' families. Some did go on to enter public life in Athens; the Athenian

orators Hyperides and Lycurgus appear on Diogenes Laertius' list
of Academy students. But the most prominent names are those
who would become known as philosophers rather than politicians and eventually succeed Plato in running the Academy. Plato's
efforts ultimately transformed Athens's key offering to the Greek
world from political hegemony to education and cultural cachet.
Plato's nephew Speusippus remained a constant presence, a trusted
deputy. Other long-term habitués occupying roles somewhere
between student and colleague included Xenocrates of Chalcedon.
After his exile from Syracuse, Dion spent much time in Athens at
the Academy. In 365 he came up with the funds to enable Plato to
act as *choregos* to a chorus of boys, paying for them to train to perform in a festival; perhaps Dion gained some credit and prestige
from this too.[2]

Diogenes Laertius' list of Plato's students at the Academy includes two women, Axiothea of Phlius and Lastheneia of Mantinea.[3]
Axiothea apparently dressed as a man in order to attend lessons
at the Academy. While the Academy training ground seems not
to have been formally off-limits, the gymnasia were not the usual
haunts of citizen-class women, especially those of the higher classes.
Plato's own private premises, separate from the public spaces of
the Academy, may have been more open to women's presence.

At some point around 367, and possibly while Plato was absent,
a new student from Macedon had arrived at the Academy, an
unprepossessing youth lacking the beauty Plato extolled and an
odd sight to the Athenians with his strange clothes and hair, speaking with a lisp.[4] Aristotle was by birth a citizen of Stageira, a small
Greek polis on the northern shore of the Aegean, not far from
Athens's strategic colony at Amphipolis. Stageira had revolted from
Athens's Delian League in 424 BCE, when Athens lost Amphipolis
to the Spartans. But now the nearby court of the increasingly powerful kings of Macedon exerted a greater influence than either
Athens or Sparta over the wider Greek world. Aristotle's father

Nicomachus had served as a doctor to King Amyntas III, a relationship which would not deter the latter's son Philip II from sacking Stageira in 348.

Like Plato, Aristotle had lost his father while still a child and it was his guardians who sent him to Athens to study at the age of seventeen. Soon it was Aristotle who asked the most challenging questions and made the most original suggestions in discussion. Aristotle's testimony and critical analysis in his own works provides the most compelling ancient guide to Plato's thought during this period.[5]

Plato's later dialogues provide some insight into the kinds of activity students undertook, notably seeking definitions using the new method of collection and division. Comic poets also satirized this activity; one, Epicrates, showed students trying to find definitions while in the grounds of the Academy:

> (B.) . . . during the Panathenaic festival, I saw a herd of young men in the exercise grounds of the Academy, and I listened to unspeakably strange discussions.

They were producing definitions of natural history and trying to distinguish between animals, trees and vegetables. In the course of these discussions they attempted to determine which category the gourd (*kolokuntē*) belongs to:

> (A.) What definition did they settle on? And what category did they put the plant into? Reveal this, if you have any information!
> (B.) At first they all stood silent and gazed at the ground for a long time, thinking the matter through.

Then suddenly, while the other boys were still staring at the ground and considering the question, one of them said it

Mosaic thought to depict Plato's Academy, showing a group of philosophers in conversation around a sundial, 1st century BCE.

was a round vegetable, another a type of grass, and a third a tree.[6]

The students are disrupted by a 'Sicilian doctor', but Plato encourages them to return to their exercise: 'The young men paid no attention. But Plato was there, and very gently and with no sign of excitement he ordered them once again to try to determine what category it belonged to. And they began drawing distinctions.' Plato also treated this method with humour, showing that it could produce unwieldy definitions which were easy to challenge. In his *Sophist*, the main speaker, a philosophical 'Visitor from Elea', produces this definition of angling, which, though a lowly activity, still generates astonishing mounds of verbiage as its distinguishing features are identified one by one:

> Within expertise as a whole one half was acquisitive; half of the acquisitive was taking possession; half of possession-taking was hunting; half of hunting was animal-hunting; half of animal-hunting was aquatic hunting; all of the lower portion of aquatic hunting was fishing; half of fishing was hunting by striking; and half of striking was hooking. And the part of hooking that involves a blow drawing a thing upward from underneath is called by a name that's derived by its similarity to the action itself, that is, it's called draw-fishing or angling – which is what we're searching for.[7]

This trial definition shows how the method proceeds, successively splitting categories in half to reach a unique description (division) and then gathering up all the steps to produce a definition (collection), which also places the concept defined within an ordered hierarchy. The process was apt to go wrong, if at any level an incorrect 'cut' was made, one which separated out only a small fraction of a class, such as humans from animals, or Greeks from barbarians.[8] The definitions it produced were unwieldy and – as Plato's own examples sometimes show – unintentionally ridiculous. One of Plato's noisiest critics, the radical street philosopher and father of Cynicism Diogenes of Sinope, was said to mock this new process:

> When Plato defined man as 'an animal with two feet and no feathers', and was held in high esteem for doing so, he

plucked a cockerel and brought it to the school and said
'This is Plato's Man'. After this, 'with flat nails' (*platuōnuchon*)
was added to the definition.[9]

Although developing definitions was an important practice,
mathematical subjects played a key role in the Academy. Later tradition had it that the Academy's doorway bore the inscription 'Let
no-one enter who does not know geometry', but the earliest sources
for this date to later antiquity.[10] Nonetheless, mathematics was a
foundational subject, and number a foundational concept, for Plato
and the Academy's students. Plato had set out an imaginary curriculum for the philosophers of Kallipolis which progressed through
various forms of work with number, starting with arithmetic and
calculation (*logistikē*) for theoretical rather than practical purposes
(7.525d). Just as with the mathematical problem presented in the
Meno, in which a member of Meno's household seeks to calculate
the lengths of the sides of a square, Plato appeared to look to the
work of Archytas; the students progress from arithmetic to two-
dimensional geometry (7.526cd), which had many practical uses for
rulers and generals, but could also take a more advanced and theoretical form. The next stage was the geometry of solids – of cubes,
for example – and then astronomy, the science of solid bodies in
rotation and movement, a subject which was treated as 'useless'
by others but which for Plato had a symbolic value as a form of
knowledge of the distant parts of the cosmos. The next stages of
the course add dimensions and motion, along with more complex proportions, in the science of harmonics, which developed
an understanding of number and proportion in sound; this, Plato
has Socrates acknowledge, is an insight of the Pythagoreans.[11] The
connection of three kinds of mean on this syllabus, the arithmetic, geometric and harmonic, was often associated with Archytas,
although he may simply have been recording a system created by
others and originally associated with musical intervals.[12]

Mathematics offered a route into understanding Platonic metaphysics. The distinction between a rough circle sketched in the sand and the mathematical definition of a circle combined with what one might picture in one's mind when circles are mentioned offered an analogy, and perhaps something more than that, between real-world objects and ideal versions of them. Through mathematical study, students might progress to understanding the Forms themselves.[13] The beauty of mathematical theorems and the order they represented held a great appeal for Plato, although he was more an admirer of mathematics than an innovator himself.

Both Isocrates and Xenophon felt that a little of the novel and arcane disciplines associated with these advanced studies might go a long way, at least as far as the education of leading citizens was concerned. Xenophon depicted Socrates himself saying so, the former using his own writing on the latter to distinguish between the teaching of Socrates and Plato, and emphasizing that the older thinker always aimed at practical advice:

> For example, he said that geometry should be studied only up to the point at which one was competent to measure a plot of land accurately, should that ever be needed for purposes of inheritance, conveyance, division, or proof of yield: and this was so easy to learn that anyone who applied his mind to the computation required would at one visit discover the size of the plot and come back from it knowing how it was measured. But he was not in favour of pursuing the study as far as those abstruse geometrical figures in which he said he could see no practical use. He was not actually unfamiliar with them, but he said they were capable of consuming a man's life to the exclusion of many other useful subjects.[14]

Xenophon's assertion of the practical bent of Socrates' teaching was at least as much a criticism of Plato's current philosophical and pedagogical practice, and the way he used Socrates as a character to present them, as a direct claim about Socrates himself.[15] He most likely wrote this when paying renewed attention to Athens in the late 360s or 350s, showing that the contest for Socrates' legacy continued.

Isocrates, the most successful educator of the time, also thought that a more traditional education was preferable to the Academy's offerings:

> I am so far from looking down on the education left to us by our ancestors that I praise even that established in our own time, I mean the geometry and astronomy and the discussions people call 'eristic', in which youths take more delight than is proper, while not one of the older men would describe them as tolerable.[16]

A Critical Approach

From the external perspectives of Xenophon and Isocrates, it might look as though Plato was providing a new form of education as leisure, a project for the wealthy who did not need to learn practical skills to earn a living for themselves.[17] The comic poets found such well-groomed and elegant Academy students an easily identifiable target for mockery, just as much as those who recruited and taught them; 'I think I'm getting a complete image of the Academy itself', concluded one description.[18]

While the Academy's students were an increasingly recognizable presence in the city, Plato was concerned with the methods they were using in their conversations and meetings. He hoped that they would make progress through a series of stages to grasp the fundamentals of reality through philosophical activity, a process he had analogized to sight in the *Republic*:

Salvator Rosa, *The Academy of Plato, c.* 1662, etching.

Therefore, Glaucon, isn't this the very practice through which dialectic achieves its goal? And although it itself belongs to the intelligible, the capacity of sight imitates it. We were saying that sight already tries to look at living things, then to the stars and finally to the sun itself. It's in this way that, whenever someone tries his hand through discussion and separately from all sense perception to reach for that which each thing really is, and does not give up until it has grasped the nature of the Good itself through thought, and so reaches the limit of the intelligible, just as the other reached the limit of the visible.[19]

At the point when he wrote this, most likely in the 370s, Plato was reaching the age at which Kallipolis' philosophers completed their own education and were ready to take their turn in using their knowledge in government. Such a role seems to have remained out of reach for Plato, who was widely perceived to be recreating the kind of aristocratic association that had led to the late fifth century oligarchies.[20] He had to content himself with critical discussion from the sidelines.

Another dialogue gives some insight into the active criticism that discussion in the Academy might involve. Plato's *Parmenides* gives a taste of what sharp philosophical discussion at the highest level might have been like, even though it is set decades before Plato's own birth, in Socrates' youth roughly in the 450s.[21] The Academy was not a passive space in which Plato's ideas were treated with reverence, but a lively intellectual environment in which students and visitors alike might challenge each other's ideas – and those of Plato himself. However, the topics discussed represent difficulties with Plato's own theories and show their development. Plato used the *Parmenides*' setting and characters to position his ideas as a response to and a development of those of the Eleatics Parmenides and Zeno, although the positions taken by the dialogue's characters might be Plato's own and those of a critic in the Academy, or even, as David Sedley has suggested, the later Plato represented by Parmenides critiquing the thought of the younger Plato represented by Socrates.

Plato imagined Parmenides travelling to Athens with his friend and fellow philosopher Zeno for a festival and to meet local teachers and students – a set-up which informally echoed his own Academy – and encountering Socrates as part of a group. The chronology is difficult; Plato's dialogue imagines that Parmenides was forty years older than Socrates, but other biographical sources place him earlier than that, reaching full adulthood in the last decade of the sixth century.[22] But the dialogue's historical concern is with the development of Plato's own thought and the debates about it in the Academy at the time he was writing. The discussion is set in a house in the potters' quarter, just outside Athens's city walls by the Dipylon, perhaps hinting that the conversation is in some way approaching the ideas of the Academy.

The narrator, Plato's younger half-brother Antiphon, arrives at the meeting while Zeno is reading from his book, which, as Zeno explains, was stolen in draft form and disseminated without his consent, before his defence of Parmenides' ideas and the problem of accounting for both unity and difference was fully formulated. Writing this, Plato revealed his own worries about his work in circulation, and the problem of the fixity of the written word.

The young Socrates believes that he has an alternative argument which accounts for the multitude of things in existence; here, Plato is putting his own ideas into the mouth of his teacher. What Socrates relates is a version of Plato's Theory of Forms.[23] But just as Zeno regretted that his early work had escaped from his control and was published and discussed before he was ready to defend it, Plato wanted to show how his own work had developed. He placed his critique in the mouth of Parmenides, representing a more mature version of himself and placing his own thought in the context of the Eleatic tradition.

Parmenides criticizes gaps in the theory. What kinds of things have related Forms? Abstract qualities such as Beauty and the Good are all very well, but is there a Form of Human, or a Form of Mud, or of Hair? Socrates has to admit some doubts on this, and Parmenides lets him off on the grounds that he is still young and developing as a philosopher. Plato was aware of the need for clarity on this topic; even in the *Republic*, the two separate accounts of the Theory of Forms do not entirely align, while the *Symposium* and the *Republic* offer different accounts of how one may come to access knowledge of the Forms.[24]

The imagined Parmenides takes Socrates to task for other flaws in his characterization of Forms, first for a vagueness about how the Form of a quality like Largeness can be indivisible yet present in many instances of large things. Then, more devastatingly for Plato's theory, he identifies a further flaw, in which once Largeness and the large things are considered together, an additional Form will be generated to explain the largeness of all this new group, and this process would (on most readings) generate an infinite series of Forms.[25] In technical terms this criticism, known now as the 'Third Man' argument, explores the problem of self-predication when it is applied to universals.

Despite his protests that his age makes such hard work impossible, Parmenides is prevailed upon to give a masterclass in what rigorous philosophical training should look like. He chooses the youngest student present, Aristotle, on the basis that his youth and inexperience will make him cooperative. By giving Parmenides' interlocutor the name of his own most promising student, Plato stretched the imaginary timescale that permitted Parmenides to talk with a young Socrates both backwards and into the future. The complex series of logical exercises Parmenides undertakes with 'Aristotle' offers an example of a thorough and rigorous philosophical work-out, perhaps appealing to the Academy's students. But it is a long way from the flirtatious wit of the Socratic dialogues.

Plato did attempt to win over the wider public through occasional public lectures, following the tradition of the earlier sophists with their exciting displays of rhetoric to paying audiences. The evidence is that Plato was less successful at public engagement. In later years, Aristotle liked to entertain his own students with an account of the negative reception of Plato's lecture 'On the Good'. One of them, Aristoxenus of Tarentum, wrote up the story as a lesson in how not to construct and deliver a lecture about difficult technical material to a broad audience:

> For each came expecting that he would learn something about the things considered to be good for humans, such as wealth, health, strength, and in summary some wonderful happiness (*eudaimonia*). But when it became evident that the arguments were about subjects such as numbers, geometry, and astronomy, and finally, that the Good is One, I think that they thought it completely contrary to common sense, and some of them belittled his claim while others found fault with it.[26]

Aristoxenus was loyal both to Aristotle and to his previous teachers in Italy, and at other points in his work appears somewhat hostile to Plato, although here he also appears to have thought poorly of the Athenian audience.[27] Aristotle appears to have used the way that Plato had lost the goodwill of his audience to explain that lectures need to be well constructed and begin with a summary – 'say what you are going to say' – and progress clearly. It is not clear where Plato delivered this infamous lecture; later sources suggest that it was at the democratic stronghold of the Piraeus, not an obvious choice for him.[28] Aristotle himself had outlasted other listeners at another less public session, when Plato had read a draft of the *Phaedo* to friends and supporters, and the audience had dwindled until Aristotle was the only one left.[29]

But Plato was unconcerned about his listeners' bemusement at his arguments, or that some of them left early. Perhaps he was aiming his remarks at a handful of his followers in the audience, to Aristotle, or to Speusippus and Xenocrates, and was unconcerned about the struggles of the wider audience. Later commentators thought the lecture 'enigmatic'.[30] But the reports, along with Aristotle's testimony of Plato's doctrine in his *Metaphysics*, are detailed enough to raise the question of whether Plato communicated a different set of doctrines in his lectures and teachings than he did in his published writing, with there being a set of 'unwritten doctrines' at the heart of his work. Given the partial and incomplete exposition of key parts of Plato's theorizing in the dialogues, that must be true to some degree; students like Aristotle, who could listen to and question Plato directly, could access his ideas very differently to someone simply reading the published dialogues. Whether there were substantive unwritten or even secret doctrines to learn from Plato and the Academy has been a matter of continuing dispute.[31] Some have argued that the dialogues written during this part of Plato's career contain the broad outlines of the ideas he was then teaching in the Academy.[32] Again Aristotle is the best guide to the way in which Plato's thought was experienced there, as an encounter between Pythagorean ideas about number and structure and the Socratic interest in definitions:

His divergence from the Pythagoreans in making the One and the Numbers separate from things, and his introduction of the Forms, were due to his inquiries in the region of definitions (for the earlier thinkers had no experience of dialectic), and his making the other entity besides the One a dyad was due to the belief that the numbers, except those which were prime, could be neatly produced out of the dyad as out of some plastic material.[33]

Aristotle gives a sense of the account of the Good that so confused the lecture audience, suggesting that those with better access to Plato were able to grasp his arguments more clearly. But Aristotle's account also suggests that Plato adjusted his theories in later years to better explain the fundamental role of numbers within them, which was now distinct from the role mathematical objects had played in the process of coming to know the Forms.[34] Throughout his late dialogues, Plato gave fresh accounts of both his metaphysics and his epistemology. In the *Sophist*, for example, as part of a thorough investigation into the philosophical use of language, he answers questions and responds to objections raised in the *Parmenides*. Once he has defined the sophist as someone who creates and communicates falsehoods and misleading images, he must deal with the objections that some (identified in the dialogue as 'late-learners') might raise to the possibility of expressing falsehood. This leads to a series of clarifications, including an argument that there are some fundamental Forms, the 'Greatest Kinds', which play a special role among the other Forms in the same way that vowels do in the alphabet.[35] For many contemporary philosophers, the central sections of the *Sophist* are Plato's richest and most rewarding – if still difficult and subject to competing interpretations – philosophical work.

The sensitivity to language Plato shows in the *Sophist* was matched across his writing by a new attention to fashions in communication which were shaping the style of literary Greek. In his later years he adopted new stylistic mannerisms, echoing the technique by which Isocrates chose words and arranged sentences to avoid 'hiatus', following a word ending with a vowel with a word starting with a vowel.[36] He also began to make more regular use of *clausulae*, using rhythmic arrangements of syllables to close sentences with the metrical form with which lines of verse were brought to satisfying closes. These stylistic changes accompany changes in the substance of the dialogues. Plato now wanted to explore ideas that went so far beyond what he had learned from Socrates that it was difficult to continue to place them in the mouth of his former teacher. So, in a series of more philosophically demanding works, Plato began to move his character Socrates into the background, while other teachers and their students dominated the conversation. The *Parmenides* had already suggested this move: Socrates only spoke in the early part of the dialogue, and the longest section, the exercises, did not involve him as a speaker.

In the *Theaetetus*, Plato's most profound investigation into the nature of knowledge, Socrates remained the main speaker, but the other main participants are mathematicians as much as philosophers. This marks another development of the Academy in this period – the growing importance of mathematics. The elderly Theodorus of Cyrene represents an older way of doing maths; he hands over the discussion to a mathematician of the next generation, the youthful Theaetetus, who engages in a new approach in which the methods of mathematics and philosophy begin to approach each other, with an emphasis on rigorous definition and formal proofs of the foundations of mathematics, rather than practical problem-solving.[37] Theaetetus had died relatively young, after falling ill on campaign in the Corinthian War, although not before his abilities had attracted attention. Plato makes his final return home through Megara the occasion for the dialogue, causing the Megarian philosopher Euclides to recollect his conversation with Socrates and read it to his colleague Terpsion.[38]

While Theaetetus was an Athenian, other mathematicians moved to Athens to work with the Academy. Eudoxus of Cnidus had previously visited the Academy as an impoverished student, walking from the Piraeus to the Academy to hear Plato talk, although he had failed to make any significant contact with him. Diogenes

Raphael, *The School of Athens*, 1511, fresco, Vatican.

Laertius reports that Plato 'snubbed' the low-status visitor.[39] Then, significantly, Eudoxus had visited Archytas in Tarentum and perhaps travelled further afield; as with so many thinkers, sifting myth from fact in his biography is impossible.

When Eudoxus returned to Athens in 368, he brought his own research group with him, a challenge to Plato's pre-eminence with their collective formidable expertise in mathematics.[40] But the group integrated well into the Academy; Philodemus quotes an account of the progress in mathematics made at this time:

It had been recognised, however, that during that time the mathematical sciences were also greatly advanced, because Plato was supervising them and posing problems that the mathematicians investigated with zeal. In this way, accordingly, this was the first time that issues related to the theory of ratios (*metrologia*) reached their peak, and the same holds for problems related to defini-tion, since Eudoxus and his students introduced changes to the old-fashioned approach of Hippocrates [of Chios].[41]

Eudoxus' emphasis on ratios moved the educational focus from arithmetic to geometry, the progression that Plato had iden-tified in the *Republic*. By working in ratios rather than restricting themselves to real numbers, mathematicians could explore more complex geometry. The demonstration that Plato had earlier used in the *Meno*, in which Socrates helped the uneducated slave solve the problem of doubling a square by leading him to recollect it, was one reflection of this aspect of mathematics.[42] But the differ-ence between arithmetic and geometric ratios also played out in political thinking; it provided a way to enable exchanges between citizens of unequal wealth or merit. Distribution by proportion rather than by strict number was touted as a fairer and more equi-table way to share out goods and honours. Xenophon showed Cyrus the Great adopting the principle of geometric equality to divide the spoils of his campaigns, while Aristotle made the concept central to his investigation of justice between citizens.[43]

Eudoxus was not interested in mathematics alone; he was also concerned with pleasure and brought to the Academy a very dif-ferent outlook from Plato's rather austere views.[44] Pleasure was a philosophical problem for Plato. While a degree of pleasure was a necessary part of human flourishing, the worry he drew from Greek tradition was that an individual's pursuit of pleasure might derail their pursuit of the Good, that it might embroil their soul in the transient joys of physical embodiment.

Encountering Eudoxus' view – that pleasure should be identi-fied with the Good – led Plato to re-examine the topic and to bring back Socrates to defend his ideas about the Good. While the

Parmenides had shown Socrates as the young student, challenging older philosophers, in the *Philebus* an elderly Socrates has his views challenged by two younger thinkers, Philebus and Protarchus, who appear to represent a group holding views similar to those of Eudoxus. Philebus is a fictional character and Protarchus, despite being identified as a son of Callias, in whose home Plato had earlier set his *Protagoras,* has left no trace in the historical record.[45] They and their supporters are in conflict with another group of 'disgruntled' thinkers, who think that there is no such thing as pleasure, merely the absence of pain.[46] Socrates urges Protarchus to reconsider the question from the perspective of this second group; he arbitrates between the two opposed positions, which seem to represent different perspectives held within the Academy, and closes the dialogue with a ranking of mental states. Even more evidently than before, Plato used his former teacher to represent himself, as a figure in some sense no longer at the cutting edge of the philosophical debate, but still with the power to arbitrate between and assess new arguments. In this final work, the *Laws,* Plato represents this as a suitable task for senior members of society.[47]

Real-World Politics Again

The internal politics of the Academy and its different groups might have been enough to occupy the ageing Plato. But several sources suggest that, in 361, he was dragged back into Syracusan politics, either in an attempt to get Dion recalled from exile and his estates returned to him, or because Dionysius II himself had summoned him.[48] The various versions of the story pile on details of the intrigues of the Syracusan court and Plato's failure to make headway in either improving the tyrant's character or ensuring Dion's return to the city. Just as with the previous visit, and perhaps through confusion with the earlier episodes, sources claim that when Plato exhausted the patience of Dionysius it was Archytas who negotiated his safe passage from the city. Plutarch goes on to embroil the Academy more broadly in Dion's subsequent actions; he represents Speusippus as a kind of *consigliere*, gathering information from the Syracusans in the city for his master on Ortygia and persuading Dion that there was enough support for him to raise an army and attack his own city. That hope was not borne out by subsequent events.

While the evidence for Plato's first visit to Sicily seems reasonably solid, and there is enough evidence of a further visit to suggest that he returned to Syracuse at least once, many of the details of the two visits in the 360s appear duplicated or confused. They may simply be subsequent biographers' attempts to connect Plato to the later events of Dion's campaign against Dionysius, which unfolded between 357 and 354, and ended with his assassination.

While Plato had made no impact in Syracusan politics, his own city was in trouble and the families of his students were struggling to support the city's military ambitions. The cost of maintaining Athens's status with its allies had drained the resources of the city's elite. Where once the wealthy could afford the cost of paying for a chorus or kitting out a trireme, and even welcomed the honour, now they struggled to pay, attempted to dodge their responsibilities by pointing to wealthier citizens who had not recently contributed, or shared the burden across several families. Citizens' expenditure, reluctant or otherwise, had not brought success in the city's military endeavours; the Second Athenian League collapsed into war between its members, and the Athenians could not support the cost of the full-scale war between the former allies which ensued in 357. Xenophon was moved to write a pamphlet suggesting ways in which the city could improve its revenues and boost its finances, largely by investing in enslaved workers to extract more value from the city's silver mines.[49] Isocrates too had advice; his *On the Peace* urged, once more, an attack on Persia. But this was unthinkable; the challenge for Athens now was holding off Philip of Macedon, whose power was growing.

A Model Society and a Model Universe

Plato appears to have paid little attention to these local concerns; perhaps his turn to the cosmic and grander scale was a further retreat from everyday preoccupations and politics. The works of his final years feature huge timescales, that is, great cycles of cosmic change, such as the great myth of the *Statesman* with its alternation between the 'Age of Zeus' and the present.[50] Returning to the *politeia* in later years, Plato connected his political thinking to the larger-scale model of cosmic order, while retaining an interest in how that order is constructed and maintained in society.[51] He imagined Socrates presenting a *politeia* very similar to that of Kallipolis to another group of interested discussants: Timaeus, a philosopher from Locri in southern Italy, Hermocrates of Syracuse, Critias of Athens and an unidentified fourth person.[52] The seriousness of their discussion is marked by the setting – unlike the *Republic*'s festival for a Thracian goddess, this meeting gathers visitors to the Great Panathenaea, Athens's most important celebration of its patron goddess.[53] Given the likely composition date, the setting is both an ironic nod to Athens's current situation and an assertion of the importance of the dialogue's theme.

Plato emphasized that this was a revision of his earlier thought. Socrates identified that he wanted more than the static model Plato had described in the *Republic* – he wanted to see the ideal city in motion, in an action such as at war. At this point, Critias identifies a story passed down in his family – a tale of an ancient version of Athens and its war with the city of Atlantis.

By placing this story in the mouth of his relative, Plato connected himself to a past Athens which went further back than the myths celebrated by the democracy and retold in the city's funeral speeches. But this story of a distant past is a prelude to the even greater timescale of Timaeus' own account of the creation of the cosmos and the life forms within it, which takes up the bulk of the dialogue. Plato connected many aspects of his thought through this 'likely story', as Timaeus introduced it; the grand sweep of the story moves from the creation of the world as an ensouled living being out of a primeval chaos by a divine creator, the Demiurge, through to the development of specific life forms, including humans, who are created by 'younger gods' under his supervision.[54] Ancient readers detected a great deal of Pythagorean influence in the account, to the extent that Plato was accused by some of plagiarism. Scholars have also debated to what extent Timaeus' story is intended as a straightforward account or as an extended metaphor. Proportion and number play a key role in the creation of the cosmos and the earth at its centre. The central claim that Timaeus makes is that these created objects imitate eternal originals; time operates to give duration to them so that they can do so. Much of the argumentation for the relationship between eternal originals and time-bound copies is obscure in the extreme, both at the macro-scale and at the micro-scale of the fundamental building blocks from which all material is made, the five Platonic solids constructed from regular triangles – the tetrahedron, octohedron, dodecahedron, icosahedron and cube. Timaeus described their interactions as they were formed into the basic substances of fire, air, earth and water, and these interacted and mixed to make more complex objects.

But Plato made no clear connection between the anthropology of Timaeus' speech and the account of a specific society in Critias' speech. Working out what connection Plato intended to make between them was challenging for ancient readers and remains so now. The connection potentially offers a rebuttal of 'two-world' criticisms of Plato's earlier political thought in the *Republic*, the apparent separation between the ideal Forms and the real-world objects which imitate them, but it is left to the reader to infer it.[55] Critias' tale further mixes the cosmic and the human scales, with Plato's imagined prehistoric Athens being destroyed by the cataclysm with which the gods sink the degraded and defeated city of Atlantis under the sea.[56]

In his final years Plato returned once more to the challenge of designing a society; this time he produced a city in which the order and piety he valued were embedded in every moment of its citizens' lives. Plato found himself talking more and more to Aristotle about politics, imagining ways in which an ideal city might be designed. Each wrote up his ideas separately, Plato's ideas taking full shape in the *politeia* of the imaginary city of Magnesia in his final work, the *Laws*. Aristotle's model *politeia* would eventually become books 7 and 8 of his *Politics*, although probably originated as a separate work. Elsewhere in the *Politics*, Aristotle would go on to criticize the writing of constitutions for imaginary cities as a way of thinking about politics and deliver some harsh criticisms of both the *Republic* and the *Laws* as he did so.[57]

Magnesia emerges from a critical discussion of existing political regimes and their tendency to decay into extreme versions of themselves – the increased concentration of power in the monarchy of Achaemenid Persia, the addiction to cultural novelty of democratic Athens – compared with the relative stability of Sparta and Egypt. This time, Plato set out not only the institutions proposed for the city, but a detailed law code. If people were like the gods' puppets, it was the rule of law that gave them some control over the 'iron pulls' of pleasure and pain.[58]

For Plato, imagining Magnesia, an ideal city to be founded on Crete, was an enjoyable project. He framed the city's law code itself in the story of three elderly men – an unnamed Athenian 'visitor', a Cretan Cleinias and a Spartan Megillus – who entertain themselves in conversation while walking from Cnossus to the mountainside cave and shrine of Zeus.[59] The world had changed since Plato wrote the *Republic* and the now defeated and dismantled Sparta was no longer such an attractive model for an ideal society. This time, Plato used his characters to explore the failings

Fragment of a papyrus text of the ninth book of Plato's *Laws*, 3rd century CE.

of Sparta, as well as its ancient strengths, and the setting on Crete acknowledged the growing popularity of its society as an exemplar of a good *politeia*.[60] Plato had used Cretan stories before: the island's mythical king Minos dispensed divine justice in the afterlife in the myth of punishment that closed the *Gorgias*.[61]

By this time, Plato needed assistance. A student, Philip of Opus, acted as his secretary; he took charge of transcribing each day's work from the wax tablets on which the text was first scratched, to a more permanent papyrus fair copy. The process was not entirely complete at Plato's death; the work was said to be still 'on the wax'.[62] Perhaps Philip went beyond copying to editing and rewriting? Some have thought him to be the author of a dialogue associated with the *Laws*, the *Epinomis*.

In the *Laws* as we have it, just as in the *Statesman*, Plato evoked a huge timescale, telling the history of Greek culture from a previous flood, tracing the redevelopment of society over a long period from the survivors of the flood on hilltops as the waters receded, through the development of agriculture and simple societies, to the building of cities such as Troy on plains, ending up with an account of the Persian Wars and the subsequent decline of Athenian democracy. Working his way through these stages gave him the opportunity to criticize others' use of these examples. Along the way he found objections to Antisthenes' use of the Homeric Cyclops, Isocrates' critique of Sparta and Xenophon's use of Cyrus the Great, while weaving them all into a grand historical narrative ending with the Persian Wars.[63]

Plato also put his love for music into this work. He emphasized the importance of collective cultural events – rituals involving singing and dancing, entertainment at symposia – to the construction of society. He imagined the different kinds of performance suitable for public choirs of different ages, the kind of choral singing and dancing old men like him would enjoy and which would instruct others. But in telling Athens's history, he lamented the forms that music had taken in Athens, the innovations in harmonization and performance style with which writers and musicians had sought to gain public approval.[64] He labelled the most developed stage of Athenian democracy as *theatrokratia*, 'rule by theatre', which rewarded populist innovation in a race to the lowest common denominator.

While Plato looked back to his own youth and idealized aspects of it to provide the regime for educating the young and training them for military service, he insisted that the culture of

Egypt, unchanging over centuries in obedience to divine com-
mandments, was a superior model to emulate.[65] Plainsong chants
to the gods, sanctioned by divine origin and centuries of use, were
superior to the 'new music' that had become fashionable in Plato's
own youth. He imagined an education system for Magnesia that
would produce young people acculturated to traditional values,
who would take their place in the elaborate choral patterns of the
city's religious and political calendar, moving through different
roles as they aged.

The *Laws* became a huge project, even longer than the *Republic*.
When it was eventually collated into a papyrus text, it spread over
twelve rolls. As the project continued, Plato imagined a detailed
legal system, a process which acts as a critical reflection on
Athenian laws and on social practices, but also focuses on Plato's
own interests. He used it to attack his intellectual opponents, especially those whose cosmological system views legal and social order
as socially constructed, and so permits relativism. This may be tar-
geted particularly at atomists like Democritus. Their implicit and
at times explicit atheism becomes a punishable offence, although
the discussants all agree that persuasion is better than threat on
this topic.[66] Homosexuality comes under close examination; while
it is not forbidden outright, the Athenian Stranger reckons there
needs to be a reconsideration of how existing social practices fail to
lead either party to virtue.[67] In this work, Plato embraced a cultural
conservatism at odds with the life he had depicted in his previous
works, even in the relatively recent *Phaedrus*. Magnesia's constitution is geared towards ensuring religious conformity and the
continuing worship of the gods. What Plato aims to demonstrate,
in the later sections of the work, is that rule by philosophers will
not be rule by atheists – still, perhaps, responding to the accusation against Socrates. He imagined the ultimate body organizing
the state as a council that meets in the quiet hours before dawn and
comprises the older magistrates, those with extensive experience

of government and diplomacy, as well as some invited juniors who are being trained for these positions.[68] Perhaps the two groups resemble a Socrates figure and a young Plato, or the older Plato and his Aristotle, who met and discussed the work regularly.

7

Legacy

The elderly Plato died after a brief illness in 348/7; his health had been declining over the previous year. Philodemus reports a story attributed to Plato's secretary Philip of Opus that while a Chaldean friend was staying with him, the elderly Plato developed a fever. Nonetheless, Plato carried on his usual kind of conversation with the Chaldean, who had brought along an enslaved Thracian woman. As she attempted to beat out a dactylic rhythm – the metre of Homeric epic – on a rattle of the kind used in ecstatic cult worship, they discussed how this non-Greek woman could not quite manage this elevated rhythm, and Plato thanked his guest for the powerful demonstration of the superiority of Greek culture.[1] Philip's story rings true to the cultural conservatism of the elderly Plato, as well as his international connections, but the biographical tradition sought more elevating stories. Just as with his birth, biographers used stories about his death to emphasize and to critique his significance, his connection to Socrates and his philosophical legacy. The sixth-century CE anonymous biographer wrote:

> Plato himself, too, shortly before his death, had a dream of himself as a swan, darting from tree to tree and causing great trouble to the fowlers, who were unable to catch him. When Simmias the Socratic heard this dream, he explained that all men would endeavour to grasp Plato's meaning,

none however would succeed, but each would interpret
him according to his own views, whether in a metaphysical
or a physical or any other sense.[2]

This most obviously connects Plato to the thoughts he gave
Socrates as he faced death, in his *Phaedo*.

The hostile tradition gives a different picture of Plato's final
days, suggesting that the old man was infested with lice, fatally
weakening him and opening him to infection.[3] That story most
likely owes more to later ideas about philosophers' squalid lifestyles
than to the facts of Plato's life, and is intended to connect Plato to
the tradition of the impoverished philosopher rejecting material
wealth, even to the Cynic tradition whose founder Diogenes had
so often clashed with him. Perhaps it is better to think of Plato following the instructions given to initiates in Orphic cults, carefully
finding his way through the underworld to the 'true Hades' he had
written about, in which his philosophical soul could escape the
cycle of reincarnation and be reunited with Socrates and his other
teachers and carry on his philosophical conversations as he had
imagined Socrates doing.[4]

Athens mourned its brilliant son, the whole city joining the
funeral procession through the Dipylon, along the broad road ending with his burial in the grounds of the Academy. The biographers
report an epitaph:

Two did Apollo bring forth, Asclepius and Plato,
The one to keep our soul healthy, the other our body.[5]

The later biographers use Plato's death to reiterate their
extravagant claim that Plato was the son of Apollo, who had also
overseen the conception and birth of the philosopher. Diogenes
Laertius is content to describe Plato as a gift of Apollo. That may
have been inscribed on his tomb near the shrine of the Muses in

the Academy, where Plato was buried after a grand procession from the city.[6]

Plato left his city an immense legacy; its international status as a centre for advanced education would give the city a purpose as its political fortunes and independence faded, first under Macedonian conquest and then with the eventual annexation of the Greek cities by the expanding Roman empire. Diogenes Laertius is more concerned with the practical matters arising from Plato's death, concerning the disposal of his property. He reports a will in which Plato left two properties, which were situated just outside Athens; one went to the younger Adeimantus, his brother's grandson. Neither of these properties is or includes the property at the Academy itself, which appears to have been handled separately; one of them adjoined the property of Speusippus' father, Eurymedon, demonstrating Plato's close contact with Potone and her family. Adeimantus also received some of Plato's property; one of the enslaved members of Plato's household, a woman named Artemis, was granted her freedom.[7]

The real question had been whom Plato would appoint to run the Academy, by now formally established as an institution that would continue at the garden near the Academy grove after his death. Competition for status in the Academy during Plato's last years showed that there were several potential candidates for the role of 'scholarch', head of school: his most brilliant student Aristotle, acknowledged by many as his true intellectual heir; another promising student, Xenocrates of Chalcedon; and his own nephew Speusippus, the son of his sister Potone. Xenocrates and Aristotle were each brilliant in different ways – Plato had once remarked that 'one needs a spur, the other a bridle' – but it was Speusippus, the oldest of the group and himself already in poor health, who won out, taking over shortly before Plato's final illness and death.[8] Aristotle, then aged 37, and Xenocrates left the city for the court of Hermias of Atarneus, on the western coast of Asia Minor.

Speusippus, who was perhaps some twenty years younger than his uncle and now approaching sixty years old, was himself an active philosopher, who had long helped and deputized for his uncle.[9] He too was writing dialogues – notably a discussion with Aristippus of Cyrene, the figure who led what would become a rival school of Socratics, the Cyrenaics. And despite his poor health and advancing age he remained an active participant in the life of the Academy, even as his own mobility failed. Diogenes Laertius reports an anecdote that demonstrates the continuing hostility of the Cynics towards the Academy: 'They say that when he was being carried in his little cart to the Academy he ran into Diogenes and wished him good health; and that he replied: "But not to you, who is clinging to life in such a condition."'[10] Speusippus led the school for eight years, but in 339, as his health failed, he invited Xenocrates to return to Athens as his successor, after a vote among the members of the Academy.[11] He then ended his own life.

The biographical tradition contains many anecdotes which are markedly hostile towards Speusippus, such as the rather cruel story in which Diogenes mocked his disability. It is as if Plato himself had been largely beyond personal criticism, but all the questions and doubts about the Academy's teachings and students could now be raised against his lower-status successor by rival educators and philosophers. Stories gathered by Diogenes Laertius accuse him of behaviour unbefitting a philosopher – dancing wildly at a wedding, throwing a puppy into a well.[12] While these stories lack credibility and in some cases are chronologically impossible, their circulation suggests that Speusippus was a target for gossip from his rivals and that Cynic criticism of the Academy outlasted Plato himself.

Speusippus in turn contributed to the memorialization of his uncle, writing an *Encomium of Plato*. Yet his recollections themselves reframed Plato's thought; Speusippus' attempts at curating his uncle's legacy may have contributed to the persistent claims that Plato had plagiarized the ideas of the Pythagoreans.[13] While much of Speusippus' work is lost, fragments and citations suggest that he took up the cosmogenic ideas of Plato's later years, expounding the development of being from the interaction of the One and Multiplicity. The fierce criticism of his work by Aristotle may not have helped its status or survival; between them, their critiques of Plato's metaphysics suggested that the Academy was edging away from the Theory of Forms in its original incarnation.[14]

While Xenocrates returned to the Academy, Aristotle did not. He travelled from Atarneus on the mainland to the island of Lesbos with Theophrastus, a young student from that island who had joined the Academy just before Aristotle left.[15] Together, they studied the animal and plant life of the island; far from an isolated self-exile, this was a hugely productive time in which Aristotle gathered the evidence from which his thought on nature would develop.[16] However, in 343 BCE he was invited by Philip of Macedon to return to his court and teach his son Alexander, then a youth of fifteen. The date of Aristotle's return to Athens is unknown, but by 335 BCE he was teaching from another of the gardens outside the city walls, the Lyceum. This too had long been used by trainers and teachers, especially Socrates – Plato had set his *Euthydemus* there – and it became the base of Aristotle's 'Peripatetic' school. But he had returned to an Athens full of political dispute and suspicion, as the city struggled to cope with subordination to the Macedonians. After Alexander's death in 323 provoked a revolt and further repression, Aristotle with his connection to Macedon was viewed with increasing hostility by the Athenians. He handed over his school to Theophrastus, under whom it flourished, and left for Chalcis in Euboea, where he died.

Plato's legacy to Athens was the development of its education industry. After the city's political importance faded under Macedonian rule and ultimately conquest by the Romans, Athens continued to enjoy immense cultural prestige. Many Romans visited the city, while one of Cicero's friends adopted Atticus ('the

Athenian') as his own third name and established a publishing business there, producing and selling manuscript copies of Greek philosophical texts produced by enslaved workers.

Some of Plato's work required rethinking in the changing political circumstances of the Hellenistic world in which cities negotiated with external rulers. Plato's political thought had been developed as a critical response to the context of classical Athens and its democracy, an independent polis where the key challenge was creating and maintaining a just and stable city in which citizens could flourish together, ensuring a good life for their own private households while sharing in the management of their community. During the fourth century, the rise of Macedon and the expansion of its empire under Philip II and Alexander showed an alternative form of regime, ruled (more or less loosely) from the top. Some major cities inside and outside mainland Greece became successful as powerful autocratic leaders directed their forces. Dionysius I of Syracuse and his son Dionysius II became exemplars for considering how this kind of rule worked. For Plato, the kings of Macedon had been his go-to exemplars for autocratic single-person rule.[17] But after the premature death of Alexander in 323, the Macedonian empire splintered into a series of kingdoms, with some of his former generals and courtiers providing their royal houses.

A popular literary device employed for for thinking about monarchical rule in this period is the letter, in which a writer might imagine how a philosopher would advise or respond to a ruler in a particular situation or context. Such letters exist for many major fourth-century and even earlier thinkers, and in some cases have been transmitted with their works, but none of them has any good claim to authenticity.[18] The corpus of Isocrates, for example, contains letters addressed to Philip of Macedon, Jason of Pherae and Dionysius II of Syracuse. The question is slightly different with Isocrates, whose undoubted works include direct addresses to rulers, including *To Philip*.

Plato, as the most famous philosopher, naturally became a character in this genre of letter and his interactions with such monarchical rulers were imagined. Letters addressed to Dionysius II of Syracuse and to Perdiccas III of Macedon found their way into the Platonic corpus. In one of them, Plato begs Dionysius for money to provide dowries for his great-nieces.[19] The 'Seventh Letter' is one of the most sophisticated examples of this genre and shows a long-term relationship between Plato, as an adviser, and the friends of Dion. But it gives more insight into how Plato's thought was interpreted by later readers than into that thought itself.[20]

Plato's doctrines continued to be debated and discussed in and beyond the Academy. They had attracted robust criticism from the outset from other Socratics. Xenophon had worked some criticism into a couple of chapters of his *Memorabilia*, which some commentators say were a late insertion.[21] Antisthenes had objected to the Theory of Forms and to Plato's use of Socrates as a mouthpiece for it, and his objections were developed by those he influenced, notably the Cynics. Aristotle had a more complex relationship with the theory, subjecting it to criticism and revision in a dedicated work *On the Forms*. He had also criticized Plato's political thought; his successors in the Lyceum continued to do the same.[22]

Speusippus's approach had opened the way for a new direction in the Academy; under a later scholarch, Arcesilaus (*c.* 315–240 BCE), this developed into a form of scepticism, approaching that devised a generation earlier by Pyrrho of Elis, who like Socrates had never produced a written version of his ideas. Scepticism took the Socratic claim of ignorance further, claiming that humans were unable to recognize the truth. By Cicero's time, this 'New Academy' was well established. Cicero's teacher Antiochus of Ascalon developed a stance somewhere between that of the sceptical Academics and another school which had arisen from the Socratic tradition and was becoming central to philosophizing in Rome, Stoicism.[23] Cicero himself saw Plato as 'a model for the politically engaged intellectual' and also for the writing of philosophy.[24] He drew extensively on Plato's political thought, applying it to the context of the Roman Republic at its time of crisis, but also adopting and adapting Plato's use of the dialogue form.

Other followers of the Platonic tradition took a more positive view of Plato's metaphysics and continued to develop his ideas. If Plato's lecture on the Good had not found an appreciative audience at the time, later Platonists leaned towards this aspect of his thought. The *Timaeus*, as the most complete statement of Plato's cosmology, remained a key text for these followers. Through translations into Latin – the most widely circulated, if incomplete, was

Unknown Florentine sculptor, 'Platonic Youth', portrait bust featuring a young man wearing a medallion illustrating Plato's *Phaedrus*, c. 1470, bronze.

that of Calcidius, probably dating from the late fourth century CE –
it became the work for which Plato was best known in later
antiquity and indeed through the mediaeval period into early
modernity.[25] Other scholars, such as Proclus in the fifth century,
wrote detailed commentaries on Plato's work that set out an interpretative tradition, that of Neoplatonism, which would go on to
dominate the reading of Plato, emphasizing a rather mystical take
on his metaphysics and particularly the presence of the 'One'.

Ideas developed from Plato's thought also influenced emerging
new religions in later antiquity. St John the Evangelist integrated
some of the language and concerns of Plato's followers into the
developing theology of Christianity; St Augustine's enthusiastic adoption embedded Plato's ideas and especially his imagery
into that tradition. Plato's works were also translated into Arabic,
although it was Aristotle who was arguably much more important
for early Islamic philosophers, such as al-Farabi (AD 870–950).
Arabic sources as well as Greek ones continued to tell anecdotes
about Plato's life.

While Plato's works never disappeared from the Christian dis-
courses of metaphysics and spirituality, the renewed interest in
Greek antiquity shown by scholars in Italy during what is conventionally labelled the Renaissance saw new translations and
commentaries, drawing on the now vast body of Latin, Greek and
Arabic scholarship. There was a renewed concern about reconcil-
ing thought from the pagan past with the Christian present. Dante's
positioning of Plato and other virtuous figures from antiquity in
Limbo, the outermost circle of Hell, represents this rapprochement,
as do glimpses of Platonism in Dante's thought, and even perhaps
the idea of a descent to the underworld.[26]

Plato's writing became more accessible to scholars during this
period; Marsilio Ficino (1433–1499), the Florentine scholar, translated the complete works into Latin, along with a commentary on
the *Phaedrus*. Ficino had done much work to reconcile Platonism

with Christianity and to ensure that Plato's dialogues could be approved reading for practising Christians. Plato's thought, with its use of image and allusion to explain complex metaphysical structures, was an important resource for those whose interests bridged philosophy and theology, such as the early modern English group known as the 'Cambridge Platonists'.[27]

Plato's erotics spoke to many readers. Ficino's interest in the *Phaedrus* lay in the central section of that dialogue and particularly the myth of the charioteer, the soul yearning to rise to the heavens. This story spoke as keenly to the culture of Renaissance Florence as it had to that of ancient Athens; same-sex relationships had a complex status – legally forbidden but eagerly pursued, they also provided a connection to the classical past.[28] A bust of a youth wearing a medallion illustrating the myth of the charioteer shows the appeal of Plato's imagery in the city of Michelangelo.[29]

Plato's association with homoeroticism and 'Greek love' would continue through allusions to Plato's works, especially the *Symposium* and *Phaedrus*, in both visual art and literature.[30] The Florentine artist Carlo Dolci (1616–1686) painted the English scholar Thomas Baines – who had travelled to the Italian city when his partner John Finch served as ambassador – reading a book by Plato, perhaps as an acknowledgement of his same-sex relationship as well as his scholarship. At the end of the nineteenth century another English traveller, Frederick Rolfe or 'Baron Corvo', would draw on Aristophanes' myth from the *Symposium* for the title of his novel about his experience of gay desire in Venice, *The Desire and Pursuit of the Whole*.[31] Plato was a presence in Mary Renault's historical and homoerotic novels *The Last of the Wine*, set in Socrates' Athens, and *The Mask of Apollo*, set largely in Syracuse in the context of the events of the *Seventh Letter*.[32]

Plato's political thought and his creation of imaginary communities inspired early modern writers themselves living through a period of colonial expansion and political change. Both Athens

Carlo Dolci, *Sir Thomas Baines*, depicted reading a work of Plato,
c. 1665–70, oil on canvas.

and the nations of early modern Europe were colonizing societies.
Writers returned to the *politeia* form, reinventing it as the utopia,
an account of an imaginary society in a far-off place whose social
and political arrangements provide a critique of the writer's own
society. Thomas More's *Utopia* (1516) draws on both the island
location of Atlantis and the social organization of Kallipolis and
Magnesia for its imagined 'No-where' society.[33] Francis Bacon's

New Atlantis (1626) is even more explicit in its debt to Plato's original, directly referencing the *Timaeus*.

Thinking about social issues through an imagined distant society is also a hallmark of speculative fiction in more recent times. Echoes of Kallipolis can be heard in many such locations, but one recent example, Jo Walton's *The Just City*, addresses questions about the city and its arrangements head-on. Imagining that the gods have created Kallipolis in time and space and transported to it any scholars who have expressed a wish to live there, Walton shows the limitations of Plato's thinking and the casual brutality of the regime he devised towards those excluded from its rule. She also satirizes the admiration for Plato shown by earlier scholars, with a focus on the limitations of Plato's inclusion of women in his society.[34]

The age of political reform in the nineteenth century renewed interest in Athens itself. While the previous century's politicians had enjoyed the anti-democratic flavour of Athenian thought, with its dismissals of the majority as a mob, a new generation of readers found inspiration in the ancient city for a new participatory politics in Athens. Although Plato's own views on democracy were at best ambivalent, his work contained a sustained investigation of its weaknesses. Reformers began to read Plato in a different way than the Platonist tradition, which focused on the ideal; George Grote, a radical political activist and historian, looked to the vivid presentation of Socrates' Athens and the competing voices with which he debated.[35]

Reformers also picked up on the possible presence of women as political actors in Kallipolis. For a brief period in the nineteenth century, during which the *Republic* took up its place as a prescribed text on Oxford's undergraduate syllabus for Literae Humaniores ('Greats'), not least because it featured a role for women, the *Republic* seemed a radical text, speaking directly from the ancient democracy of Athens to the newly democratizing imperial powers of the era.[36] However, by the mid-twentieth century it was clear that Plato might not so much have liberated his readers from the cave as provided their rulers with tools for keeping them there. Responding to the advent of totalitarianism in Europe, critics began to point to Plato and his Kallipolis as antecedents for societies that controlled all aspects of citizens' lives. Karl Popper placed Plato's text at the beginning of a tradition that led inexorably to Nazi Germany, a tradition in which the ideal society both controlled all aspects of individuals' lives and provided compelling narratives to persuade its people to accept and even enjoy this.[37] Other thinkers, notably Leo Strauss and his influential followers, have been keen to oppose Plato's ideas to those of the present day, to assert that a return to Plato's pre-modern world of ideas might rescue us from the confusion and decline of modern culture.[38] Plato's political thinking continues to resist easy assimilation to present-day ideologies.

We finish Plato's life where we began, with his work finding a new relevance in the twentieth and twenty-first centuries, as Western philosophy makes connections with the disciplines of mathematics and theoretical physics, just as he had envisaged, if not perhaps in ways he had foreseen. Just as Plato saw mathematics as a discipline of certainty and rigour, a key step on the path to knowledge, modern thinkers have turned to mathematical theory as the ultimate form of knowledge. French philosopher Alain Badiou rewrote the *Republic* to feature contemporary set theory as a reconceptualization of the Theory of Forms.[39] But where does that leave the discussions of Socrates and Plato? American philosopher Rebecca Newberger Goldstein imagined Plato in a dialogic encounter with the technology gurus of Google, staking a claim for the value of philosophy alongside science, words against numbers, human dialogue against machine-based algorithms.[40] How would he argue for his theory of recollection in a society where Wikipedia is waiting online for all to access? While, Goldstein noted, Plato 'initiated a process that has taken us beyond him', nonetheless he made a compelling character for her to use to present the importance of philosophy as a discipline, of interpersonal discussion, for humans and their society. Perhaps Plato could, as she thought, walk into and join any seminar discussion today. Some even hope to explore that possibility through the use of artificial intelligence chatbots trained on Plato's surviving works.

Those works have been transmitted over the centuries in many forms, from the wax tablets from which Philip of Opus transcribed the manuscript of the *Laws* through handwritten papyrus scrolls, and from books bound from leaves of vellum or paper painstakingly copied by scribes to printed versions, and now online editions, with translations and commentaries in many languages. It is possible to search for key terms and to trace themes across the work of Plato and his contemporaries in comprehensive databases, to analyse his changing use of language in greater detail, and to read fragments of sources such as Philodemus' *History of the Academy* newly recovered through the use of new scanning and machine-learning technologies. Yet perhaps nothing brings us closer to Plato himself than rereading the dialogues into which he poured his affection for his teacher Socrates, and for his family and friends, and his desire to transform communities like Athens for the better. While his Academy sat at the edge of the city, both it and Plato himself were nonetheless enmeshed in Athenian civic life.

REFERENCES

Abbreviations

APPP	Westerink, Leendert Gerrit, *Anonymous Prolegomena to Platonic Philosophy*, 2nd edn (Dilton Marsh, 2011)
Arist.	Aristotle
Met.	*Metaphysics*
NE	*Nicomachean Ethics*
Pol.	*Politics*
[Arist.]	pseudo-Aristotle
Ath. Pol.	*Constitution of the Athenians*
MXG	*Melissus, Xenophanes, Gorgias*
Diels	Diels, Hermann, ed., *Poetarum philosophorum fragmenta* (Berlin, 1901)
DK	Diels, Hermann, and Walther Kranz, eds, *Die Fragmente der Vorsokratiker: griechisch und deutsch*, 6th edn (Berlin, 1974)
DL	Diogenes Laertius, *Lives of Eminent Philosophers*
DS	Diodorus Siculus, *Library of History*
Hdt.	Herodotus *Histories*
IG	*Inscriptiones Graecae*
OLP	Griffin, Michael J., *Olympiodorus, Life of Plato and On Plato First Alcibiades 1–9* (London, 2015)
PHA	Philodemus *History of the Academy*, PHerc 1021
Pl.	Plato
Apol.	*Apology*
Crat.	*Cratylus*
Grg.	*Gorgias*
Menex.	*Menexenus*
Phd.	*Phaedo*
Phdr.	*Phaedrus*
Plt.	*Statesman*
Prm.	*Parmenides*
Prt.	*Protagoras*
Rep.	*Republic*
Tht.	*Theaetetus*
Tim.	*Timaeus*
[Pl.]	pseudo-Plato

SSR	Giannantoni, Gabriele, *Socratis et Socraticorum reliquiae* (Naples, 1990)
Thuc.	Thucydides *History of the Peloponnesian War*
Xen.	Xenophon
Anab.	*Anabasis*
Apol.	*Apology*
Cyr.	*Cyropaedia*
Hell.	*Hellenica*
Lac. Pol.	*Constitution of the Spartans*
Mem.	*Memorabilia*
Oec.	*Oeconomicus*
Smp.	*Symposium*
[Xen.]	pseudo-Xenophon

Introduction

1 Alfred North Whitehead, *Process and Reality: An Essay in Cosmology* (New York, 1979), p. 63.
2 Pl. *Rep.* 7.514a–517a; see Chapter Five.
3 Pierre Vidal-Naquet, *The Atlantis Story: A Short History of Plato's Myth*, trans. Janet Lloyd (Exeter, 2007).
4 C. S. Lewis, *The Last Battle: A Story for Children*, ed. Pauline Baynes (London, 1956); one might note that Lewis's evocation of a Christian Neoplatonism was contemporary with the rise of 'Oxford philosophy', resistant to metaphysics of a spiritual bent.
5 Gareth B. Matthews, 'Plato and Narnia', in *The Chronicles of Narnia and Philosophy: The Lion, the Witch, and the Worldview*, ed. Gregory Bassham, Jerry Gregory and William Irwin (Chicago, IL, 2005), pp. 169–79.
6 Pl. *Plt.* 270b–274e; see Chapters Four and Five.
7 Virginia Woolf, *Moments of Being: Unpublished Autobiographical Writings*, ed. Jeanne Schulkind (London, 1976), p. 104.
8 Debra Nails, *The People of Plato: A Prosopography of Plato and Other Socratics* (Indianapolis, IN, 2002); Robin Waterfield, *Plato of Athens: A Life in Philosophy* (Oxford, 2023).
9 Quentin Skinner, 'Meaning and Understanding in the History of Ideas', *History and Theory*, VIII/1 (1969), pp. 3–53.
10 Translation and commentary in Paul Kalligas et al., eds, *Plato's Academy: Its Workings and Its History* (Cambridge, 2021). Revised and expanded Greek text (with German translation): Kilian Josef Fleischer, *Philodem, Geschichte der Akademie: Einführung, Ausgabe, Kommentar* (Leiden, 2023); text cited from this source is from the principal papyrus recovered, PHerc 1021.
11 Pamela Mensch and Jim Miller, *Diogenes Laertius: Lives of the Eminent Philosophers* (New York, 2018), is the most accurate and accessible edition.
12 Ryan C. Fowler, *Imperial Plato: Albinus, Maximus, Apuleius: Text and Translation, with an Introduction and Commentary* (Las Vegas, NV, 2016).
13 Michael J. Griffin, ed. and trans., *Olympiodorus: Life of Plato and On Plato First Alcibiades 1–9* (London, 2015); APPP.
14 Alice Swift Riginos, *Platonica: The Anecdotes Concerning the Life and Writings of Plato* (Leiden, 1976).

15 See the Suda On Line, currently at www.cs.uky.edu/~raphael/sol/sol-html/
index.html, accessed 20 February 2024.
16 [Pl.] *Twelfth Letter* 359e3.
17 Rudolf Hercher, *Epistolographi Graeci* [1871] (Amsterdam, 1965).
18 Patricia A. Rosenmeyer, *Ancient Epistolary Fictions: The Letter in Greek
Literature* (Cambridge, 2001); for a more positive take on the Platonic
epistles, see Glenn R. Morrow, *Plato's Epistles: A Translation with Critical
Essays and Notes* (Indianapolis, IN, 1962).
19 Myles F. Burnyeat and Michael Frede, *The Pseudo-Platonic Seventh Letter*,
ed. Dominic Scott (Oxford, 2015), pp. 5–13.
20 Ibid., pp. 41–57.
21 Ibid.; Malcolm Schofield, 'Plato and Practical Politics', in *The Cambridge
History of Greek and Roman Political Thought*, ed. Christopher J. Rowe and
Malcolm Schofield (Cambridge, 2000), pp. 293–302.
22 Helen Morales, ed., *Greek Fiction: Chariton Callirhoe; Longus Daphnis and
Chloe; Anonymous Letters of Chion* (London, 2011).
23 Burnyeat and Frede, *Seventh Letter*, pp. 15–25; Michael Frede, *The Historiography of Philosophy*, ed. Katerina Ierodiakonou (Oxford, 2021).

1 A Wartime Childhood

1 Thuc. 2.47.3–4, trans. Thomas Hobbes in *Thucydides: The Peloponnesian
War*, ed. David Grene [1629] (Chicago, IL, 1989).
2 Thuc. 2.65.6; Plutarch *Pericles* 36. Athenians named rather than numbered
their years, using the given name of one of the annual archons who admin-
istered the city (the 'eponymous archon'), rather than a sequential number.
These years ran roughly from our April to April, so that for many events in
Athenian history we cannot give a single date in our system of numbering
years. See Robert Hannah, *Greek and Roman Calendars: Constructions of
Time in the Classical World* (London, 2005).
3 Plutarch *Pericles* 33–5.
4 The exact date of Plato's birth is unknown – see below.
5 Pl. *Prt.* 314e–315a.
6 DL 3.3; *APPP* 2.8–11; Debra Nails, *The People of Plato: A Prosopography of
Plato and Other Socratics* (Indianapolis, IN, 2002), pp. 53–4.
7 DL 3.4, citing a lost work by Hellenistic biographer Alexander Polyhistor,
the *Successions of Philosophers*. But biography in this period often involved
finding signs and patterns in an author's life consonant with his work; see
James A. Notopoulos, 'The Name of Plato', *Classical Philology*, XXXIV/2
(1939), pp. 135–45.
8 DL 3.3; PHA 2.35–8.
9 *APPP* 2.5–8.
10 Nails, *People of Plato*, pp. 246–7; Robin Waterfield, *Plato of Athens: A Life in
Philosophy* (Oxford, 2023), pp. 1–3, although Waterfield's case rests on the
'Seventh Letter'.
11 DL 3.2; not quite the equivalent of sharing a birthday, as the seventh day in
every month was sacred to Apollo.
12 DL 3.2; *APPP* 2.11–15; *OLP* 2.20–24.
13 Robert Parker, *Polytheism and Society at Athens* (Oxford, 2007), pp. 13–14.

14 Cicero *De Divinatione* 1.36, 78; APPP 2.16–24.
15 Parker, *Polytheism and Society at Athens*, pp. 290–316.
16 [Arist.] *Ath. Pol.* 3.3–5.
17 Pl. *Rep.* 2.381d–e.
18 Pl. *Rep.* 2.377b–c.
19 DL 3.1.
20 Thomas G. Rosenmeyer, 'The Family of Critias', *American Journal of Philology*, LXX/4 (1949), pp. 404–10; Nails, *People of Plato*, pp. 106–11.
21 Apollodorus *Library* 3.14.6.
22 Pl. *Rep.* 2.377a–378b.
23 Felix Jacoby, *Atthis: The Local Chronicles of Ancient Athens* (Oxford, 1949); Phillip Harding, *The Story of Athens: The Fragments of the Local Chronicles of Attika* (London, 2008), pp. 73–81; Carol Atack, 'The Discourse of Kingship in Classical Athenian Thought', *Histos*, VIII (2014), pp. 329–62.
24 Hellanicus Fragment 23 Jacoby; Hdt. 5.65.4.
25 Pl. *Tim.* 20d–27b. On Solon's reforms see Paul Cartledge, *Democracy: A Life* (Oxford, 2016), pp. 49–59.
26 See Chapter Four on Plato's encounters with Pythagoreanism.
27 Perictione *On the Harmony of Women*, Fragment 4 (Stobaeus *Anthology* 4.28.19 = T 142.17–145.6), trans. Dorota Dutsch, *Pythagorean Women Philosophers: Between Belief and Suspicion* (Oxford, 2020), pp. 228–32.
28 Ibid.; Caterina Pellò, *Pythagorean Women* (Cambridge, 2022).
29 Xen. *Oec.* 7–10; see Sarah B. Pomeroy, *Xenophon, Oeconomicus: A Social and Historical Commentary* (Oxford, 1994); Josine Blok, *Citizenship in Classical Athens* (Cambridge, 2017); and Carol Atack, 'Citizenship and Gender', in *A Cultural History of Democracy in Antiquity*, ed. Carol Atack and Paul Cartledge (London, 2021), pp. 115–35 on citizen women's lives in Athens.
30 Pl. *Euthydemus* 291b.
31 Aristophanes *Lysistrata* 638–47.
32 Aristophanes *Thesmophoriazusae* 330; Marcel Detienne and Jean-Pierre Vernant, eds, *The Cuisine of Sacrifice among the Greeks*, trans. Paula Wissing (Chicago, IL, 1989), pp. 129–47.
33 Rosenmeyer, 'The Family of Critias'; Mary Louise Gill, 'Plato's Unfinished Trilogy: *Timaeus–Critias–Hermocrates*', in *Plato's Styles and Characters: Between Literature and Philosophy*, ed. Gabriele Cornelli (Berlin, 2016), pp. 33–45.
34 Pl. *Tim.* 20d–21a.
35 Pl. *Tim.* 22b.
36 Pl. *Charmides* 158a.
37 Thuc. 1.96.
38 John K. Davies, *Athenian Propertied Families, 600–300 BC* (Oxford, 1971), p. 330; Nails, *People of Plato*, pp. 124–5.
39 Vincent Azoulay, *Pericles of Athens*, trans. Janet Lloyd (Princeton, NJ, 2014).
40 Plutarch *Pericles* 13.
41 Hdt. 1.5, 1.202.
42 Nails, *People of Plato*, p. 258; Hdt. 7.151.
43 Paul Cartledge, 'Fowl Play: A Curious Lawsuit in Classical Athens', in *Nomos: Essays in Athenian Law, Politics and Society*, ed. Paul Cartledge, Paul Millett and Stephen Todd (Cambridge, 2002), pp. 41–61; Antiphon Fragments 57–9 Thallheim.

44 Aristophanes *Acharnians* 62–3.
45 Plutarch *Pericles* 13.
46 Pl. *Rep.* 5.464bd.

2 Education in a Divided City

1 Thuc. 2.45.2.
2 Aristophanes *Wasps* 98.
3 The version of the *Clouds* transmitted to us in the manuscript tradition is a revision, never performed, dating from a few years later; for details and a comparison of the versions, see Kenneth James Dover, ed., *Aristophanes: Clouds* (Oxford, 1968), pp. lxxx–xcviii.
4 Aristophanes *Clouds* 961–1111.
5 *Dissoi Logoi*, in André Laks and Glenn W. Most, *Early Greek Philosophy*, vol. VIII: *Sophists: Part 1* (Cambridge, MA, 2016), pp. 164–207; Geoffrey E. R. Lloyd, *Polarity and Analogy: Two Types of Argumentation in Early Greek Thought* (Cambridge, 1966).
6 [Pl.] *Alcibiades* I 106e. The attribution of this dialogue to Plato has been much debated. Denyer treats it as genuine; Nicholas Denyer, *Plato: Alcibiades* (Cambridge, 2001).
7 APPP 2.30–36; see Chapter Five for Plato's account of the tripartite soul.
8 DL 3.4, echoed by Apuleius *De Platone* 1.2, OLP 2.32–5 and other later sources. However, Riginos observes that the name is likely taken from the teacher in the pseudo-Platonic dialogue *Amatores*; Alice Swift Riginos, *Platonica: The Anecdotes Concerning the Life and Writings of Plato* (Leiden, 1976), p. 40.
9 Xen. *Lac. Pol.* 2.1–2; Pl. *Laches*.
10 [Xen.] *Constitution of the Athenians* 2.10; Daniela Marchiandi, 'In the Shadow of Athena Polias: The Divinities of the Academy, the Training of Politai and Death in Service to Athens', in *Plato's Academy: Its Workings and Its History*, ed. Paul Kalligas et al. (Cambridge, 2021), pp. 11–27.
11 Pausanias 1.29.2–15.
12 Paul Cartledge, *Democracy: A Life* (Oxford, 2016).
13 As transmitted by the fourth-century Athenian historian Kleidemos, reported by Athenaeus (FGrH 323 F15 = Ath. 13.609cd); Pausanias *Description of Greece* 1.30.1.
14 R. E. Wycherley, 'Peripatos: The Athenian Philosophical Scene – II', *Greece and Rome*, IX/1 (1962), pp. 2–21.
15 Plutarch *Life of Theseus* 31–2; DS 13.107; cf. Isocrates *Helen* 1; *Plato's Academy*, ed. Kalligas et al.
16 Sophocles *Oedipus at Colonus* 694–705; Pausanias *Description of Greece* 1.30.2.
17 Plutarch *Life of Cimon* 13.
18 Plutarch *Solon* 23.
19 DL 3.4–5; other later sources expanded this to include victories at various of the four most prestigious games; Riginos, *Platonica*, pp. 41–2.
20 Thuc. 6.16.2–3.
21 Pl. *Euthydemus* 271c–272b; see Chapter Five.
22 On the delicate balance between acceptable and unacceptable homosocial relationships in classical Greece see Kenneth James Dover, *Greek Homosexuality* (London, 2016); James N. Davidson, *The Greeks and Greek Love*:

A Radical Reappraisal of Homosexuality in Ancient Greece (London, 2007); and Mark Masterson, Nancy Sorkin Rabinowitz and James Robson, eds, *Sex in Antiquity: Exploring Gender and Sexuality in the Ancient World* (New York, 2015).

23 Daniela Marchiandi and A. Caruso, 'L'accademia', in *Topografia di Atene: sviluppo urbano e monumenti dalle origini al iii secolo D. C. tomo 4, Ceramico, dipylon e accademia*, ed. Emanuele Greco (Athens, 2014), pp. 1465–510; Marchiandi, 'In the Shadow of Athena Polias'.

24 Aristophanes *Clouds* 972–80.

25 Ibid., 961–8.

26 Pl. *Laches* 180cd.

27 DL 3.5, Apuleius *De Platone* 1.2. The details are suspect; see Riginos, *Platonica*, pp. 43–4.

28 Euripides *Suppliant Women* 350–53; Carol Atack, *The Discourse of Kingship in Classical Greece* (London, 2020), pp. 47–9; Günther Zuntz, *The Political Plays of Euripides* (Manchester, 1963).

29 Thuc. 5.84.1–3, 116.4.

30 Eric Csapo, 'The Politics of the New Music', in *Music and the Muses: The Culture of Mousike in the Classical Athenian City*, ed. Penelope Murray and Peter Wilson (Oxford, 2004), pp. 207–48; Armand d'Angour, 'Euripides and the Sound of Music', in *A Companion to Euripides*, ed. Laura McClure (Hoboken, NJ, 2017), pp. 428–43.

31 Pl. *Laws* 3.700b–701a.

32 DL 3.4–5; Pl. *Laws* 3.700c–701b; Aristophanes *Clouds* 972.

33 Pl. *Laws* 4.700e–701a, trans. Tom Griffith in *Plato: The Republic*, ed. Giovanni R.F. Ferrari (Cambridge, 2000).

34 Pl. *Ion* 535ad.

35 Daniela Cammack, 'Deliberation and Discussion in Classical Athens', *Journal of Political Philosophy*, XXIX/2 (2021), pp. 135–66; Josiah Ober, *Mass and Elite in Democratic Athens: Rhetoric, Ideology, and the Power of the People* (Princeton, NJ, 1989).

36 Aristophanes *Clouds* 1038–42.

37 On Anaxagoras' thought, see G. S. Kirk, J. E. Raven and Malcolm Schofield, *The Presocratic Philosophers: A Critical History with a Selection of Texts*, 2nd edn (Cambridge, 1983), pp. 353–5; Martin Ostwald, *From Popular Sovereignty to the Sovereignty of Law: Law, Society, and Politics in Fifth-Century Athens* (Berkeley, CA, 1986), pp. 530–32; and for a more detailed exposition Malcolm Schofield, *An Essay on Anaxagoras* (Cambridge, 1980).

38 Pl. *Apol.* 26d.

39 Protagoras DK 80 B1. See Mauro Bonazzi, 'Protagoras', in *The Stanford Encyclopedia of Philosophy*, ed. Edward N. Zalta and Uri Nodelman, https://plato.stanford.edu, accessed 21 May 2024.

40 Pl. *Tht.* 152a; see Myles F. Burnyeat, intro. and trans., and M. J. Levett, trans., *The Theaetetus of Plato* (Indianapolis, IN, 1990), and Chapter Six. It is impossible to know when Plato encountered the ideas of fifth-century intellectuals, the subjects of his works written decades after they had taught in Athens.

41 Malcolm Schofield, ed., and Tom Griffith, trans., *Plato: Gorgias, Menexenus, Protagoras* (Cambridge, 2010), p. xxvi.

42 DL 9.51. See David Sedley, 'The Atheist Underground', in *Politeia in Greek and Roman Philosophy*, ed. Verity Harte and Melissa Lane (Cambridge, 2013), pp. 329–48, who notes the poor quality of much evidence for early atheism.

43 Aristophanes *Clouds* 658–99.

44 DS 12.53.2–5.

45 Gorgias DK 82 B11, B11a.

46 Gorgias *Helen* 21 (DK 82 B11).

47 Pausanias *Description of Greece* 6.17.9, 10.18.7; E. R. Dodds, *Gorgias: A Revised Text* (Oxford, 1959), p. 9.

48 Pl. *Grg.* 456c.

49 Thuc. 5.89, trans. Jeremy Mynott, *Thucydides: The War of the Peloponnesians and the Athenians* (Cambridge, 2013).

50 Thuc. 6.8.3–24.4.

51 Plutarch *Alcibiades* 17.

52 Pl. *Smp.* 219c.

53 Thuc. 6.27–9; Andocides *On the Mysteries* 34–42.

54 See Ostwald, *Popular Sovereignty*, pp. 536–50, for analysis and Debra Nails, *The People of Plato: A Prosopography of Plato and Other Socratics* (Indianapolis, IN, 2002), pp. 17–20, for an assessment of the links to Plato's family and Socrates' circle.

55 Andocides *On the Mysteries* 16.

56 Although it was possible for slaves to be initiated; the only requirement was the entry fee and the ability to speak Greek.

57 Pl. *Laches* 180e–181a.

58 Nails, *People of Plato*, p. 247.

59 Pl. *Lysis* 203a–204b.

60 Pl. *Charmides* 154b.

61 Thucydides 1.56.2–66, 119; G.E.M. de Ste. Croix, *The Origins of the Peloponnesian War* (London, 1972).

62 Pl. *Charmides* 155d.

63 DL 3.5.

64 See OLP 2.20–24, and Chapter One.

65 DL 3.5; Socrates becomes a poet at Pl. *Phd.* 60d–61c, with 84e–85b.

66 Xenophon's Socratic dialogues often have a loose dramatic date in the 400s when Xenophon himself knew Socrates. While Plato set many of his dialogues in the previous decades, Xenophon gives a possibly more historical picture of the Socratic circle; see George R. Boys-Stones and Christopher J. Rowe, *The Circle of Socrates: Readings in the First-Generation Socratics* (Indianapolis, IN, 2013); Martin Hammond, trans., and Carol Atack, intro. and notes, *Memories of Socrates: Xenophon's 'Memorabilia' and 'Apology'* (Oxford, 2023).

67 Xen. *Mem.* 4.2.1–6, possibly also the Euthydemus mentioned at Pl. *Smp.* 222b.

68 See Nails, *People of Plato*, pp. 209–10; Aristophanes *Clouds* 63–7 with note by Dover, *Clouds*, p. 102. Pericles' father was called Xanthippus and the name is not frequently found in the records.

69 Xen. *Oec.* 2.3. Sarah Pomeroy notes that, while Socrates' minimal assets cited here should have placed him in the lowest socio-economic group of Athenian citizens, the *thetes*, Plato depicts him serving as a hoplite (Sarah

B. Pomeroy, *Xenophon, Oeconomicus: A Social and Historical Commentary* (Oxford, 1994), pp. 223–4).

70 Pl. *Tht.* 149a–c, 150a–151d. The claim Plato gives to Socrates here – that his intellectual midwifery is of greater importance than the physical midwifery of his mother – has been seen by Luce Irigaray and others as part of a misogynist devaluation of women; Luce Irigaray, *Speculum of the Other Woman*, trans. Gillian C. Gill (Ithaca, NY, 1985), and see Chapter Five.

71 Pl. *Apol.* 20c–22e.

72 Pl. *Apol.* 38a.

73 For example John Beversluis, *Cross-Examining Socrates: A Defense of the Interlocutors in Plato's Early Dialogues* (Cambridge, 2000).

74 Pl. *Charmides* 176ab.

75 Voula Tsouna, *Plato's 'Charmides': An Interpretative Commentary* (Cambridge, 2022), pp. 291–9.

3 The Trial and Death of Socrates

1 Thuc. 8.1–2, trans. Thomas Hobbes in *Thucydides: The Peloponnesian War*, ed. David Grene [1629] (Chicago, IL, 1989).

2 [Arist.] *Ath. Pol.* 29–33; P. J. Rhodes, *A Commentary on the Aristotelian Athenaion Politeia* (Oxford, 1993), pp. 362–415; Claude Mossé, 'Le Thème de la *patrios politeia* dans la pensée grecque du ivème siècle', *Eirene*, XVI (1978), pp. 81–9. On Plato's own use of the *patrios politeia* theme, see Carol Atack, 'Ancestral Constitutions in Fourth-Century BCE Athenian Political Argument: Genre and Re-Invention', MPhil Dissertation, University of Cambridge, 2010.

3 Aristophanes *Knights* 551–80.

4 Thuc. 8.66.1–67.3.

5 Thuc. 8.97.2.

6 Thuc. 7.19–20; Plutarch *Theseus* 32.

7 Thuc. 7.27–45.

8 There is little concrete evidence of a formal programme during the late fifth century, but youth military service was formalized and institutionalized in the fourth century.

9 Pl. *Laws* 6.760b–762d.

10 Pl. *Rep.* 2.367e–368a.

11 Arist. *Met.* A.6.987a31–b7; DL 3.6; David N. Sedley, *Plato's 'Cratylus'* (Cambridge, 2003), pp. 16–18, arguing against Charles H. Kahn, *Plato and the Socratic Dialogue: The Philosophical Use of a Literary Form* (Cambridge, 1996), pp. 81–3; Phillip Sidney Horky, *Plato and Pythagoreanism* (New York, 2013), pp. 125–66.

12 Arist. *Met.* A.987a31–3.

13 G. B. Kerferd, *The Sophistic Movement* (Cambridge, 1981).

14 Hermogenes also appears in Xenophon's Socratic works and appears to have provided him with eyewitness testimony for his *Apology*.

15 Cosmic etymologies Pl. *Crat.* 388d–390a; ethical etymologies 411a–421c; see Sedley, *Plato's 'Cratylus'*, pp. 66–74, 113–22.

16 22 B12, B91 DK; Charles H. Kahn, *The Art and Thought of Heraclitus* (Cambridge, 1979); G. S. Kirk, J. E. Raven and Malcolm Schofield, *The*

Presocratic Philosophers: A Critical History with a Selection of Texts, 2nd edn (Cambridge, 1983), pp. 181–212.

17 Pl. *Tht.* 179c–183c uses the language of flux, though never this precise phrase.

18 Arist. *Met.* Γ.5.101a10–13.

19 That Hermogenes 'escorts' (*propempsei*) Cratylus (Pl. *Crat.* 440e5) hints at the god Hermes Psychopompos, who led souls to the underworld.

20 Pl. *Crat.* 440b2–c1, translation adapted from C.D.C. Reeve, *Plato: Cratylus* (Indianapolis, IN, 1999).

21 DL 9.41, 46. See Michael Gagarin and Paul Woodruff, *Early Greek Political Thought from Homer to the Sophists* (Cambridge, 1995) and C.C.W. Taylor, *The Atomists: Leucippus and Democritus: Fragments* (Toronto, 1999). Only scant fragments of Democritus' work survive, and the authenticity of many of them is disputed. For an introduction to Democritus and other Presocratics, see James Warren, *Presocratics: Natural Philosophers before Socrates* (Berkeley, CA, 2007).

22 Although Plato never explicitly cites Democritus by name (DL 9.40).

23 [Arist.] *MXG* 979a12–13. Translation adapted from Daniel W. Graham, *The Texts of Early Greek Philosophy: The Complete Fragments and Selected Testimonies of the Major Presocratics* (New York, 2010).

24 The full text is not preserved, but Sextus Empiricus quotes or summarizes the argument (*Against the Professors* 7.65–87 = DK 82 B3).

25 Pl. *Crat.* 384b; DL 9.53–4.

26 Aristophanes *Clouds* 659–99.

27 Xen. *Hell.* 1.4.8–20.

28 Pl. *Apol.* 32bc; Xen. *Hell.* 1.7.15.

29 Xen. *Hell.* 1.6.26–38.

30 Plutarch *Alcibiades* 35–6.

31 Xenophon *Anab.* 1–2; see Chapter Two.

32 Pl. *Meno* 80b, translation from David N. Sedley and Alex G. Long, *Meno and Phaedo* (Cambridge, 2011).

33 Pl. *Meno* 90b–95a.

34 Xen. *Hell.* 2.2.3–4.

35 Xen. *Hell.* 2.2.22–4.

36 Pl. *Apol.* 32ce.

37 Scholars have long debated whether this 'Seventh Letter' is by Plato, or another author, and when it might have been written. Its level of detail seems to suggest actual knowledge of Plato's life, and so many have thought that it must have been written by someone who knew Plato, not long after the events described – perhaps a student who knew Plato later in his life. Others, however, have pointed to some odd details in the ideas attributed to Plato in the work. Myles Burnyeat thought that the account of Greek religion was more in line with later thought and practice, from the Hellenistic or even imperial period. Michael Frede argued that there are no genuine letters from philosophers and rulers of the fourth century surviving in the literary tradition; Myles F. Burnyeat and Michael Frede, *The Pseudo-Platonic Seventh Letter*, ed. Dominic Scott (Oxford, 2015). For arguments for the letter's authenticity see Glenn R. Morrow, *Plato's Epistles: A Translation with Critical Essays and Notes* (Indianapolis, IN, 1962); Robin Waterfield, *Plato of Athens: A Life in Philosophy* (Oxford, 2023).

38 [Pl.] *Seventh Letter* 324bd.
39 Friedrich Schleiermacher, *Schleiermacher's Introduction to the Dialogues of Plato*, ed. and trans. William Dobson (Bristol, 1992); see Jacob Howland, 'Glaucon's Fate: Plato's *Republic* and the Drama of the Soul', *Proceedings of the Boston Area Colloquium in Ancient Philosophy*, XXIX/1 (2014), pp. 113–36; Mark Henderson Munn, *The School of History: Athens in the Age of Socrates* (Berkeley, CA, 2000).
40 See Lysias 12, *Against Eratosthenes*, for an account of his family's suffering. Plato would later set his *Republic* in their home; see Chapter Five.
41 Xen. *Mem.* 1.2.12–16.
42 Xen. *Mem.* 1.2.32–7.
43 Debra Nails, *The People of Plato: A Prosopography of Plato and Other Socratics* (Indianapolis, IN, 2002), p. 88.
44 See Critias DK 88 B25; David Sedley, 'The Atheist Underground', in *Politeia in Greek and Roman Philosophy*, ed. Verity Harte and Melissa Lane (Cambridge, 2013), pp. 329–48.
45 Pl. *Apol.* 32ce; Xen *Mem.* 4.4.3; [Pl.] *Seventh Letter* 324e–325a.
46 Xen. *Hell.* 2.3.18–56.
47 Xen. *Hell.* 2.4.19. Some have speculated that Glaucon perished during this period (Munn, *School of History*; Howland, 'Glaucon's Fate').
48 Julia L. Shear, *Polis and Revolution: Responding to Oligarchy in Classical Athens* (Cambridge, 2011).
49 [Pl.] *Seventh Letter* 325bc.
50 Xen. *Anab.* 2.6.
51 [Pl.] *Seventh Letter* 325ab.
52 Pl. *Euthyphro* 2a.
53 Xen. *Mem.* 2.9.1–8.
54 Xen. *Mem.* 1.1.1; other sources for the charges include DL 2.40 (purporting to be the formal prosecution affidavit), Pl. *Apol.* 24b.
55 Martin Ostwald, *From Popular Sovereignty to the Sovereignty of Law: Law, Society, and Politics in Fifth-Century Athens* (Berkeley, CA, 1986), pp. 528–36.
56 DL 9.52–5; DK 80 B4 .
57 Kirk, Raven and Schofield, *Presocratic Philosophers*, pp. 352–84.
58 Ideas associated with the philosopher Archelaus of Athens; see Gábor Betegh, 'Archelaus on Cosmogony and the Origins of Social Institutions', *Oxford Studies in Ancient Philosophy*, LI (2016), pp. 1–40.
59 Pl. *Apol.* 18ac.
60 DL 2.40–41.
61 Two different views on the trial: I. F. Stone, *The Trial of Socrates* (London, 1988); Paul Cartledge, *Ancient Greek Political Thought in Practice* (Cambridge, 2009), pp. 76–90.
62 Xen. *Apol.* 1–3.
63 Pl. *Apol.* 20e–21a.
64 Pl. *Apol.* 38bc. DL reports stories that Plato himself intervened and made a public speech in court at this point (DL 2.41) but this seems unlikely.
65 Pl. *Apol.* 38c; Xen. *Apol.* 23; DL 2.42.
66 Pl. *Phd.* 60d–61d.
67 Pl. *Crito* 45ac.
68 Pl. *Phd.* 59b.

69 Glenn W. Most, 'A Cock for Asclepius', *Classical Quarterly*, XLIII/1 (1993), pp. 96–111.
70 Homer *Odyssey* 11.487–91.
71 Pl. *Apol.* 40c6–10.
72 Pl. *Apol.* 40e4–41a6.
73 Hdt. 8.65.
74 Pl. *Phd.* 60ab; Xen. *Smp.* 2.9–10.
75 Aeschines SSR VIA 70 = Cic. *On the Invention of Rhetoric* 1.52–3. For a positive account of Xanthippe, see Christine de Pizan's *The Book of the City of Ladies*, trans. Rosalind Brown-Grant (London, 1999).
76 Patricia A. Rosenmeyer, *Ancient Epistolary Fictions: The Letter in Greek Literature* (Cambridge, 2001).
77 Suda s.v. Platon (Adler π1707).
78 Plutarch *Spartan Sayings* 14/*Moralia* 227f.
79 Mogens Herman Hansen, *The Athenian Democracy in the Age of Demosthenes: Structure, Principles, and Ideology* (Bristol, 1999), pp. 246–65.
80 [Pl.] *Seventh Letter* 325ce.

4 Plato outside Athens

1 Cicero *De Finibus* 5.50.
2 Cicero *De Republica* 1.16.
3 DL 3.6.
4 OLP 1.139–44.
5 Aulus Gellius *Noctes Atticae* 7.10.1–4.
6 Pl. *Tht.* 142a–143b; Pl. *Phd.* 59b.
7 Isocrates *Against the Sophists, Helen* 1.
8 G. S. Kirk, J. E. Raven and Malcolm Schofield, *The Presocratic Philosophers: A Critical History with a Selection of Texts*, 2nd edn (Cambridge, 1983); Reginald E. Allen, *Plato's Parmenides* (Minneapolis, MN, 1997).
9 DL 9.21, 23.
10 On Parmenides, see Kirk, Raven and Schofield, *Presocratic Philosophers*, pp. 239–62; on Plato's reading of him, Mary Margaret McCabe, *Plato and His Predecessors: The Dramatisation of Reason* (Cambridge, 2000).
11 Parmenides DK 20 B8, trans. André Laks and Glenn W. Most, *Early Greek Philosophy*, vol. V: *Western Greek Thinkers, Part 2* (Cambridge, MA, 2016).
12 See Kirk, Raven and Schofield, *Presocratic Philosophers*, pp. 263–79.
13 Plutarch *Pericles* 26; Kirk, Raven and Schofield, *Presocratic Philosophers*, pp. 390–401; Benjamin Harriman, *Melissus and Eleatic Monism* (Cambridge, 2019).
14 Xen. *Hell.* 4.2.1–8; DL 2.51. This may have been the motivation for the Athenians to exile Xenophon, who settled on an estate in the Peloponnese not far from Olympia (Xen. *Anab.* 5.3.7–13).
15 Reported at DL 3.9; Aelian *Var. Hist.* 7.14; Alice Swift Riginos, *Platonica: The Anecdotes Concerning the Life and Writings of Plato* (Leiden, 1976), pp. 51–2. Although Aristoxenus was writing in the late fourth century BCE, he was a hostile witness to Plato and the Academy.
16 Armand J. d'Angour, 'Archinus, Eucleides and the Reform of the Athenian Alphabet', *Bulletin of the Institute of Classical Studies*, XLIII/1 (1999), pp. 109–30.

17 See Lysias 30 *Against Nicomachus.*

18 The 390s and 380s were the peak of Lysias' speechwriting career; on the problems of chronology see S. C. Todd, ed., *A Commentary on Lysias, Speeches 1–11* (Oxford, 2007), pp. 10–17.

19 [Plutarch] *Life of Isocrates* 837ab.

20 Rosalind Thomas, *Oral Tradition and Written Record in Classical Athens* (Cambridge, 1989), pp. 15–94, describes increasing literacy and use of written documents in democratic practice in Athens during Plato's life.

21 Pl. *Phdr.* 275de, translation adapted from Reginald Hackforth, *Plato's Phaedrus* (Cambridge, 1952).

22 Pl. *Prt.* 316cd; DL 9.52.

23 Xen. *Mem.* 4.2.1.

24 DL 6.5. On works titled *Hypomnemata* in Greek, see Myles F. Burnyeat and Michael Frede, *The Pseudo-Platonic Seventh Letter*, ed. Dominic Scott (Oxford, 2015).

25 See Danielle S. Allen, *Why Plato Wrote* (Oxford, 2010). It is possible that the earliest Socratic dialogues pre-date their subject's death, but given their commemorative function, this may not have been the case.

26 DL 2.38–9.

27 George R. Boys-Stones and Christopher J. Rowe, *The Circle of Socrates: Readings in the First-Generation Socratics* (Indianapolis, IN, 2013). The authoritative collection of fragments and testimony is Gabriele Giannantoni, *Socratis et Socraticorum reliquiae* (Naples, 1990).

28 Cicero *De Inventione* 1.51–2 = Aeschines SSR VI A 70. On Aeschines' contribution to the erotic aspects of Socratic dialogue see Charles H. Kahn, 'Aeschines and Socratic Eros', in *The Socratic Movement*, ed. P. A. Vander Waerdt (Ithaca, NY, 1994), pp. 87–106.

29 Xen. *Mem.* 2.6, 3.10.

30 While some have thought that Xenophon's earliest written works date to the 390s, his Socratic dialogues appear to post-date the Spartan defeat at 371, and a subsequent re-engagement with Athens.

31 Xen. *Mem.* 3.6.

32 Allen, *Why Plato Wrote*, pp. 89–107.

33 DL 3.35, APP 3.28–31; see Charles H. Kahn, 'On Platonic Chronology', in *New Perspectives on Plato, Modern and Ancient*, ed. Julia Annas and Christopher J. Rowe (Washington, DC, 2002), pp. 93–127.

34 Pl. *Apol.* 25a.

35 Pl. *Apol.* 21a.

36 Xen. *Apol.* 1.

37 See Penelope Murray, *Plato on Poetry* (Cambridge, 1996); Charles H. Kahn, *Plato and the Socratic Dialogue: The Philosophical Use of a Literary Form* (Cambridge, 1996).

38 Pl. *Ion* 530a1–4.

39 Myles F. Burnyeat, 'First Words: A Valedictory Lecture', *Proceedings of the Cambridge Philological Society*, XLIII (1998), pp. 1–20.

40 Pl. *Ion* 533d–535a.

41 Pl. *Ion* 535a.

42 Malcolm Schofield, *How Plato Writes: Perspectives and Problems* (Cambridge, 2023), pp. 42–51. Reading the dialogues through the framework

of narratology provides many insights into how Plato subtly communicates authority; see Margalit Finkelberg, *The Gatekeeper: Narrative Voice in Plato's Dialogues* (Leiden, 2019).

43 Xen. *Anab.* 3.1.5–8.
44 On the Pythagoreans see the essays in *A History of Pythagoreanism*, ed. Carl A. Huffman (Cambridge, 2014), and on Plato's use of Pythagorean sources Phillip Sidney Horky, *Plato and Pythagoreanism* (New York, 2013).
45 DL 8.1–3.
46 He is identified as a teacher of Simmias and Cebes at Pl. *Phd.* 61d.
47 Aetius II.7.7 (DK 44 A 16); DL 8.85; Daniel W. Graham, 'Philolaus', in *A History of Pythagoreanism*, ed. Huffman, pp. 46–68 at pp. 56–8; Kirk, Raven and Schofield, *Presocratic Philosophers*, pp. 342–4.
48 Archytas Fr. 1, trans. Huffman, ed., *A History of Pythagoreanism*.
49 See Graham, 'Philolaus', pp. 49–53.
50 DL 8.79.
51 [Pl.] *Twelfth Letter*, DL 8.80–81. Many commentators concur that these letters are forgeries intended to authenticate faked works attributed to the Pythagorean Ocellus; see Burnyeat and Frede, *Seventh Letter*, pp. 15–26; Riginos, *Platonica*, pp. 169–74.
52 Pl. *Apol.* 41ac.
53 Timon Fr. 54 Diels; DL transmits separate stories at 3.9 and 8.85; see Riginos, *Platonica*, pp. 169–74.
54 The composition date of the *Gorgias* is subject to controversy. While some conventional methods of stylometry suggest that it is not an 'early' dialogue, and sits somewhere between 'early' dialogues like the *Charmides* and 'middle' dialogues like the *Republic*, its lack of a narrative frame and other features of its language and argument made both Malcolm Schofield and Charles Kahn identify it as an earlier work than others had supposed; Malcolm Schofield, ed., and Tom Griffith, trans., *Plato: Gorgias, Menexenus, Protagoras* (Cambridge, 2010); Charles H. Kahn, 'On the Relative Date of the Gorgias and the Protagoras', *Oxford Studies in Ancient Philosophy*, VI (1988), pp. 69–102.
55 Pl. *Grg.* 447d.
56 Pl. *Grg.* 481d.
57 Plato gives Callicles a group of friends whose historicity is confirmed by documentary sources (Pl. *Grg.* 487c); see E. R. Dodds, *Gorgias: A Revised Text* (Oxford, 1959), p. 282; Debra Nails, *The People of Plato: A Prosopography of Plato and Other Socratics* (Indianapolis, IN, 2002), pp. 75–6; John K. Davies, *Athenian Propertied Families, 600–300 BC* (Oxford, 1971), p. 291.
58 Davies, *Athenian Propertied Families*, p. 330, noting that Demos vanishes from records after holding a command in 390.
59 Dodds, *Gorgias*, pp. 13–14; Dodds also insists on the historicity of both Polus and Callicles.
60 Pl. *Grg.* 462b11; possibly alluded to at Pl. *Phdr.* 267b.
61 Pl. *Grg.* 524d–525a, 526cd.
62 Thuc. 4.58–65.
63 Isocrates [Plutarch] *Lives of the Ten Orators* 836f: Antisthenes DL 6.1.
64 Pindar *Olympian* 1; *Pythian* 1.

65 Thuc. 6.4.3–4, 6.5.3; Hdt. 7.155.
66 Valerius Maximus *Memorable Words and Sayings* 9.12.
67 Plutarch *Dion* 4.
68 [Pl.] *Seventh Letter* 326bd.
69 Pl. *Rep.* 9.574d1–575a7.
70 DL 3.18–19; Plutarch *Dion* 5; PHA X.9–22; Riginos, *Platonica*, pp. 86–92.
71 The enslaved philosopher is a topos of ancient literature; see Page DuBois, *Slaves and Other Objects* (Chicago, IL, 2008), pp. 153–69.
72 DL 3.20.
73 DL 3.21–2. The letter quoted is probably a fabrication.

5 Establishing an Academy

1 Xen. *Hell.* 5.1.29–33, Pl. *Menex.* 245c.
2 Isocrates *Panegyricus* 19–20, probably written later than its dramatic date. Just as with Plato's works, one cannot deduce the composition date of Isocrates' works from their purported dramatic date; see Yun Lee Too, *The Rhetoric of Identity in Isocrates: Text, Power, Pedagogy* (Cambridge, 1995).
3 Isocrates *Panegyricus* 47–8.
4 Confusingly, the two separate but adjacent entities – Plato's premises and the civic training ground – are often conflated in both ancient sources and modern scholarship. See Eutychia Lygouri-Tolia, 'The Gymnasium of the Academy and the School of Plato', in *Plato's Academy: Its Workings and Its History*, ed. Paul Kalligas et al. (Cambridge, 2021), pp. 46–64.
5 Debra Nails, *The People of Plato: A Prosopography of Plato and Other Socratics* (Indianapolis, IN, 2002), pp. 247–8, argues for a later date, possibly 384, rather than 387, in line with her later dating of Plato's birth; Robin Waterfield, *Plato of Athens: A Life in Philosophy* (Oxford, 2023), agrees, adding that Plato could not have undertaken his first journey to Sicily until the King's Peace was in place. See also Mauro Bonazzi, *Platonism: A Concise History from the Early Academy to Late Antiquity*, trans. Sergio Knipe (Cambridge, 2023), pp. 3–5. On synchronisms and their role in ancient historiography, see Dennis C. Feeney, *Caesar's Calendar: Ancient Time and the Beginnings of History* (Berkeley, CA, 2007).
6 Pausanias *Description of Greece* 1.30.2.
7 Pausanias *Description of Greece* 1.29.4.
8 Thuc. 2.37–45; Lysias 2.3–16.
9 On the genre and rhetoric of the Athenian funeral speech see Nicole Loraux, *The Invention of Athens*, trans. Alan Sheridan (New York, 2006).
10 *Menex.* 244d–246a; Pierre Vidal-Naquet, 'Platon, l'Histoire et les Historiens', in *Histoire et structure. A la mémoire de Victor Goldschmidt*, ed. J. Brunschwig, C. Imbert and A. Roger (Paris, 1985), pp. 147–60. See Malcolm Schofield, ed., and Tom Griffith, trans., *Plato: Gorgias, Menexenus, Protagoras* (Cambridge, 2010), pp. xix, 130–31.
11 DL 6.15–18 contains a catalogue of his work.
12 DL 6.1, 6.13.
13 DL 6.1; see Susan Hukill Prince, *Antisthenes of Athens: Texts, Translations, and Commentary* (Ann Arbor, MI, 2015).
14 Isocrates *Helen* 6.

15 Pl. *Euthydemus* 271a–272d; Mary Margaret McCabe, *Platonic Conversations* (Oxford, 2015), pp. 125–37.
16 Schofield and Griffith, *Gorgias, Menexenus, Protagoras*, p. xxv.
17 Pl. *Prt.* 314e–315c.
18 This vivid scene is thought to have inspired Raphael's School of Athens fresco in the papal apartments in the Vatican; Glenn W. Most, 'Reading Raphael: "The School of Athens" and Its Pre-Text', *Critical Inquiry*, XXIII/1 (1996), pp. 145–82; see also Tim Rood, Carol Atack and Tim Phillips, *Anachronism and Antiquity* (London, 2020), pp. 198–206.
19 Pl. *Prt.* 315ab.
20 On philosophical dialogues as anachronistic communities, see Rood, Atack and Phillips, *Anachronism and Antiquity*, pp. 206–18.
21 One of the details that led Athenaeus to complain about anachronism in the work.
22 Carol Atack, 'Plato's Queer Time: Dialogic Moments in the Life and Death of Socrates', *Classical Receptions Journal*, XII/1 (2020), pp. 10–31.
23 Pl. *Prt.* 320c–323d, 338e–342a.
24 DL 3.37, Aristoxenus; Anton-Herman Chroust, 'Plato's Detractors in Antiquity', *Review of Metaphysics*, XVI/1 (1962), pp. 98–118.
25 Pl. *Prt.* 358ad.
26 Pl. *Prt.* 361e–362.
27 Good treatments include Nicholas Denyer, 'The Political Skill of Protagoras', in *Politeia in Greek and Roman Philosophy*, ed. Verity Harte and M. S. Lane (Cambridge, 2013), pp. 155–67.
28 Pl. *Prt.* 355e–357e.
29 Pl. *Euthydemus* 291a; Pl. *Phd.* 88c–89b.
30 Charles H. Kahn, 'On Platonic Chronology', in *New Perspectives on Plato, Modern and Ancient*, ed. Julia Annas and Christopher J. Rowe (Washington, DC, 2002), pp. 93–127.
31 Carl A. Huffman, ed., *A History of Pythagoreanism* (Cambridge, 2014).
32 Dominic Scott, 'Platonic Anamnesis Revisited', *Classical Quarterly*, XXXVII/2 (1987), pp. 346–66; Dominic Scott, *Plato's Meno* (Cambridge, 2006).
33 Pl. *Meno* 80d.
34 Pl. *Meno* 81cd.
35 Pl. *Meno* 82b–85c; see Scott, *Plato's Meno*, pp. 98–100.
36 Archytas A14, A15; Carl A. Huffman, *Archytas of Tarentum: Pythagorean, Philosopher and Mathematician King* (Cambridge, 2005), pp. 371–2; Alice Swift Riginos, *Platonica: The Anecdotes Concerning the Life and Writings of Plato* (Leiden, 1976), pp. 141–5.
37 See David N. Sedley and Alex G. Long, *Meno and Phaedo* (Cambridge, 2011), and David Ebrey, *Plato's 'Phaedo': Forms, Death, and the Philosophical Life* (Cambridge, 2023).
38 DL 2.105.
39 Pl. *Phd.* 61d.
40 Pl. *Phd.* 85ab.
41 Pl. *Phd.* 109b.
42 Pl. *Phd.* 114bc.
43 Pl. *Phd.* 73c–76c.
44 Sedley and Long, *Meno and Phaedo*, pp. x–xi.

45 Antisthenes Fr. 134 = DL 6.11.

46 Xen. *Hell.* 5.4.20–24.

47 See the prospectus for the league, *IG* II² 43, displayed in Athens's Epigraphic Museum; and 'Decree Inviting States to Join the Second Athenian League, 378/7 BC', *Attic Inscriptions Online*, www.atticinscriptions.com, accessed 14 October 2023.

48 Pl. *Phd.* 108b, 113e.

49 Xen. *Lac. Pol.* 2; see Noreen Humble, *Xenophon of Athens: A Socratic on Sparta* (Cambridge, 2022). Two accounts of the Spartan *politeia* are attributed to Plato's relative Critias (Critias 88 B2, 6 DK), but the attribution is not secure.

50 On political *realia* in Plato see Malcolm Schofield, 'Plato and Practical Politics', in *The Cambridge History of Greek and Roman Political Thought*, ed. Christopher J. Rowe and Malcolm Schofield (Cambridge, 2000), pp. 293–302.

51 Myles F. Burnyeat, 'First Words: A Valedictory Lecture', *Proceedings of the Cambridge Philological Society*, XLIII (1998), pp. 1–20.

52 Pl. *Rep.* 1.331d.

53 Pl. *Rep.* 1.336a–338c.

54 Pl. *Rep.* 5.453d; Homer *Odyssey* 5.400–459.

55 Pl. *Rep.* 4.432be; Homer *Odyssey* 19.379–475.

56 Roger Brock, *Greek Political Imagery from Homer to Aristotle* (London, 2013), pp. 69–82.

57 Pl. *Rep.* 2.372ad.

58 Pl. *Rep.* 7.540e–541b.

59 Dionysius of Halicarnassus *Lysias* 1; Paul Cartledge, 'Urbicide in the Ancient Greek World, 480–330 BCE', in *The Cambridge World History of Genocide*, vol. I: *Genocide in the Ancient, Medieval and Premodern Worlds*, ed. Ben Kiernan, T. M. Lemos and Tristan S. Taylor (Cambridge, 2023), pp. 235–56.

60 Thuc. 5.116.

61 Malcolm Schofield, *How Plato Writes: Perspectives and Problems* (Cambridge, 2023), pp. 139–62.

62 See Leo Strauss, *The City and Man* (Chicago, IL, 1977); Myles Burnyeat, *Explorations in Ancient and Modern Philosophy*, vol. III (Cambridge, 2012).

63 Pl. *Rep.* 5.458e–459b; Xen. *Lac. Pol.* 1.6–10.

64 Xen. *Lac. Pol.* 2. See Paul Cartledge, 'Spartan Wives: Liberation or Licence?', *Classical Quarterly*, XXXI/1 (1981), pp. 84–105.

65 Pl. *Rep.* 5.473cd.

66 Geoffrey Bakewell, 'Mining Plato's Cave: Silver Mining, Slavery, and Philosophical Education', *Polis*, XL/3 (2023), pp. 436–56.

67 Xen. *Hell.* 6.2.4–23; see Carol Atack, *Xenophon* (*Greece and Rome*, New Surveys in the Classics) (Cambridge, 2024).

68 Pl. *Rep.* 8.547b–549b.

69 Pl. *Rep.* 10.620cd.

70 Kenneth James Dover, *Plato: Symposium* (Cambridge, 1980), p. 10. On Thebes's history see Paul Cartledge, *Thebes: The Forgotten City of Ancient Greece* (London, 2020).

71 Pl. *Smp.* 177d, 178e.

72 Daniela Marchiandi, 'In the Shadow of Athena Polias: The Divinities of the Academy, the Training of Politai and Death in Service to Athens', in *Plato's Academy*, ed. Kalligas et al., pp. 11–27.

73 Pl. *Smp.* 176e–177a; Fiona Hobden, *The Symposion in Ancient Greek Society and Thought* (Cambridge, 2013).

74 For a critical feminist reading of Diotima's speech, see Luce Irigaray, 'Sorcerer Love: A Reading of Plato's *Symposium*, Diotima's Speech', *Hypatia*, III/3 (1988), pp. 32–44.

75 Nails, *People of Plato*, p. 314, suggests 418–416 as a dramatic date, and suggests on that basis that Lysias already had a reputation as an orator then, although she also notes (p. 191) that his reputation developed after the return of the democracy in 403.

76 See Martha C. Nussbaum, *The Fragility of Goodness: Luck and Ethics in Greek Tragedy and Philosophy* (Cambridge, 2001), pp. 228–31, citing the epigram attributed to Plato at DL 3.30.

77 Pl. *Phdr.* 229be.

78 DS 15.73.5.

79 Plutarch *Dion* 8–9; [Pl.] *Seventh Letter* 327c–329b, W. H. Porter, *Plutarch: Life of Dion, with Introduction and Notes* (Dublin, 1952), pp. 61–3.

80 DL 3.21.

81 [Pl.] *Seventh Letter* 329be.

82 DL 4.11.

83 See Myles F. Burnyeat and Michael Frede, *The Pseudo-Platonic Seventh Letter*, ed. Dominic Scott (Oxford, 2015).

84 Hdt. 1.29–33; Xenophon *Hiero*.

85 DL 3.21–2, Aristoxenus Fr. 50 = Athenaeus 12.545a, Cicero *De Senectute* 12.39–41; Huffman, *Archytas of Tarentum: Pythagorean, Philosopher and Mathematician King*, pp. 307–40.

86 Matthias Haake, 'The Academy in Athenian Politics and Society between Integration and Disintegration: The First Eighty Years (387/6–306/5)', in *Plato's Academy*, ed. Kalligas et al., pp. 65–88 at pp. 73–4.

87 DS 15.81.5.

88 The subject of a much later epistolary novel, the *Letters of Chion*; see Helen Morales, ed., *Greek Fiction: Chariton Callirhoe; Longus Daphnis and Chloe; Anonymous Letters of Chion* (London, 2011).

89 DS 16.6.3–4, 16.9–13.

6 The Academy Flourishes

1 Matthias Haake, 'The Academy in Athenian Politics and Society between Integration and Disintegration: The First Eighty Years (387/6–306/5)', in *Plato's Academy: Its Workings and Its History*, ed. Paul Kalligas et al. (Cambridge, 2021), pp. 65–88 at p. 87.

2 Plutarch *Dion* 17.5; DL 3.3.

3 DL 3.46; Philodemus *History of the Academy* VI.26–7.

4 DL 5.1, 5.9; see Mauro Bonazzi, *Platonism: A Concise History from the Early Academy to Late Antiquity*, trans. Sergio Knipe (Cambridge, 2023), pp. 7–8.

5 Arist. *Met.* A.6, *Pol.* 2.1–5, *On the Ideas*.

6 Epicrates Fr. 11 = Athenaeus *Deipnosophistae* 2.59d, translation adapted from S. Douglas Olson, *Athenaeus: The Learned Banqueters* (Cambridge, MA, and London, 2006–12). See Bonazzi, *Platonism*, pp. 8–11.

7 Pl. *Sophist* 221bc, trans. Nicholas P. White, *Plato: Sophist* (Indianapolis, IN, 1993).

8 Pl. *Plt.* 262b–263a.

9 DL 6.40.

10 The Greek text appears in a *scholion* (comment by a scholar) on a manuscript copy of Aelius Aristides; further ancient sources are listed in Alice Swift Riginos, *Platonica: The Anecdotes Concerning the Life and Writings of Plato* (Leiden, 1976), pp. 138–9, and Henri-Dominique Saffrey, 'Ἀγεωμέτρητος Μηδεὶς Εἰσίτω. Une inscription légendaire', *Revue des Études Grecques*, LXXXI/384–5 (1969), pp. 67–87.

11 Pl. *Rep.* 7.530d.

12 Archytas Fr. 2 = Porphyry *On Ptolemy's Harmonics* 1.5; Carl A. Huffman, *Archytas of Tarentum: Pythagorean, Philosopher and Mathematician King* (Cambridge, 2005), pp. 162–81.

13 Myles F. Burnyeat, *Explorations in Ancient and Modern Philosophy*, vol. III (Cambridge, 2022), pp. 5–72.

14 Xen. *Mem.* 4.7.2–3, trans. Martin Hammond and Carol Atack, *Memories of Socrates: Xenophon's 'Memorabilia' and 'Apology'* (Oxford, 2023).

15 On Xenophon as a critic of Plato see my introduction and notes in Hammond and Atack, *Memories of Socrates*; Louis-André Dorion and Michele Bandini, *Xénophon: Mémorables*, 3 vols (Paris, 2000–2011), explores Xenophon's references to Plato in greater detail.

16 Isocrates *Panathenaicus* 26.

17 See Haake, 'The Academy in Athenian Politics', pp. 73–4.

18 Antiphanes Fr. 35 = Athenaeus 12.545a; Haake, 'The Academy in Athenian Politics', p. 77.

19 Pl. *Rep.* 7.532ab.

20 Matthias Haake, 'Doing Philosophy? Soziales Kapital versus politischer Mißkredit? Zur Funktionalität und Dysfunktionalität von Philosophie im sozialen und politischen Raum des klassichen Athen', in *Rollenbilder in der Athenischen Demokratie: Medien, Gruppen, Räume im politischen und sozialen System*, ed. Christian Mann, Matthias Haake and Ralf von den Hoff (Wiesbaden, 2009), pp. 113–45.

21 Margalit Finkelberg, *The Gatekeeper: Narrative Voice in Plato's Dialogues* (Leiden, 2019), pp. 38–44. I am grateful to David Sedley for sight of his draft paper 'Forms in the *Parmenides* and *Timaeus*'.

22 DL 9.23.

23 Pl. *Prm.* 128e–129c.

24 Pl. *Rep.* 10.596e–597d. Plato needs there to be Forms of manufactured objects in this argument, so that he can contrast the original, which exists in nature, with the three-dimensional copy made by a carpenter and the two-dimensional copy of that copy made by a painter depicting the carpenter's work. But this version of the theory may simply be offering a more graspable analogy for the relationship between Forms and objects in the ordinary world.

25 Pl. *Prm.* 132ab; see Constance C. Meinwald, *Plato's Parmenides* (New York and Oxford, 1991).

26 Aristoxenus *Elements of Harmonics* 30–31.

27 Aristoxenus' works, beyond his writings on musical theory, included lives of Socrates and Plato, and a summary of Pythagorean philosophy and life; see

Carl A. Huffman, 'The Peripatetics on the Pythagoreans', in *A History of Pythagoreanism*, ed. Carl A. Huffman (Cambridge, 2014), pp. 274–95 at pp. 285–95.

28 Themistius 21.245cd. See Konrad Gaiser, 'Plato's Enigmatic Lecture "on the Good"', *Phronesis*, xxv/1 (1980), pp. 5–37; Riginos, *Platonica*, pp. 124–6; W.K.C. Guthrie, *A History of Greek Philosophy*, vol. v: *The Later Plato and the Academy* (Cambridge, 1978), pp. 424–6.

29 DL 3.37, attributing the anecdote to Favorinus.

30 Simplicius *In Aristotelis Physica* 453, 25–31.

31 See John M. Dillon, *The Heirs of Plato: A Study of the Old Academy (347–274 BC)* (Oxford, 2003), pp. 16–29, and Harold F. Cherniss, *The Riddle of the Early Academy* (Berkeley, CA, 1945), pp. 1–30. Identifying and expounding Plato's unwritten doctrines preoccupied researchers of the Tübingen School, and the possibility of gaps between exoteric writing and esoteric principles has also featured in Straussian interpretations of Plato.

32 See for example Kenneth M. Sayre, *Plato's Late Ontology: A Riddle Resolved* (Las Vegas, NV, 2005).

33 Arist. *Met.* A.6.987b29–988a1, translation adapted from David Ross, *Aristotle's Metaphysics* (Oxford, 1924).

34 There is less emphasis on number in Aristotle's other account of the theory, in *Metaphysics* M.4. See Carlos G. Steel, 'Plato as Seen by Aristotle', in *Aristotle's Metaphysics Alpha: Symposium Aristotelicum*, ed. Carlos G. Steel and Oliver Primavesi (Oxford, 2012), pp. 167–200.

35 Pl. *Sophist* 254d–255e; see Lesley Brown, 'The Sophist on Statements, Predication and Falsehood', in *The Oxford Handbook of Plato*, ed. Gail Fine (Oxford, 2019), pp. 309–36.

36 Leonard Brandwood, 'Stylometry and Chronology', in *The Cambridge Companion to Plato*, 2nd edn, ed. David Ebrey and Richard Kraut (Cambridge, 2022), pp. 90–120.

37 Vassilis Karasmanis, 'Plato and the Mathematics of the Academy', in *Plato's Academy*, ed. Kalligas et al., pp. 108–52 at pp. 110–11.

38 Debra Nails, *The People of Plato: A Prosopography of Plato and Other Socratics* (Indianapolis, IN, 2002), pp. 274–7; Burnyeat and other scholars have argued that Theaetetus died in a later battle, after a longer career as mathematician and teacher (Myles F. Burnyeat, intro. and trans., and M. J. Levett, trans., *The Theaetetus of Plato* (Indianapolis, IN, 1990), p. 3).

39 DL 8.87. The story of Eudoxus' extensive travels may, like similar stories attached to Plato, simply reflect a claim to intellectual authority.

40 DL 8.90 gives this as the date of Eudoxus' 'flourishing'.

41 PHA Y.1–12.

42 Pl. *Meno* 82a–85c.

43 Xen. *Cyr.* 2.2.17–23; Arist. *NE* 5.5.

44 DL 8.88.

45 Nails, *People of Plato*, p. 238; Myles F. Burnyeat, 'Fathers and Sons in Plato's "Republic" and "Philebus"', *Classical Quarterly*, LIV/1 (2004), pp. 80–87.

46 Pl. *Philebus* 44b; Dillon, *The Heirs of Plato*, pp. 67–76.

47 In the roles of the third chorus (book 2) and the Nocturnal Council (book 12). I thank Malcolm Schofield for this suggestion.

48 DL 3.23; [Pl.] *Seventh Letter* 345c–350b; Plutarch *Dion* 18–21.

49 Xenophon *Poroi*, likely written around 355; see Robin Waterfield, trans., and Paul Cartledge, notes, *Xenophon: Hiero the Tyrant and Other Treatises* (London, 1997).
50 Pl. *Plt.* 268e74e.
51 Melissa Lane, *Of Rule and Office: Plato's Ideas of the Political* (Princeton, NJ, 2023).
52 Often assumed to be Plato himself; see Mary Louise Gill, 'Plato's Unfinished Trilogy: Timaeus–Critias–Hermocrates', in *Plato's Styles and Characters: Between Literature and Philosophy*, ed. Gabriele Cornelli (Berlin, 2016), pp. 33–45.
53 Pl. *Tim.* 26e.
54 Pl. *Tim.* 29c; Myles F. Burnyeat, 'Εικως Μυθος', *Rhizai*, II/2 (2005), pp. 143–65.
55 See Thomas K. Johansen, *Plato's Natural Philosophy: A Study of the 'Timaeus–Critias'* (Cambridge, 2004) and Sarah Broadie, *Nature and Divinity in Plato's 'Timaeus'* (Cambridge, 2012), for two thoughtful readings.
56 Pl. *Critias* 120d–121c.
57 Arist. *Politics* 2 considers the usefulness of ideal *politeiai* as a way of thinking through political problems.
58 Pl. *Laws* 1.644d–645a; Malcolm Schofield, *How Plato Writes: Perspectives and Problems* (Cambridge, 2023), pp. 251–74.
59 Pl. *Laws* 1.625ab.
60 The idealized Cretan *politeia* explored in fourth-century Athenian texts, such as that of Aristotle's *Politics* 2.10, replaces the political realities of Crete with an ahistorical unified single narrative.
61 Pl. *Grg.* 523a–527e. See Chapter Four.
62 DL 3.37.
63 This conjectural history takes up book 3; see Carol Atack, '"An Origin for Political Culture": *Laws* 3 as Political Thought and Intellectual History', *Polis*, XXXVII/3 (2020), pp. 468–84.
64 Pl. *Laws* 3.700a–701b.
65 Pl. *Laws* 2.656d–657c; 7.799a.
66 Pl. *Laws* 10.890bd; Robert Mayhew, *Plato Laws X* (Oxford, 2008), pp. 76–7.
67 Pl. *Laws* 8.836c–837a.
68 Pl. *Laws* 12.961a–962e.

7 Legacy

1 PHA 4.35-5.19; see Kilian Josef Fleischer, *Philodem, Geschichte der Akademie: Einführung, Ausgabe, Kommentar* (Leiden, 2023), p. 172 for text, pp. 569–70 for commentary. The Greek text, as currently deciphered, is clear that the slave was playing a rattle, not an *aulos*, a wind instrument which would have provided a drone accompaniment to song. Plato's date of death is given at PHA 2.35–8.
2 APPP 1.29–35, translation Leendert Gerrit Westerink.
3 DL 3.40; see Alice Swift Riginos, *Platonica: The Anecdotes Concerning the Life and Writings of Plato* (Leiden, 1976), pp. 196–7, and a similar claim about Speusippus DL 4.4.
4 Pl. *Apol.* 40e–41c; on Orphic texts, see Gábor Betegh, *The Derveni Papyrus: Cosmology, Theology and Interpretation* (Cambridge, 2004).

5 *OLP* 2.166–7, translation Michael Griffin.
6 DL 3.45; PHA 2.30–31.
7 DL 3.41–3.
8 DL 4.6; see Mauro Bonazzi, *Platonism: A Concise History from the Early Academy to Late Antiquity*, trans. Sergio Knipe (Cambridge, 2023), pp. 11–14; John M. Dillon, *The Heirs of Plato: A Study of the Old Academy (347–274 BC)* (Oxford, 2003).
9 The catalogue of his works includes short treatises, dialogues on a range of ethical and other topics; DL 4.4–5; Debra Nails, *The People of Plato: A Prosopography of Plato and Other Socratics* (Indianapolis, IN, 2002), pp. 271–2.
10 DL 4.2.
11 DL 5.1.
12 DL 4.1.
13 Dillon, *The Heirs of Plato*, pp. 40–64.
14 Bonazzi, *Platonism*, pp. 11–21.
15 DL 4.2.
16 On Aristotle's biological writings and his time on Lesbos, see Armand Marie Leroi, *The Lagoon: How Aristotle Invented Science* (London, 2015).
17 Pl. *Rep.* 1.336a; Pl. *Grg.* 470d–471d.
18 Myles F. Burnyeat and Michael Frede, *The Pseudo-Platonic Seventh Letter*, ed. Dominic Scott (Oxford, 2015), pp. 3–13.
19 [Pl.] *Thirteenth Letter* 361ce.
20 The failings of the summary of Plato's philosophy in the 'Seventh Letter' are set out in Burnyeat and Frede, *Seventh Letter*.
21 Xen. *Mem.* 3.8–9.
22 See Gail Fine, *On Ideas: Aristotle's Criticism of Plato's Theory of Forms* (Oxford, 1993), and Lloyd P. Gerson, *From Plato to Platonism* (Ithaca, NY, 2013). The latter notes scholarly disagreement on the extent to which Aristotle rejects or revises Plato's metaphysics in his own work.
23 Malcolm Schofield, ed., *Aristotle, Plato and Pythagoreanism in the First Century BC: New Directions for Philosophy* (Cambridge, 2013).
24 Malcolm Schofield, 'Cicero and Plato', in *The Cambridge Companion to Cicero's Philosophy*, ed. Jed W. Atkins and Thomas Bénatouïl (Cambridge, 2021), pp. 88–102.
25 Christina Hoenig, *Plato's 'Timaeus' and the Latin Tradition* (Cambridge, 2018).
26 Dante *Inferno* IV.130–35.
27 Sarah Hutton, *British Philosophy in the Seventeenth Century* (Oxford, 2015), pp. 136–59.
28 Michael Rocke, *Forbidden Friendships: Homosexuality and Male Culture in Renaissance Florence* (New York, 1996).
29 Marsilio Ficino, 'Argumentum et commentarius in Phaedrum', in Michael J. B. Allen, *Marsilio Ficino and the Phaedran Charioteer* (Berkeley, CA, 1981).
30 Alastair Blanshard, *Sex: Vice and Love from Antiquity to Modernity* (Oxford, 2010).
31 Frederick Rolfe, *The Desire and Pursuit of the Whole* (London, 1993). Although an expurgated version was originally published in 1934, the full original was only published in this edition.

32 Mary Renault, *The Last of the Wine* (London, 1956); *The Mask of Apollo* (London, 1966).
33 See Thomas More, Henry Neville and Francis Bacon, *Three Early Modern Utopias*, ed. Susan Bruce (Oxford, 1999).
34 Jo Walton, *The Just City* (London, 2015).
35 George Grote, *Plato and the Other Companions of Sokrates* (London, 1865).
36 Myles F. Burnyeat, 'The Past in the Present: Plato as Educator of Nineteenth-Century Britain', in *Philosophers on Education: Historical Perspectives*, ed. Amélie Rorty (London, 1998), pp. 353–73.
37 Karl R. Popper, *The Open Society and Its Enemies*, vol. I: *The Spell of Plato*, 5th edn (London, 1966).
38 For example, Leo Strauss, *Studies in Platonic Political Philosophy* (Chicago, IL, 1983).
39 Alain Badiou, *Plato's 'Republic'*, trans. Susan Spitzer (Cambridge, 2012).
40 Rebecca Goldstein, *Plato at the Googleplex: Why Philosophy Won't Go Away* (London, 2014).

BIBLIOGRAPHY

Primary Sources

Burnyeat, Myles, intro. and trans., and M. J. Levett, trans., *The Theaetetus of Plato* (Indianapolis, IN, 1990)

Cooper, John, and D. S. Hutchinson, eds, *Plato: Complete Works* (Indianapolis, IN, 1997)

Fleischer, Kilian Josef, *Philodem, Geschichte der Akademie: Einführung, Ausgabe, Kommentar* (Leiden, 2023)

Fowler, Ryan C., *Imperial Plato: Albinus, Maximus, Apuleius: Text and Translation, with an Introduction and Commentary* (Las Vegas, NV, 2016)

Griffin, Michael, *Olympiodorus: Life of Plato and On Plato First Alcibiades 1–9* (London, 2015)

Hammond, Martin, trans., and Carol Atack, intro. and notes, *Memories of Socrates: Xenophon's 'Memorabilia' and 'Apology'* (Oxford, 2023)

Kalligas, Paul, and Voula Tsouna, trans., with notes by Myrto Hatzimichali, 'Philodemus' *History of the Philosophers: Plato and the Academy* (PHerc. 1021 and 164)' in *Plato's Academy: Its Workings and Its History*, ed. Paul Kalligas et al. (Cambridge, 2021), pp. 276–383.

Mensch, Pamela, and Jim Miller, *Diogenes Laertius: Lives of the Eminent Philosophers* (New York, 2018)

Morrow, Glenn R., *Plato's Epistles: A Translation with Critical Essays and Notes* (Indianapolis, IN, 1962)

Schofield, Malcolm, ed., and Tom Griffith, trans., *Plato: Gorgias, Menexenus, Protagoras* (Cambridge, 2010)

—, *Plato: The Laws* (Cambridge, 2016)

Waterfield, Robin, trans., and Paul Cartledge, notes, *Xenophon: Hiero the Tyrant and Other Treatises* (London, 1997)

Westerink, Leendert Gerrit, *Anonymous Prolegomena to Platonic Philosophy*, 2nd edn (Dilton Marsh, 2011)

Secondary Literature

Allen, Danielle, *Why Plato Wrote* (Oxford, 2010)

Atack, Carol, 'Plato's Queer Time: Dialogic Moments in the Life and Death of Socrates', *Classical Receptions Journal*, XII/1 (2020), pp. 10–31

Azoulay, Vincent, *Pericles of Athens*, trans. Janet Lloyd (Princeton, NJ, 2014)

Badiou, Alain, *Plato's Republic*, trans. Susan Spitzer (Cambridge, 2012)

Betegh, Gábor, *The Derveni Papyrus: Cosmology, Theology and Interpretation* (Cambridge, 2004)

Blanshard, Alastair, *Sex: Vice and Love from Antiquity to Modernity* (Oxford, 2010)

Bonazzi, Mauro, *The Sophists* (*Greece and Rome*, New Surveys in the Classics) (Cambridge, 2020)

——, *Platonism: A Concise History from the Early Academy to Late Antiquity*, trans. Sergio Knipe (Cambridge, 2023)

Boys-Stones, George R., and Christopher J. Rowe, *The Circle of Socrates: Readings in the First-Generation Socratics* (Indianapolis, IN, 2013)

Broadie, Sarah, *Nature and Divinity in Plato's 'Timaeus'* (Cambridge, 2012)

Brock, Roger, *Greek Political Imagery from Homer to Aristotle* (London, 2013)

Burnyeat, Myles, *Explorations in Ancient and Modern Philosophy*, vol. III (Cambridge, 2022)

Burnyeat, Myles F., and Michael Frede, *The Pseudo-Platonic Seventh Letter*, ed. Dominic Scott (Oxford, 2015)

Cartledge, Paul, *Spartan Reflections* (London, 2001)

——, 'Fowl Play: A Curious Lawsuit in Classical Athens', in *Nomos: Essays in Athenian Law, Politics and Society*, ed. Paul Cartledge, Paul Millett and Stephen Todd (Cambridge, 2002), pp. 41–61

——, *Democracy: A Life*, revd edn (Oxford, 2018)

Davies, John, *Athenian Propertied Families, 600–300 BC* (Oxford, 1971)

Dillon, John, *The Heirs of Plato: A Study of the Old Academy (347–274 BC)* (Oxford, 2003)

DuBois, Page, *Slaves and Other Objects* (Chicago, IL, 2008)

Dutsch, Dorota, *Pythagorean Women Philosophers: Between Belief and Suspicion* (Oxford, 2020)

Ebrey, David, *Plato's 'Phaedo': Forms, Death, and the Philosophical Life* (Cambridge, 2023)

——, and Richard Kraut, eds, *The Cambridge Companion to Plato*, 2nd edn (Cambridge, 2022)

Ferrari, G.R.F., ed., *The Cambridge Companion to Plato's 'Republic'* (Cambridge, 2007)

Fine, Gail, *On Ideas: Aristotle's Criticism of Plato's Theory of Forms* (Oxford, 1993)

——, ed., *The Oxford Handbook of Plato*, 2nd edn (Oxford, 2019)

Finkelberg, Margalit, *The Gatekeeper: Narrative Voice in Plato's Dialogues* (Leiden, 2019)

Gerson, Lloyd P., *From Plato to Platonism* (Ithaca, NY, 2013)

Giannantoni, Gabriele, *Socratis et Socraticorum reliquiae* (Naples, 1990)

Gill, Mary Louise, 'Plato's Unfinished Trilogy: Timaeus–Critias–Hermocrates', in *Plato's Styles and Characters: Between Literature and Philosophy*, ed. Gabriele Cornelli (Berlin, 2016), pp. 33–45

Goldstein, Rebecca, *Plato at the Googleplex: Why Philosophy Won't Go Away* (London, 2014)

Grote, George, *Plato and the Other Companions of Sokrates* (London, 1865)

Haake, Matthias, 'The Academy in Athenian Politics and Society between Integration and Disintegration: The First Eighty Years (387/6–306/5)', in *Plato's Academy: Its Workings and Its History*, ed. Paul Kalligas et al. (Cambridge, 2021), pp. 65–88

Hansen, Mogens Herman, *The Athenian Democracy in the Age of Demosthenes: Structure, Principles, and Ideology*, 2nd edn (Bristol, 1999)

Harding, Phillip, *The Story of Athens: The Fragments of the Local Chronicles of Attika* (London, 2008)

Hobden, Fiona, *The Symposion in Ancient Greek Society and Thought* (Cambridge, 2013)

Horky, Phillip Sidney, *Plato and Pythagoreanism* (New York, 2013)

Huffman, Carl A., *Archytas of Tarentum: Pythagorean, Philosopher and Mathematician King* (Cambridge, 2005)

——, ed., *A History of Pythagoreanism* (Cambridge, 2014)

Humble, Noreen, *Xenophon of Athens: A Socratic on Sparta* (Cambridge, 2022)

Kahn, Charles H., *Plato and the Socratic Dialogue: The Philosophical Use of a Literary Form* (Cambridge, 1996)

Kalligas, Paul, et al., eds, *Plato's Academy: Its Workings and Its History* (Cambridge, 2021)

Kirk, G. S., J. E. Raven and Malcolm Schofield, *The Presocratic Philosophers: A Critical History with a Selection of Texts*, 2nd edn (Cambridge, 1983)

Lane, Melissa, *Of Rule and Office: Plato's Ideas of the Political* (Princeton, NJ, 2023)

McCabe, Mary Margaret, *Plato and His Predecessors: The Dramatisation of Reason* (Cambridge, 2000)

Masterson, Mark, Nancy Sorkin Rabinowitz and James Robson, eds, *Sex in Antiquity: Exploring Gender and Sexuality in the Ancient World* (New York, 2015)

Nails, Debra, *The People of Plato: A Prosopography of Plato and Other Socratics* (Indianapolis, IN, 2002)

Ober, Josiah, *Mass and Elite in Democratic Athens: Rhetoric, Ideology, and the Power of the People* (Princeton, NJ, 1989)

Popper, Karl R., *The Open Society and Its Enemies*, vol. I: *The Spell of Plato*, 5th edn (London, 1966)

Riginos, Alice Swift, *Platonica: The Anecdotes Concerning the Life and Writings of Plato* (Leiden, 1976)

Schofield, Malcolm, *Plato: Political Philosophy* (Oxford, 2006)

——, *How Plato Writes: Perspectives and Problems* (Cambridge, 2023)

Sedley, David, 'The Atheist Underground', in *Politeia in Greek and Roman Philosophy*, ed. Verity Harte and Melissa Lane (Cambridge, 2013), pp. 329–48

Shear, Julia L., *Polis and Revolution: Responding to Oligarchy in Classical Athens* (Cambridge, 2011)

Steel, Carlos G., 'Plato as Seen by Aristotle', in *Aristotle's Metaphysics Alpha: Symposium Aristotelicum*, ed. Carlos G. Steel and Oliver Primavesi (Oxford, 2012), pp. 167–200

Strauss, Leo, *The City and Man* (Chicago, IL, 1977)

Thomas, Rosalind, *Oral Tradition and Written Record in Classical Athens* (Cambridge, 1989)

Tsouna, Voula, *Plato's 'Charmides': An Interpretative Commentary* (Cambridge, 2022)

Vidal-Naquet, Pierre, *The Atlantis Story: A Short History of Plato's Myth*, trans. Janet Lloyd (Exeter, 2007)

Warren, James, *Presocratics: Natural Philosophers before Socrates* (Berkeley, CA, 2007)

Waterfield, Robin, *Plato of Athens: A Life in Philosophy* (Oxford, 2023)

ACKNOWLEDGEMENTS

Thank you to Paul Cartledge for inviting me to write this book, to Malcolm Schofield for encouragement and support throughout and without whom this would have been impossible, and to Vivian Constantinopoulos, commissioning editor of the series, and Emma Devlin at Reaktion, and the Reaktion editorial and production team. This book owes much to continuing dialogues: with the Cambridge community of scholars in ancient philosophy from whom I have learned so much in our weekly reading seminars, with the conference and seminar audiences to whom I've presented my research, and with friends far and wide. Thanks to Newnham College for providing me with an academic community and home base, and for funding research travel and reproduction costs for many of the images in this book through its Senior Member Research Fund. Especial thanks to Alex van Someren for his logistical support for adventures in the psychogeography of Plato's Greece, and for everything else.

PHOTO ACKNOWLEDGEMENTS

The author and publishers wish to express their thanks to the sources listed below for illustrative material and/or permission to reproduce it. Some locations of artworks are also given below, in the interest of brevity:

Alamy Stock Photo: pp. 143 (K. J. Donell), 114–15 (Erin Babnik); American Numismatic Society, New York: p. 113; Antikensammlung, Staatliche Museen zu Berlin (CC BY-SA 4.0): pp. 38, 45; Cambridge University Library: p. 183; photo Carol Atack: p. 26; © S. Ballard 2024: pp. 10–11, 12; © The Fitzwilliam Museum, University of Cambridge: pp. 23, 197; © The Fitzwilliam Museum, University of Cambridge, reproduced by courtesy of the Master and Fellows of Corpus Christi College, Cambridge: p. 153; iStock.com: p. 6 (brunocoelhopt); The J. Paul Getty Museum, Los Angeles: pp. 52, 121; The Metropolitan Museum of Art, New York: pp. 40, 46, 91, 155, 168; Musei Vaticani, Vatican City: p. 176; Wikimedia Commons: pp. 71 (Musée du Louvre, Paris; photo Eric Gaba/Sting, CC BY-SA 2.5), 129 (photo Tomisti, CC BY-SA 3.0), 160 (Glyptothek, Munich; photo Bibi Saint-Pol, public domain), 163 (Museo Archeologico Nazionale, Naples; photo Jebulon, public domain), 194 (Museo Nazionale del Bargello, Florence; photo MenkinAlRire, CC BY-SA 4.0).

INDEX

Page numbers in *italics* refer to illustrations